Practical Education
Vol. I

by

Maria Edgeworth And Richard Lovell Edgeworth

Practical Education
Vol. I
by Maria Edgeworth And Richard Lovell Edgeworth

ISBN: 978-93-67140-86-4

Published by

DOUBLE 9 BOOKS
2/13-B, Ansari Road
Daryaganj, New Delhi – 110002
info@double9books.com
www.double9books.com
Tel. 011-40042856

This book is under public domain

ABOUT THE AUTHOR

Maria Edgeworth and her father, Richard Lovell Edgeworth, were prominent Anglo-Irish writers known for their contributions to literature and education. Richard was deeply interested in education and developed progressive ideas about teaching, which influenced Maria's work. He authored several texts on education and wrote children's books, emphasizing moral instruction and practical knowledge.

Maria Edgeworth, novels, such as "Castle Rackrent" and "Belinda," explored themes of class, gender, and social reform, showcasing her keen observation of Irish society. Maria's writing often reflected her advocacy for women's education and empowerment, challenging societal norms of her time.

Their book - "Practical Education" explores innovative educational methods, emphasizing practical learning, moral development, and the importance of tailoring education to individual needs and societal context.

Together, they collaborated on several projects, reflecting their shared belief in the power of education to transform society. Their contributions laid the groundwork for future writers and educators, highlighting the interplay between literature and social reform.

CONTENTS

PREFACE

We shall not imitate the invidious example of some authors, who think it necessary to destroy the edifices of others, in order to clear the way for their own. We have no peculiar system to support, and, consequently, we have no temptation to attack the theories of others; and we have chosen the title of Practical Education, to point out that we rely entirely upon practice and experience.

To make any progress in the art of education, it must be patiently reduced to an experimental science: we are fully sensible of the extent and difficulty of this undertaking, and we have not the arrogance to imagine, that we have made any considerable progress in a work, which the labours of many generations may, perhaps, be insufficient to complete; but we lay before the publick the result of our experiments, and in many instances the experiments themselves. In pursuing this part of our plan, we have sometimes descended from that elevation of style, which the reader might expect in a quarto volume; we have frequently been obliged to record facts concerning children which may seem trifling, and to enter into a minuteness of detail which may appear unnecessary. No anecdotes, however, have been admitted without due deliberation; nothing has been introduced to gratify the idle curiosity of others, or to indulge our own feelings of domestic partiality.

In what we have written upon the rudiments of science, we have pursued an opposite plan; so far from attempting to teach them in detail, we refer our readers to the excellent treatises on the different branches of science, and on the various faculties of the human mind, which are to be found in every language. The chapters that we have introduced upon these subjects, are intended merely as specimens of the manner in which we think young children should be taught. We have found from experience, that an early knowledge of the first principles of science may be given in conversation, and may be insensibly acquired from the usual incidents of life: if this knowledge be carefully associated with the technical terms which common use may preserve in the memory, much of the difficulty of subsequent instruction may be avoided.

The sketches we have hazarded upon these subjects, may to some appear too slight, and to others too abstruse and tedious. To those who have explored the vast mines of human knowledge, small specimens appear trifling and contemptible, whilst the less accustomed eye is somewhat dazzled and confused by the appearance even of a small collection: but to the most enlightened minds, new combinations may be suggested by a new arrangement of materials, and the curiosity and enthusiasm of the inexperienced may be awakened, and excited to accurate and laborious researches.

With respect to what is commonly called the education of the heart, we have endeavoured to suggest the easiest means of inducing useful and agreeable habits, well regulated sympathy and benevolent affections. A witty writer says, "Il est permis d'ennuyer en moralites d'ici jusqu' a Constantinople." Unwilling to avail ourselves of this permission, we have sedulously avoided declamation, and, wherever we have been obliged to repeat ancient maxims, and common truths, we have at least thought it becoming to present them in a new dress.

On religion and politics we have been silent, because we have no ambition to gain partisans, or to make proselytes, and because we do not address ourselves exclusively to any sect or to any party. The scrutinizing eye of criticism, in looking over our table of contents, will also, probably, observe that there are no chapters on courage and chastity. To pretend to teach courage to Britons, would be as ridiculous as it is unnecessary; and, except amongst those who are exposed to the contagion of foreign manners, we may boast of the superior delicacy of our fair countrywomen; a delicacy acquired from domestic example, and confirmed by publick approbation. Our opinions concerning the female character and understanding, have been fully detailed in a former publication; [1] and, unwilling to fatigue by repetition, we have touched but slightly upon these subjects in our chapters on Temper, Female Accomplishments, Prudence, and Economy.

We have warned our readers not to expect from us any new theory of education, but they need not apprehend that we have written without method, or that we have thrown before them a heap of desultory remarks and experiments, which lead to no general conclusions, and which tend to the establishment of no useful principles. We assure them that we have worked upon a regular plan, and where we have failed of executing our design, it has not been for want of labour or attention. Convinced that it is the duty and the interest of all who write, to inquire what others have said and thought upon the subject of which they treat, we have examined attentively the works of others, that we might collect whatever knowledge they contain, and that we might neither arrogate inventions which do not belong to us, nor weary the public by repetition. Some useful and ingenious essays may probably have escaped our notice; but we flatter ourselves, that our readers will not find reason to accuse us of negligence, as we have perused with diligent attention every work upon education, that has obtained the sanction of time or of public approbation, and, though we have never bound ourselves to the letter, we hope that we have been faithful to the spirit, of their authors. Without incumbering ourselves with any part of their systems which has not been authorized by experience, we have steadily attempted immediately to apply to practice such of their ideas as we have thought useful; but whilst we have used the thoughts of others, we have been anxious to avoid mean plagiarism, and wherever we have borrowed, the debt has been carefully acknowledged.

The first hint of the chapter on Toys was received from Dr. Beddoes; the sketch of an introduction to chemistry for children was given to us by Mr. Lovell Edgeworth; and the rest of the work was resumed from a design formed and begun twenty years ago. When a book appears under the name of two authors, it is natural to inquire what share belongs to each of them. All that relates to the art of teaching to read in the chapter on Tasks, the chapters on Grammar and Classical Literature, Geography, Chronology, Arithmetic, Geometry, and Mechanics, were written by Mr. Edgeworth, and the rest of the book by Miss Edgeworth. She was encouraged and enabled to write upon this important subject, by having for many years before her eyes the conduct of a judicious mother in the education of a large family. The chapter on Obedience, was written from Mrs. Edgeworth's notes, and was exemplified by her successful practice in the management of her children; the whole manuscript was submitted to her judgment, and she revised parts of it in the last stage of a fatal disease.

[1] Letters for Literary Ladies.

CHAPTER I
TOYS

"Why don't you play with your playthings, my dear? I am sure that I have bought toys enough for you; why can't you divert yourself with them, instead of breaking them to pieces?" says a mother to her child, who stands idle and miserable, surrounded by disjointed dolls, maimed horses, coaches and one-horse chairs without wheels, and a nameless wreck of gilded lumber.

A child in this situation is surely more to be pitied than blamed; for is it not vain to repeat, "Why don't you play with your playthings," unless they be such as he can play with, which is very seldom the case; and is it not rather unjust to be angry with him for breaking them to pieces, when he can by no other device render them subservient to his amusement? He breaks them, not from the love of mischief, but from the hatred of idleness; either he wishes to see what his playthings are made of, and how they are made; or, whether he can put them together again, if the parts be once separated. All this is perfectly innocent; and it is a pity that his love of knowledge and his spirit of activity should be repressed by the undistinguishing correction of a nursery maid, or the unceasing reproof of a French governess.

The more natural vivacity and ingenuity young people possess, the less are they likely to be amused with the toys which are usually put into their hands. They require to have things which exercise their senses or their imagination, their imitative, and inventive powers. The glaring colours, or the gilding of toys, may catch the eye, and please for a few minutes, but unless some use can be made of them, they will, and ought, to be soon discarded. A boy, who has the use of his limbs, and whose mind is untainted with prejudice, would, in all probability, prefer a substantial cart, in which he could carry weeds, earth and stones, up and down hill, to the finest frail coach and six that ever came out of a toy-shop: for what could he do with the coach after having admired, and sucked the paint, but drag it cautiously along the carpet of a drawing-room, watching the wheels, which will not turn, and seeming to sympathize with the just terrors of the lady and gentleman within, who are certain of being overturned every five minutes? When he is tired of this, perhaps, he may set about to unharness horses which were never meant to be unharnessed; or to currycomb their woollen manes and tails, which usually come off during the first attempt.

That such toys are frail and useless, may, however, be considered as evils comparatively small: as long as the child has sense and courage to destroy the toys, there is no great harm done; but, in general, he is taught to set a value upon them totally independent of all ideas of utility, or of any regard to his own real feelings. Either he is conjured to take particular care of them, because they cost a great deal of money; or else he is taught to admire them as miniatures of some of the fine things on which fine people pride themselves: if no other bad consequence were to ensue, this single circumstance of his being guided in his choice by the opinion of others is dangerous. Instead of attending to his own sensations, and learning from his own experience, he acquires the habit of estimating his pleasures by the taste and judgment of those who happen to be near him.

"I liked the cart best," says the boy, "but mamma and every body said that the coach was the prettiest; so I chose the coach." —Shall we wonder if the same principle afterwards governs him in the choice of "the toys of age?"

A little girl, presiding at her baby tea-table, is pleased with the notion that she is like her mamma; and, before she can have any idea of the real pleasures of conversation and society, she is confirmed in the persuasion, that tattling and visiting are some of the most enviable privileges of grown people; a set of beings whom she believes to be in possession of all the sweets of happiness.

Dolls, beside the prescriptive right of ancient usage, can boast of such an able champion in Rousseau, that it requires no common share of temerity to attack them. As far as they are the means of inspiring girls with a taste for neatness in dress, and with a desire to make those things for themselves, for which women are usually dependent upon milliners, we must acknowledge their utility; but a watchful eye should be kept upon the child, to mark the first symptoms of a love of finery and fashion. It is a sensible remark of a late female writer, that whilst young people work, the mind will follow the hands, the thoughts are occupied with trifles, and the industry is stimulated by vanity.

Our objections to dolls are offered with great submission and due hesitation. With more confidence we may venture to attack baby-houses; an unfurnished baby-house might be a good toy, as it would employ little carpenters and seamstresses to fit it up; but a completely furnished baby-house proves as tiresome to a child, as a finished seat is to a young nobleman. After peeping, for in general only a peep can be had into each apartment, after being thoroughly satisfied that nothing is wanting, and that consequently there is nothing to be done, the young lady lays her doll upon the state bed, if the doll be not twice as large as the bed, and falls fast asleep in the midst of her felicity.

Before dolls, baby-houses, coaches, and cups and saucers, there comes a set of toys, which are made to imitate the actions of men and women, and the notes or noises of birds and beasts. Many of these are ingenious in their construction, and happy in their effect, but that effect unfortunately is transitory. When the wooden woman has churned her hour in her empty churn; when the stiff backed man has hammered or sawed till his arms are broken, or till his employers are tired; when the gilt lamb has ba-ad, the obstinate pig squeaked, and the provoking cuckoo cried cuckoo, till no one in the house can endure the noise; what remains to be done? — Wo betide the unlucky little philosopher, who should think of inquiring why the woman churned, or how the bird cried cuckoo; for it is ten to one that in prosecuting such an inquiry, just when he is upon the eve of discovery, he snaps the wire, or perforates the bellows, and there ensue "a death-like silence, and a dread repose."

The grief which is felt for spoiling a new plaything might be borne, if it were not increased, as it commonly is, by the reproaches of friends; much kind eloquence, upon these occasions, is frequently displayed, to bring the sufferer to a proper sense of his folly, till in due time the contrite corners of his mouth are drawn down, his wide eyes fill with tears, and, without knowing what he means, he promises never to be so silly any more. The future safety of his worthless playthings is thus purchased at the expense of his understanding, perhaps of his integrity: for children seldom scrupulously adhere to promises, which they have made to escape from impending punishment.

We have ventured to object to some fashionable toys; we are bound at least to propose others in their place; and we shall take the matter up soberly from the nursery.

The first toys for infants should be merely such things as may be grasped without danger, and which might, by the difference of their sizes, invite comparison: round ivory or wooden sticks should be put into their little hands; by degrees they will learn to lift them to their mouths, and they will distinguish their sizes: square and circular bits of wood, balls, cubes, and triangles, with holes of different sizes made in them, to admit the sticks, should be their playthings. No greater apparatus is necessary for the amusement of the first months of an infant's life. To ease the pain which they feel from cutting teeth, infants generally carry to their mouths whatever they can lay their hands upon; but they soon learn to distinguish those bodies which relieve their pain, from those which gratify their palate; and, if they are left to themselves, they will always choose what is painted in preference to every thing else; nor must we attribute the look of delight with which they seize toys that are painted red, merely to the pleasure which their eye takes in the bright colour, but to the love of the sweet taste which they suck from the paint. What injury may be done to the health by the quantity of lead which is thus swallowed, we will not pretend to determine, but we refer to a medical name of high authority, [2] whose cautions probably will not be treated with neglect. To gratify the eye with glittering objects, if this be necessary, may be done with more safety by toys of tin and polished iron: a common steel button is a more desirable plaything to a young child than many expensive toys; a few such buttons tied together, so as to prevent any danger of their being swallowed, would continue for some time a source of amusement.

When a nurse wants to please or to pacify a child, she stuns its ear with a variety of noises, or dazzles its eye with glaring colours or stimulating light. The eye and the ear are thus fatigued without advantage, and the temper is hushed to a transient calm by expedients, which in time must lose their effect, and which can have no power over confirmed fretfulness. The pleasure of exercising their senses, is in itself sufficient to children without any factitious stimulus, which only exhausts their excitability, and renders them incapable of being amused by a variety of common objects, which would naturally be their entertainment. We do not here speak of the attempts made to sooth a child who is ill; "to charm the sense of pain," so far as it can be done by diverting the child's attention from his own sufferings to outward objects, is humane and reasonable, provided our compassion does not induce in the child's mind the expectation of continual attendance, and that impatience of temper which increases bodily suffering. It would be in vain to read lectures on philosophy to a nurse, or to expect stoicism from an infant; but, perhaps, where mothers pay attention themselves to their children, they will be able to prevent many of the consequences of vulgar prejudice and folly. A nurse's wish is to have as little trouble as possible with the child committed to her charge, and at the same time to flatter the mother, from whom she expects her reward. The appearance of extravagant fondness for the child, of incessant attention to its humour, and absurd submission to its caprices, she imagines to be the surest method of recommending herself to favour. She is not to be imposed upon by the faint and affected rebukes of the fond mother, who exclaims, "Oh, nurse, indeed you *do* spoil that child sadly!—Oh, nurse, upon my word she governs you entirely!—Nurse, you must not let her have her own way always.—Never mind her crying, I beg, nurse."—Nurse smiles, sees that she has gained her point, and promises what she knows it is not expected she should perform. Now if, on the contrary, she perceived that the mother was neither to be flattered nor pleased by these means, one motive for spoiling the child would immediately cease: another strong one would, it is true, still remain. A nurse wishes to save herself trouble, and she frequently consults her own convenience when she humours an infant. She hushes it to sleep, that she may leave it safely; she stops it from crying, that she may not hear an irritating noise, that she may relieve herself as soon as possible from the painful weakness of compassion, or that she may avoid the danger of being interrogated by the family as to the cause of the disturbance. It is less trouble to her to yield to caprice and ill-humour than to prevent or cure it, or at least she thinks it is so. In reality it is not; for an humoured child in time plagues its attendant infinitely more than it would have done with reasonable management. If it were possible to convince nurses of this, they would sacrifice perhaps the convenience of a moment to the peace of future hours, and they would not be eager to quell one storm, at the hazard of being obliged to endure twenty more boisterous; the candle would then no more be thrust almost into the infant's eyes to make it take notice of the light through the mist of tears, the eternal bunch of keys would not dance and jingle at every peevish summons, nor would the roarings of passion be overpowered by insulting songs, or soothed by artful caresses; the child would then be caressed and amused when he looks smiling and good-humoured, and all parties would be much happier.

Practical education begins very early, even in the nursery. Without the mountebank pretence, that miracles can be performed by the turning of a straw, or the dictatorial anathematizing tone, which calls down vengeance upon those who do not follow to an iota the injunctions of a theorist, we may simply observe, that parents would save themselves a great deal of trouble, and their children some pain, if they would pay some attention to their early education. The temper acquires habits much earlier than is usually apprehended; the first impressions which infants receive, and the first habits which they learn from their nurses, influence the temper and disposition long after the slight causes which produced them are forgotten. More care and judgment than usually fall to the share of a nurse are necessary, to cultivate the disposition which infants show, to exercise their senses, so as neither to suffer them to become indolent and torpid from want of proper objects to occupy their attention, nor yet to exhaust their senses by continual excitation. By ill-timed restraints or injudicious incitements, the nurse frequently renders the child obstinate or passionate. An infant should never be interrupted in its operations; whilst it wishes to use its hands, we should not be impatient to make it walk; or when it is pacing, with all the attention to its centre of gravity that is exerted by a rope-dancer, suddenly arrest its progress, and insist upon its pronouncing the scanty vocabulary which we have compelled it to learn. When children are busily trying experiments upon objects within their reach, we should not, by way of saving them trouble, break the course of their ideas, and totally prevent them from acquiring knowledge by their own experience. When a foolish nurse sees a child attempting to reach or lift any thing, she runs immediately, "Oh, dear love, it can't do it, it can't!—I'll do it for it, so I will!"—If the child be trying the difference between pushing and pulling, rolling or sliding, the powers of the wedge or the lever, the officious nurse hastens instantly to display her own knowledge of the mechanic powers: "Stay, love, stay; that is not the way to do it—I'll show it the right way—see here—look at me love."—Without interrupting a child in the moment of action, proper care might previously be taken to remove out of its way those things which can really hurt it, and a just degree of attention must be paid to its first experiments upon hard and heavy, and more especially upon sharp, brittle, and burning bodies; but this degree of care should not degenerate into cowardice; it is better that a child should tumble down or burn its fingers, than that it should not learn the use of its limbs and its senses. We should for another reason take care to put all dangerous things effectually out of the child's reach, instead of saying perpetually, "Take care, don't touch that!—don't do that!—let that alone!" The child, who scarcely understands the words, and not at all the reason of these prohibitions, is frightened by the tone and countenance with which they are uttered and accompanied; and he either becomes indolent or cunning; either he desists from exertion, or seizes the moment to divert himself with forbidden objects, when the watchful eye that guards them is withdrawn. It is in vain to encompass the restless prisoner with a fortification of chairs, and to throw him an old almanack to tear to pieces, or an old pincushion to explore; the enterprising adventurer soon makes his escape from this barricado, leaves his goods behind him, and presently is again in what the nurse calls mischief.

Mischief is with nurses frequently only another name for any species of activity which they find troublesome; the love which children are supposed to have for pulling things out of their places, is in reality the desire of seeing things in motion, or of putting things into different situations. They will like to put the furniture in a room in its proper place, and to arrange every thing in what we call order, if we can make these equally permanent sources of active amusement; but when things are once in their places, the child has nothing more to do, and the more quickly each chair arrives at its destined situation, the sooner comes the dreaded state of idleness and quiet.

A nursery, or a room in which young children are to live, should never have any furniture in it which they can spoil; as few things as possible should be left within their reach which they are not to touch, and at the same time they should be provided with the means of amusing themselves, not with painted or gilt toys, but with pieces of wood of various shapes and sizes, which they may build up and pull down, and put in a variety of different forms and positions; balls, pulleys, wheels, strings, and strong little carts, proportioned to their age, and to the things which they want to carry in them, should be their playthings.

Prints will be entertaining to children at a very early age; it would be endless to enumerate the uses that may be made of them; they teach accuracy of sight, they engage the attention, and employ the imagination. In 1777 we saw L——, a child of two years old, point out every piece of furniture in the French prints of Gil Blas; in the print of the Canon at Dinner, he distinguished the knives, forks, spoons, bottles, and every thing upon the table: the dog lying upon the mat, and the bunch of keys hanging at Jacintha's girdle; he told, with much readiness, the occupation of every figure in the print, and could supply, from his imagination, what is supposed to be hidden by the foremost parts of all the objects. A child of four years old was asked, what was meant by something that was very indistinctly represented as hanging round the arm of a figure in one of the prints of the London Cries. He said it was a glove; though it had as little resemblance to a glove, as to a ribbon or a purse. When he was asked how he knew that it was a glove, he answered, "that it ought to be a glove, because the woman had one upon her other arm, and none upon that where the thing was hanging." Having seen the gown of a female figure in a print hanging obliquely, the same child said, "The wind blows that woman's gown back." We mention these little circumstances from real life, to show how early prints may be an amusement to children, and how quickly things unknown, are learnt by the relations which they bear to what was known before. We should at the same time observe, that children are very apt to make strange mistakes, and hasty conclusions, when they begin to reason from analogy. A child having asked what was meant by some marks in the forehead of an old man in a print; and having been told, upon some occasion, that old people were wiser than young ones, brought a print containing several figures to his mother, and told her that *one*, which he pointed to, was wiser than all the rest; upon inquiry, it was found that he had formed this notion from seeing that one figure was wrinkled, and that the others were not.

Prints for children should be chosen with great care; they should represent objects which are familiar; the resemblances should be accurate, and the manners should be attended to, or at least, the general moral that is to be drawn from them. The attitude of Sephora, the boxing lady in Gil Blas, must appear unnatural to children who have not lived with termagant heroines. Perhaps, the first ideas of grace, beauty, and propriety, are considerably influenced by the first pictures and prints which please children. Sir Joshua Reynolds tells us, that he took a child with him through a room full of pictures, and that the child stopped, with signs of aversion, whenever it came to any picture of a figure in a constrained attitude.

Children soon judge tolerably well of proportion in drawing, where they have been used to see the objects which are represented: but we often give them prints of objects, and of animals especially, which they have never seen, and in which no sort of proportion is observed. The common prints of animals must give children false ideas. The mouse and the elephant are nearly of the same size, and the crocodile and whale fill the same space in the page. Painters, who put figures of men amongst their buildings, give the idea of the proportionate height immediately to the eye: this is, perhaps, the best scale we can adopt; in every print for children this should be attended to. Some idea of the relative sizes of the animals they see represented would then be given, and the imagination would not be filled with chimeras.

After having been accustomed to examine prints, and to trace their resemblance to real objects, children will probably wish to try their own powers of imitation. At this moment no toy, which we could invent for them, would give them half so much pleasure as a pencil. If we put a pencil into their hands even before they are able to do any thing with it but make random marks all over a sheet of paper, it will long continue a real amusement and occupation. No matter how rude their first attempts at imitation may be; if the attention of children be occupied, our point is gained. Girls have generally one advantage at this age over boys, in the exclusive possession of the scissors: how many camels, and elephants with amazing trunks, are cut out by the industrious scissors of a busy, and therefore happy little girl, during a winter evening, which passes so heavily, and appears so immeasurably long, to the idle.

Modelling in clay or wax might probably be a useful amusement about this age, if the materials were so prepared, that the children could avoid being every moment troublesome to others whilst they are at work. The making of baskets, and the weaving of sash-line, might perhaps be employment for children; with proper preparations, they might at least be occupied with these things; much, perhaps, might not be produced by their labours, but it is a great deal to give early habits of industry. Let us do what we will, every person who has ever had any experience upon the subject, must know that it is scarcely possible to provide sufficient and suitable occupations for young children: this is one of the first difficulties in education. Those who have never tried the experiment, are astonished to find it such a difficult and laborious business as it really is, to find employments for children from three to six years old. It is perhaps better, that our pupils should be entirely idle, than that they should be half employed. "My dear, have you nothing to do?" should be spoken in sorrow rather than in anger. When they see other people employed and happy, children feel mortified and miserable to have nothing to do. Count Rumford's was an excellent scheme for exciting sympathetic industry amongst the children of the poor at Munich; in the large hall, where the elder children were busy in spinning, there was a range of seats for the younger children, who were not yet permitted to work; these being compelled to sit idle, and to see the busy multitude, grew extremely uneasy in their own situation, and became very anxious to be employed. We need not use any compulsion or any artifice; parents in every family, we suppose, who think of educating their own children, are employed some hours in the day in reading, writing, business, or conversation; during these hours, children will naturally feel the want of occupation, and will, from sympathy, from ambition and from impatience of insupportable ennui, desire with anxious faces, "to have something to do." Instead of loading them with playthings, by way of relieving their misery, we should honestly tell them, if that be the truth, "I am sorry I cannot find any thing for you to do at present. I hope you will soon be able to employ yourself. What a happy thing it will be for you to be able, by and by, to read, and write and draw; then you will never be forced to sit idle."

The pains of idleness stimulate children to industry, if they are from time to time properly contrasted with the pleasures of occupation. We should associate cheerfulness, and praise, and looks of approbation, with industry; and, whenever young people invent employments for themselves, they should be assisted as much as possible, and encouraged. At that age when they are apt to grow tired in half an hour of their playthings, we had better give them playthings only for a very short time, at intervals in the day; and, instead of waiting till they are tired, we should take the things away before they are weary of them. Nor should we discourage the inquisitive genius from examining into the structure of their toys, whatever they may be. The same ingenious and active dispositions, which prompt these inquiries, will secure children from all those numerous temptations to do mischief, to which the idle are exposed. Ingenious children are pleased with contrivances which answer the purposes for which they are intended: and they feel sincere regret whenever these are injured or destroyed: this we mention as a further comfort and security for parents, who, in the company of young mechanics, are apt to tremble for their furniture. Children who observe, and who begin to amuse themselves with *thought*, are not so actively hostile in their attacks upon inanimate objects. We were once present at the dissection of a wooden cuckoo, which was attended with extreme pleasure by a large family of children; and it was not one of the children who broke the precious toy, but it was the father who took it to pieces. Nor was it the destruction of the plaything which entertained the company, but the sight of the manner in which it was constructed. Many guesses were made by all the spectators about the internal structure of the cuckoo, and the astonishment of the company was universal, when the bellows were cut open, and the simple contrivance was revealed to view; probably, more was learnt from this cuckoo, than was ever learnt from any cuckoo before. So far from being indifferent to the destruction of this plaything, H— — the little girl of four years old, to whom it belonged, remembered, several months afterwards, to remind her father of his promise to repair the mischief he had done.

"Several toys, which are made at present, are calculated to give pleasure merely by exciting surprise, and of course give children's minds such a tone, that they are afterwards too fond of *similar useless baubles*." [3] This species of delight is soon over, and is succeeded by a desire to triumph in the ignorance, the credulity, or the cowardice, of their companions. Hence that propensity to play tricks, which is often injudiciously encouraged by the smiles of parents, who are apt to mistake it for a proof of wit and vivacity. They forget, that "gentle dulness ever loved a joke;" and that even wit and vivacity, if they become troublesome and mischievous, will be feared, and shunned. Many juggling tricks and puzzles are highly ingenious; and, as far as they can exercise the invention or the patience of young people, they are useful. Care, however, should be taken, to separate the ideas of deceit and of ingenuity, and to prevent children from glorying in the mere possession of a secret.

Toys which afford trials of dexterity and activity, such as tops, kites, hoops, balls, battledores and shuttlecocks, ninepins, and cup-and-ball, are excellent; and we see that they are consequently great and lasting favourites with children; their senses, their understanding, and their passions, are all agreeably interested and exercised by these amusements. They emulate each other; but, as some will probably excel at one game, and some at another, this emulation will not degenerate into envy. There is more danger that this hateful passion should be created in the minds of young competitors at those games, where it is supposed that some *knack* or *mystery* is to be learned before they can be played with success. Whenever children play at such games, we should point out to them how and why it is that they succeed or fail: we may show them, that, in reality, there is no *knack* or *mystery* in any thing, but that from certain causes certain effects will follow; that, after trying a number of experiments, the circumstances essential to success may be discovered; and that all the ease and dexterity, which we often attribute to the power of natural genius, is simply the consequence of practice and industry. This sober lesson may be taught to children without putting it into grave words or formal precepts. A gentleman once astonished a family of children by his dexterity in playing at bilboquet: he caught the ball nine or ten times successively with great rapidity upon the spike: this success appeared miraculous; and the father, who observed that it had made a great impression upon the little spectators, took that opportunity to show the use of spinning the ball, to make the hole at the bottom ascend in a proper direction. The nature of centrifugal motion, and its effect, in preserving the *parallelism* of *motion*, if we may be allowed the expression, was explained, not at once, but at different intervals, to the young audience. Only as much was explained at a time as the children could understand, without fatiguing their attention, and the abstruse subject was made familiar by the mode of illustration that was adopted.

It is surprising how much children may learn from their playthings, when they are judiciously chosen, and when the habit of reflection and observation is associated with the ideas of amusement and happiness. A little boy of nine years old, who had had a hoop to play with, asked "why a hoop, or a plate, if rolled upon its edge, keeps up as long as it rolls, but falls as soon as it stops, and will not stand if you try to make it stand still upon its edge?" Was not the boy's understanding as well employed whilst he was thinking of this phenomenon, which he observed whilst he was beating his hoop, as it could possibly have been by the most learned preceptor?

When a pedantic schoolmaster sees a boy eagerly watching a paper kite, he observes, "What a pity it is that children cannot be made to mind their grammar as well as their kites!" And he adds, perhaps, some peevish ejaculation on the natural idleness of boys, and that pernicious love of play against which he is doomed to wage perpetual war. A man of sense will see the same thing with a different eye; in this pernicious love of play he will discern the symptoms of a love of science, and, instead of deploring the natural idleness of children, he will admire the activity which they display in the pursuit of knowledge. He will feel that it is his business to direct this activity, to furnish his pupil with materials for fresh combinations, to put him or to let him put himself, in situations where he can make useful observations, and acquire that experience which cannot be bought, and which no masters can communicate.

It will not be beneath the dignity of a philosophic tutor to consider the different effects, which the most common plays of children have upon the habits of the understanding and temper. Whoever has watched children putting together a dissected map, must have been amused with the trial between Wit and Judgment. The child, who quickly perceives resemblances, catches instantly at the first bit of the wooden map, that has a single hook or hollow that seems likely to answer his purpose; he makes, perhaps, twenty different trials before he hits upon the right; whilst the wary youth, who has been accustomed to observe differences, cautiously examines with his eye the whole outline before his hand begins to move; and, having exactly compared the two indentures, he joins them with sober confidence, more proud of never disgracing his judgment by a fruitless attempt, than ambitious of rapid success. He is slow, but sure, and wins the day.

There are some plays which require presence of mind, and which demand immediate attention to what is actually going forward, in which children, capable of the greatest degree of abstract attention, are most apt to be defective. They have many ideas, but none of them ready, and their knowledge is useless, because it is recollected a moment too late. Could we, in suitably dignified language, describe the game of "birds, beasts, and fishes," we should venture to prescribe it as no very painful remedy for these absent and abstracted personages. When the handkerchief or the ball is thrown, and when his bird's name is called for, the absent little philosopher is obliged to collect his scattered thoughts instantaneously, or else he exposes himself to the ridicule of naming, perhaps, a fish or a beast, or any bird but the right. To those children, who, on the contrary, are not sufficiently apt to abstract their attention, and who are what Bacon calls "birdwitted," we should recommend a solitary-board. At the solitary-board they must withdraw their thoughts from all external objects, hear nothing that is said, and fix their attention solely upon the figure and the pegs before them, else they will never succeed; and, if they make one errour in their calculations, they lose all their labour. Those who are precipitate, and not sufficiently attentive to the consequences of their own actions, may receive many salutary lessons at the draught or chess-board—happy, if they can learn prudence and foresight, by frequently losing the battle.

We are not quite so absurd as to imagine, that any great or permanent effects can be produced by such slight causes as a game at draughts, or at a solitary-board, but the combination of a number of apparent trifles, is not to be neglected in education.

We have never yet mentioned what will probably first occur to those who would invent employments for children. We have never yet mentioned a garden; we have never mentioned those great delights to children, a spade, a hoe, a rake, and a wheelbarrow. We hold all these in proper respect; but we did not sooner mention them, because, if introduced too early, they are useless. We must not expect, that a boy six or seven years old, can find, for any length of time, sufficient daily occupation in a garden: he has not strength for hard labour; he can dig soft earth; he can weed groundsel, and other weeds, which take no deep root in the earth; but after he has weeded his little garden, and sowed his seeds, there must be a suspension of his labours. Frequently children, for want of something to do, when they have sowed flower-seeds in their crooked beds, dig up the hopes of the year to make a new walk, or to sink a well in their garden. We mention these things, that parents may not be disappointed, or expect more from the occupation of a garden, than it can, at a very early age, afford. A garden is an excellent resource for children, but they should have a variety of other occupations: rainy days will come, and frost and snow, and then children must be occupied within doors. We immediately think of a little set of carpenter's tools, to supply them with active amusement. Boys will probably be more inclined to attempt making models, than drawings of the furniture which appears to be the most easy to imitate; they will imagine that, if they had but tools, they could make boxes, and desks, and beds, and chests of drawers, and tables and chairs innumerable. But, alas! these fond imaginations are too soon dissipated. Suppose a boy of seven years old to be provided with a small set of carpenter's tools, his father thinks perhaps that he has made him completely happy; but a week afterwards the father finds dreadful marks of the file and saw upon his mahogany tables; the use of these tools is immediately interdicted until a bench shall be procured. Week after week passes away, till at length the frequently reiterated speech of "Papa, you bid me put you in mind about my bench." "Papa" has its effect, and the bench appears. Now the young carpenter thinks he is quite set up in the world, and projects carts and boxes, and reading-desks and writing-desks for himself and for his sisters, if he have any; but when he comes to the execution of his plans, what new difficulties, what new wants arise! the wood is too thick or too thin; it splits, or it cannot be cut with a knife; wire, nails, glue, and above all, the means of heating the glue, are wanting. At last some frail machine, stuck together with pegs or pins, is produced, and the workman is usually either too much ridiculed, or too much admired. The step from pegging to mortising is a very difficult step, and the want of a mortising-chisel is insuperable: one tool is called upon to do the duty of another, and the pricker comes to an untimely end in doing the hard duty of the punch; the saw wants setting; the plane will plane no longer; and the mallet must be used instead of the hammer, because the hammer makes so much noise, that the ladies of the family have voted for its being locked up. To all these various evils the child submits in despair; and finding, after many fruitless exertions, that he cannot make any of the fine things he had projected, he throws aside his tools, and is deterred by these disappointments from future industry and ingenuity. Such are the consequences of putting excellent tools into the hands of children before they can possibly use them: but the tools which are useless at seven years old, will be a most valuable present at eleven or twelve, and for this age it will be prudent to reserve them. A rational toy-shop should be provided with all manner of carpenter's tools, with wood properly prepared for the young workman, and with screws, nails, glue, emery-paper, and a variety of articles which it would be tedious to enumerate; but which, if parents could readily meet within a convenient assemblage, they would willingly purchase for their children. The trouble of hunting through a number of different shops, prevents them at present from purchasing such things; besides, they may not perhaps be sufficiently good carpenters to know distinctly every thing that is necessary for a young workman.

Card, pasteboard, substantial but not sharp-pointed scissors, wire, gum and wax, may, in some degree, supply the want of carpenter's tools at that early age when we have observed that the saw and plane are useless. Models of common furniture should be made as toys, which should take to pieces, so that all their parts, and the manner in which they are put together, might be seen distinctly; the names of the different parts should be written [4] or stamped upon them: by these means the names will be associated with realities; children will retain them in their memory, and they will neither learn by rote technical terms, nor will they be retarded in their progress in mechanical invention by the want of language. Before young people can use tools, these models will amuse and exercise their attention. From models of furniture we may go on to models of architecture; pillars of different orders, the roofs of houses, the manner of slating and tiling, &c. Then we may proceed to models of simple machines, choosing at first such as can be immediately useful to children in their own amusements, such as wheelbarrows, carts, cranes, scales, steelyards, jacks, and pumps, which children ever view with eager eyes.

From simple, it will be easy to proceed gradually to models of more complicated, machinery: it would be tiresome to give a list of these; models of instruments used by manufacturers and artists should be seen; many of these are extremely ingenious; spinning-wheels, looms, paper-mills, wind-mills, water-mills, might with great advantage be shown in miniature to children.

The distracting noise and bustle, the multitude of objects which all claim the attention at once, prevent young people from understanding much of what they see, when they are first taken to look at large manufactories. If they had previously acquired some general idea of the whole, and some particular knowledge of the different parts, they would not stare when they get into these places; they would not "stare round, see nothing, and come home content," bewildered by the sight of cogs and wheels; and the explanations of the workmen would not be all jargon to them; they would understand some of the technical terms, which so much alarm the intellects of those who hear them for the first time.

We may exercise the ingenuity and judgment of children by these models of machines, by showing them first the thing to be done, and exciting them to invent the best means of doing it; afterwards give the models as the reward for their ingenuity, and let them compare their own inventions with the contrivances actually in use amongst artificers; by these means, young people may be led to compare a variety of different contrivances; they will discern what parts of a machine are superfluous, and what inadequate, and they will class particular observations gradually under general principles. It may be thought, that this will tend to give children only mechanical invention, or we should call it, perhaps, the invention of machines; and those who do not require this particular talent, will despise it as unnecessary in what are called the liberal professions. Without attempting to compare the value of different intellectual talents, we may observe, that they are all in some measure dependent upon each other. Upon this subject we shall enlarge more fully when we come to consider the method of cultivating the memory and invention.

Chemical toys will be more difficult to manage than mechanical, because the materials, requisite to try many chemical experiments, are such as cannot safely be put into the hands of children. But a list of experiments, and of the things necessary to try them, might easily be drawn out by a chemist who would condescend to such a task; and if these materials, with proper directions, were to be found at a rational toy-shop, parents would not be afraid of burning or poisoning their children in the first chemical lessons. In some families, girls are taught the confectionary art; might not this be advantageously connected with some knowledge of chemistry, and might not they be better taught than by Mrs. Raffeld or Mrs. Glass? [5] Every culinary operation may be performed as an art, probably, as well by a cook as by a chemist; but, if the chemist did not assist the cook now and then with a little science, epicures would have great reason for lamentation. We do not, by any means, advise that girls should be instructed in confectionary arts, at the hazard of their keeping company with servants. If they learn any thing of this sort, there will be many precautions necessary to separate them from servants: we do not advise that these hazards should be run; but if girls learn confectionary, let them learn the principles of chemistry, which may assist in this art. [6]

Children are very fond of attempting experiments in dying, and are very curious about vegetable dyes; but they can seldom proceed for want of the means of boiling, evaporating, distilling, and subliming. Small stills, and small tea-kettles and lamps, would be extremely useful to them: these might be used in the room with the children's parents, which would prevent all danger: they should continue to be the property of the parents, and should be produced only when they are wanted. No great apparatus is necessary for showing children the first simple operations in chemistry: such as evaporation, crystalization, calcination, detonation, effervescence, and saturation. Water and fire, salt and sugar, lime and vinegar, are not very difficult to be procured; and a wine-glass is to be found in every house. The difference between an acid and alkali should be early taught to children; many grown people begin to learn chemistry, without distinctly knowing what is meant by those terms.

In the selection of chemical experiments for young people, it will be best to avoid such as have the appearance of jugglers tricks, as it is not our purpose to excite the amazement of children for the moment, but to give them a permanent taste for science. In a well known book, called "Hooper's *Rational Recreations*," there are many ingenious experiments; but through the whole work there is such a want of an enlarged mind, and such a love of magic and deception appears, as must render it not only useless, but unsafe, for young people, in its present state. Perhaps a selection might be made from it in which these defects might be avoided: such titles as *"The real apparition: the confederate counters: the five beatitudes*: and *the book of fate,"* may be changed for others more *rational*. Receipts for *"Changing winter into spring,"* for making *"Self-raising pyramids, inchanted mirrors,* and *intelligent flies,"* might be omitted, or explained to advantage. Recreation the 5th, "To tell by the dial of a watch at what hour any person intends to rise;" Recreation the 12th, "To produce the appearance of a phantom on a pedestal placed on the middle of a table;" and Recreation the 30th, "To write several letters which contain no meaning, upon cards; to make them, after they have been twice shuffled, give an answer to a question that shall be proposed;" as for example, "What is love?" scarcely come under the denomination of Rational Recreations, nor will they much conduce to the end proposed in the introduction to Hooper's work; that is to say, in his own words, "To enlarge and fortify the mind of man, that he may advance with tranquil steps through the flowery paths of investigation, till arriving at some noble eminence, he beholds, with awful astonishment, the boundless regions of science, and becomes animated to attain a still more lofty station, whilst his heart is incessantly rapt with joys of which the groveling herd have no conception."

Even in those chemical experiments in this book, which are really ingenious and entertaining, we should avoid giving the old absurd titles, which can only confuse the understanding, and spoil the taste of children. The tree of Diana, and "Philosophic wool," are of this species. It is not necessary to make every thing marvellous and magical, to fix the attention of young people; if they are properly educated, they will find more amusement in discovering, or in searching for the cause of the effects which they see, than in a blind admiration of the juggler's tricks.

In the papers of the Manchester Society, in Franklin's letters, in Priestley's and Percival's works, there may be found a variety of simple experiments which require no great apparatus, and which will at once amuse and instruct. All the papers of the Manchester Society, upon the repulsion and attraction of oil and water, are particularly suited to children, because they state a variety of simple facts; the mind is led to reason upon them, and induced to judge of the different conclusions which are drawn from them by different people. The names of Dr. Percival, or Dr. Wall, will have no weight with children; they will compare only the reasons and experiments. Oil and water, a cork, a needle, a plate, and a glass tumbler, are all the things necessary for these experiments. Mr. Henry's experiments upon the influence that fixed air has on vegetation, and several of Reaumur's experiments, mentioned in the memoirs of the French Academy of Sciences, are calculated to please young people much, and can be repeated without expense or difficulty.

To those who acquire habits of observation, every thing that is to be seen or heard, becomes a source of amusement. Natural history interests children at an early age; but their curiosity and activity is often repressed and restrained by the ignorance or indolence of their tutors. The most inquisitive genius grows tired of repeating, "Pray look at this—What is it? What can the use of this be?" when the constant answer is, "Oh! it's nothing worth looking at, throw it away, it will dirty the house." Those who have attended to the ways of children and parents, well know that there are many little inconveniences attending their amusements, which the sublime eye of the theorist in education overlooks, which, nevertheless, are essential to practical success. "It will dirty the house," puts a stop to many of the operations of the young philosopher; nor is it reasonable that his experiments should interfere with the necessary regularity of a well ordered family. But most well ordered families allow their horses and their dogs to have houses to themselves; cannot one room be allotted to the children of the family? If they are to learn chemistry, mineralogy, botany, or mechanics; if they are to take sufficient bodily exercise without tormenting the whole family with noise, a room should be provided for them. We mention exercise and noise in particular, because we think they will, to many, appear of the most importance.

To direct children in their choice of fossils, and to give them some idea of the general arrangements of mineralogy, toy-shops should be provided with specimens of ores, &c. properly labelled and arranged, in drawers, so that they may be kept in order. Children should have empty shelves in their cabinets, to be filled with their own collections; they will then know how to direct their researches, and how to dispose of their treasures. If they have proper places to keep things in, they will acquire a taste for order by the best means, by feeling the use of it: to either sex, this taste will be highly advantageous. Children who are active and industrious, and who have a taste for natural history, often collect, with much enthusiasm, a variety of pebbles and common stones, which they value as great curiosities, till some surly mineralogist happens to see them, and condemns them all with one supercilious "pshaw!" or else a journey is to be taken, and there is no way in making up the heterogeneous, cumbersome collection, which must, of course, be abandoned. Nay, if no journey is to be taken, a visitor, perhaps, comes unexpectedly; the little naturalist's apartment must be vacated on a few minutes notice, and the labour of years falls a sacrifice, in an instant, to the housemaid's undistinguishing broom.

It may seem trifling to insist so much upon such slight things, but, in fact, nothing can be done in education without attention to minute circumstances. Many who have genius to sketch large plans, have seldom patience to attend to the detail which is necessary for their accomplishment. This is a useful, and therefore, no humiliating drudgery.

With the little cabinets, which we have mentioned, should be sold cheap microscopes, which will unfold a world of new delights to children; and it is very probable that children will not only be entertained with looking at objects through a microscope, but they will consider the nature of the magnifying glass. They should not be rebuffed with the answer, "Oh, it's only a common magnifying glass," but they should be encouraged in their laudable curiosity; they may easily be led to try slight experiments in optics, which will, at least, give the habits of observation and attention. In Dr. Priestley's History of Vision, many experiments may be found, which are not above the comprehension of children of ten or eleven years old; we do not imagine that any science can be taught by desultory experiments, but we think that a taste for science may early be given by making it entertaining, and by exciting young people to exercise their reasoning and inventive faculties upon every object which surrounds them. We may point out that great discoveries have often been made by attention to slight circumstances. The blowing of soap bubbles, as it was first performed as a scientific experiment by the celebrated Dr. Hook, before the Royal Society, makes a conspicuous figure in Dr. Priestley's chapter on the reflection of light; this may be read to children, and they will be pleased when they observe that what at first appeared only a trifling amusement, has occupied the understanding, and excited the admiration, of some great philosophers.

Every child observes the colours which are to be seen in panes of glass windows: in Priestley's History of Vision, there are some experiments of Hook's and Lord Brereton's upon these colours, which may be selected. Buffon's observations upon blue and green shadows, are to be found in the same work, and they are very entertaining. In Dr. Franklin's letters, there are numerous experiments, which are particularly suited to young people; especially, as in every instance he speaks with that candour and openness to conviction, and with that patient desire to discover truth, which we should wish our pupils to admire and imitate.

The history of the experiments which have been tried in the progress of any science, and of the manner in which observations of minute facts have led to great discoveries, will be useful to the understanding, and will gradually make the mind expert in that mental algebra, on which both reasoning and invention (which is, perhaps, only a more rapid species of reasoning) depend. In drawing out a list of experiments for children, it will, therefore, be advantageous to place them in that order which will best exhibit their relative connection; and, instead of showing young people the steps of a discovery, we should frequently pause to try if they can invent. In this, our pupils will succeed often beyond our expectations; and, whether it be in mechanics, chemistry, geometry, or in the arts, the same course of education will be found to have the same advantages. When the powers of reason have been cultivated, and the inventive faculty exercised; when general habits of voluntary exertion and patient perseverance, have been acquired, it will be easy, either for the pupil himself, or for his friends, to direct his abilities to whatever is necessary for his happiness. We do not use the phrase, *success in the world*, because, if it conveys any distinct ideas, it implies some which are, perhaps, inconsistent with real happiness.

Whilst our pupils occupy and amuse themselves with observation, experiment, and invention, we must take care that they have a sufficient variety of manual and bodily exercises. A turning-lathe, and a work-bench, will afford them constant active employment; and when young people can invent, they feel great pleasure in the execution of their own plans. We do not speak from vague theory; we have seen the daily pleasures of the work-bench, and the persevering eagerness with which young people work in wood, and brass, and iron, when tools are put into their hands at a proper age, and when their understanding has been previously taught the simple principles of mechanics. It is not to be expected that any exhortations we could use, could prevail upon a father, who happens to have no taste for mechanics, or for chemistry, to spend any of his time in his children's laboratory, or at their work-bench; but in his choice of a tutor, he may perhaps supply his own defects; and he will consider, that even by interesting himself in the daily occupations of his children, he will do more in the advancement of their education, than can be done by paying money to a hundred masters.

We do not mean to confine young people to the laboratory or the work-bench, for exercise; the more varied exercises, the better. Upon this subject we shall speak more fully hereafter: we have in general recommended all trials of address and dexterity, except games of chance, which we think should be avoided, as they tend to give a taste for gambling; a passion, which has been the ruin of so many young men of promising talents, of so many once happy families, that every parent will think it well worth his while to attend to the smallest circumstances in education, which can prevent its seizing hold of the minds of his children.

In children, as in men, a taste for gaming arises from the want of better occupation, or of proper emotion to relieve them from the pains and penalties of idleness; both the vain and indolent are prone to this taste from different causes. The idea of personal merit is insensibly connected with what is called *good luck,* and before avarice absorbs every other feeling, vanity forms no inconsiderable part of the charm which fixes such numbers to the gaming-table. Indolent persons are fond of games of chance, because they feel themselves roused agreeably from their habitual state of apathy, or because they perceive, that at these contests, without any mental exertion, they are equal, perhaps superior, to their competitors.

Happy they, who have early been inspired with a taste for science and literature! They will have a constant succession of agreeable ideas; they will find endless variety in the commonest objects which surround them; and feeling that every day of their lives they have sufficient amusement, they will require no extraordinary excitations, no holyday pleasures. They who have learnt, from their own experience, a just confidence in their own powers; they who have tasted the delights of well-earned praise, will not lightly trust to *chance,* for the increase of self-approbation; nor will those pursue, with too much eagerness, the precarious triumphs of fortune, who know, that in their usual pursuits, it is in their own power to command success proportioned to their exertions. Perhaps it may be thought, that we should have deferred our eulogium upon literature till we came to speak of Tasks; but if there usually appears but little connection in a child's mind, between books and toys, this must be attributed to his having had bad books and bad toys. In the hands of a judicious instructer, no means are too small to be useful; every thing is made conducive to his purposes, and instead of useless baubles, his pupils will be provided with play things which may instruct, and with occupations which may at once amuse and improve the understanding.

It would be superfluous to give a greater variety of instances of the sorts of amusements which are advantageous; we fear that we have already given too many, and that we have hazarded some observations, which will be thought too pompous for a chapter upon Toys. We intended to have added to this chapter an inventory of the present most fashionable articles in our toy-shops, and *a list of the new assortment,* to speak in the true style of an advertisement; but we are obliged to defer this for the present; upon a future occasion we shall submit it to the judgment of the public. A revolution, *even in toy-shops,* should not be attempted, unless there appear a moral certainty that we both may, and can, change for the better. The danger of doing too much in education, is greater even than the danger of doing too little. As the merchants in France answered to Colbert, when he desired to know "how he could best assist them," children might, perhaps, reply to those who are most officious to amuse them, "Leave us to ourselves."

[2] Dr. Fothergill.

[3] Dr. Beddoes.

[4] We are indebted to Dr. Beddoes for this idea.

[5] We do not mean to do injustice to Mrs. Raffeld's professional skill.

[6] V. Diderot's ingenious preface to "Chymie de gout et de l'odorat."

CHAPTER II
TASKS

"Why don't you get your task, instead of playing with your playthings from morning till night? You are grown too old now to do nothing but play. It is high time you should learn to read and write, for you cannot be a child all your life, child; so go and fetch your *book*, and learn your *task*."

This angry apostrophe is probably addressed to a child, at the moment when he is intent upon some agreeable occupation, which is now to be stigmatized with the name of Play. Why that word should all at once change its meaning; why that should now be a crime, which was formerly a virtue; why he, who had so often been desired to *go and play*, should now be reviled for his obedience, the young casuist is unable to discover. He hears that he is no longer a child: this he is willing to believe; but the consequence is alarming. Of the new duties incumbent upon his situation, he has but yet a confused idea. In his manly character, he is not yet thoroughly perfect: his pride would make him despise every thing that is childish, but no change has yet been wrought in the inward man, and his old tastes and new ambition, are in direct opposition. Whether to learn to read, be a dreadful thing or not, is a question he cannot immediately solve; but if his reasoning faculty be suspended, there is yet a power secretly working within him, by which he will involuntarily be governed. This power is the power of association: of its laws, he is, probably, not more ignorant than his tutor; nor is he aware that whatever word or idea comes into his mind, with any species of pain, will return, whenever it is recalled to his memory, with the same feelings. The word Task, the first time he hears it, is an unmeaning word, but it ceases to be indifferent to him the moment he hears it pronounced in a terrible voice. "Learn your task," and "fetch your book," recur to his recollection with indistinct feelings of pain; and hence, without further consideration, he will be disposed to dislike both books and tasks; but his feelings are the last things to be considered upon this occasion; the immediate business, is to teach him to read. A new era in his life now commences. The age of learning begins, and begins in sorrow. The consequences of a bad beginning, are proverbially ominous; but no omens can avert his fate, no omens can deter his tutor from the undertaking; the appointed moment is come; the boy is four years old, and he must learn to read. Some people, struck with a panic fear, lest their children should never learn to read and write, think that they cannot be in too great a hurry to teach them. Spelling-books, grammars, dictionaries, rods and masters, are collected; nothing is to be heard of in the house but tasks; nothing is to be seen but tears.

"No tears! no tasks! no masters! nothing upon compulsion!" say the opposite party in education. "Children must be left entirely at liberty; they will learn every thing better than you can teach them; their memory must not be overloaded with trash; their reason must be left to grow."

Their reason will never grow, unless it be exercised, is the reply; their memory must be stored whilst they are young, because, in youth, the memory is most tenacious. If you leave them at liberty for ever, they will never learn to spell; they will never learn Latin; they will never learn Latin grammar; yet, they must learn Latin grammar, and a number of other disagreeable things; therefore, we must give them tasks and task-masters.

In all these assertions, perhaps, we shall find a mixture of truth and errour; therefore, we had better be governed by neither party, but listen to both, and examine arguments unawed by authority. And first, as to the panic fear, which, though no argument, is a most powerful motive. We see but few examples of children so extremely stupid as not to have been able to learn to read and write between the years of three and thirteen; but we see many whose temper and whose understanding have been materially injured by premature or injudicious instruction; we see many who are disgusted, perhaps irrecoverably, with literature, whilst they are fluently reading books which they cannot comprehend, or learning words by rote, to which they affix no ideas. It is scarcely worth while to speak of the vain ambition of those who long only to have it said, that their children read sooner than those of their neighbours do; for, supposing their utmost wish to be gratified, that their son could read before the age when children commonly articulate, still the triumph must be of short duration, the fame confined to a small circle of "foes and friends," and, probably, in a few years, the memory of the phenomenon would remain only with his doting grandmother. Surely, it is the use which children make of their acquirements which is of consequence, not the possessing them a few years sooner or later. A man, who, during his whole life, could never write any thing that was worth reading, would find it but poor consolation for himself, his friends, or the public, to reflect, that he had been in joining-hand before he was five years old.

As it is usually managed, it is a dreadful task indeed to learn, and, if possible, a more dreadful task to teach to read. With the help of counters, and coaxing, and gingerbread, or by dint of reiterated pain and terror, the names of the four-and-twenty letters of the alphabet, are, perhaps, in the course of some weeks, firmly fixed in the pupil's memory. So much the worse; all these names will disturb him, if he have common sense, and at every step must stop his progress. To begin with the vowels: each of these have several different sounds, and, consequently, ought to have several names, or different signs, to distinguish them in different circumstances. In the first lesson of the spelling book, the child begins with a-b, makes ab; b-a makes ba. The inference, if any general inference can be drawn from this lesson, is, that when *a* comes before *b*, it has one sound, and after *b*, it has another sound; but this is contradicted by and by, and it appears that *a* after *b*, has various sounds, as in *ball*, in *bat*, in *bare*. The letter *i* in *fire*, is *i*, as we call it in the alphabet, but in fir, it is changed; in *pin*, it is changed again; so that the child, being ordered to affix to the same sign a variety of sounds and names, and not knowing in what circumstances to obey, and in what to disregard the contradictory injunctions imposed upon him, he pronounces sounds at hazard, and adheres positively to the last ruled case, or maintains an apparently sullen, or truly philosophic and sceptical silence. Must *e* in *pen*, and *e* in *where*, and *e* in *verse*, and *e* in *fear*, all be called *e* alike? The child is patted on the head for reading *u* as it ought to be pronounced in *future*; but if, remembering this encouragement, the pupil should venture to pronounce *u* in *gun*, and *bun*, in the same manner, he will, inevitably, be disgraced. Pain and shame, impress precepts upon the mind: the child, therefore, is intent upon remembering the new sound of *u* in *bun*; but when he comes to *busy*, and *burial*, and *prudence*, his last precedent will lead him fatally astray, and he will again be called a *dunce*. O, in the exclamation *Oh!* is happily called by its alphabetical name; but in *to*, we can hardly know it again, and in *morning* and *wonder*, it has a third and a fourth additional sound. The amphibious letter *y*, which is either a vowel or a consonant, has one sound in one character, and two sounds in the other; as a consonant, it is pronounced as in *yesterday*; in *try*, it is sounded as *i*; in *any*, and in the termination of many other words, it is sounded like *e*. Must a child know all this by intuition, or must it be whipt into him? But he must know a great deal more, before he can read the most common words. What length of time should we allow him for learning, when *c* is to be sounded like *k*, and when like *s*? and how much longer time shall we add for learning, when *s* shall be pronounced *sh*, as in *sure*, or *z*, as in *has*; the sound of which last letter *z*, he cannot, by any conjuration, obtain from the name *zed*, the only name by which he has been taught to call it? How much time shall we allow a patient tutor for teaching a docile pupil, when *g* is to be sounded soft, and when hard? There are many carefully worded rules in the spelling-books, specifying before what letters, and in what situations, *g* shall vary in sound; but, unfortunately, these rules are difficult to be learned by heart, and still more difficult to understand. These laws, however positive, are not found to be of universal application, or at least, a child has not always wit or time to apply them upon the spur of the occasion. In coming to the words *ingenious gentleman, get a good grammar,* he may be puzzled by the nice distinctions he is to make in pronunciation in cases apparently similar; but he has not yet become acquainted with all the powers of this privileged letter: in company with *h,* it assumes the character of *f,* as in *tough;* another time he meets it, perhaps, in the same company, in the same place, and, as nearly as possible, in the same circumstances, as in the word *though;* but now *g* is to become a silent letter, and is to pass incognito, and the child will commit an unpardonable errour, if he claimed the incognito as his late acquaintance *f.* Still, all these are slight difficulties; a moment's reflection must convince us, that by teaching the common names of every consonant in the alphabet, we prepare a child for misery, when he begins to spell or read. A consonant, as sayeth the spelling-book, is a letter which cannot be pronounced without a vowel before or after it: for this reason, *B,* is called *be,* and *L, el;* but why the vowel should come first in the one case, or last in the second, we are not informed; nor are we told why the names of some letters have no resemblance whatever to their sounds, either with a vowel before or after them. Suppose, that after having learned the alphabet, a child was to read the words

> *Here is some apple-pye.*
> He would pronounce the letters thus:
> *Acheare ies esoeme apepeele pewie.*

With this pronunciation the child would never decipher these simple words. It will be answered, perhaps, that no child is expected to read as soon as he has learnt his alphabet: a long initiation of monosyllabic, dissyllabic, trissyllabic, and polysyllabic words is previously to be submitted to; nor, after this inauguration, are the novices capable of performing with propriety the ceremony of reading whole words and sentences. By a different method of teaching, all this waste of labour and of time, all this confusion of rules and exceptions, and all the consequent confusion in the understanding of the pupil, may be avoided.

In teaching a child to read, every letter should have a precise single sound annexed to its figure; this should never vary. Where two consonants are joined together, so as to have but one sound, as ph, sh, &c. the two letters should be coupled together by a distinct invariable mark. Letters that are silent should be marked in such a manner as to point out to the child that they are not to be sounded. Upon these simple rules our method of teaching to read has been founded. The signs or marks, by which these distinctions are to be effected, are arbitrary, and may be varied as the teacher chooses; the addition of a single point above or below the common letters is employed to distinguish the different sounds that are given to the same letter, and a mark underneath such letters as are to be omitted, is the only apparatus necessary. These marks were employed by the author in 1776, before he had seen Sheridan's, or any similar dictionary; he has found that they do not confuse children as much as figures, because when dots are used to distinguish sounds, there is only a change of place, and no change of form: but any person that chooses it, may substitute figures instead of dots. It should, however, be remembered, that children must learn to distinguish the figures before they can be useful in discriminating the words.

All these sounds, and each of the characters which denote them, should be distinctly known by a child before we begin to teach him to read. And here at the first step we must entreat the teacher to have patience; to fix firmly in her mind, we say *her* mind, because we address ourselves to mothers; that it is immaterial whether a child learns this alphabet in six weeks or in six months; at all events, let it not be inculcated with restraint, or made tiresome, lest it should retard the whole future progress of the pupil. We do not mean to recommend the custom of teaching in play, but surely a cheerful countenance is not incompatible with application.

The three sounds of the letter (a) should first be taught; they may be learned by the dullest child in a week, if the letters are shown to him for a minute or two, twice a day. Proper moments should be chosen when the child is not intent upon any thing else; when other children have appeared to be amused with reading; when the pupil himself appears anxious to be instructed. As soon as he is acquainted with the sounds of (*a*) and with their distinguishing marks, each of these sounds should be formed into syllables, with each of the consonants; but we should never name the consonants by their usual names; if it be required to point them out by sounds, let them resemble the real sounds or powers of the consonants; but in fact it will never be *necessary* to name the consonants separately, till their powers, in combination with the different vowels, be distinctly acquired. It will then be time enough to teach the common names of the letters. To a person unacquainted with the principles upon which this mode of teaching is founded, it must appear strange, that a child should be able to read before he knows the names of his letters; but it has been ascertained, that the names of the letters are an incumbrance in teaching a child to read.

Vowels. Sounded as in	Dipthongs. Sounded as in	Consonants & double Consonants.
a — fate	ea — ocean	c as in cap
à — fat		ç — city
á — fall	ew — few	ch — child
e — mere		ch — machine
è — met	ia — filial	g — got
e — her		ĝ — age
è — where	ie — Daniel	ng — long
i — fine		ing — thing
ï — in	io — minion	le — able
i — bird		re — acre
ī — machine	oi — voice	ph — physic
o — throne		s — has
ò — on	ou — found	sh — she
o — love		sion — fusion
o — move	ow — now	th — the
u — pure		ti — christian
ü — busy	ua — asuage	tion — nation
u — sun		wh — who
u — full	ui — languid	ough — tough
y — by		
y — ably	oy — joy	

Consonants.

ba ca da fa ga ha ja ka la ma

na pa qua ra sa ta va wa ya za

(˛) This mark under a Letter shews that it is not to be pronounced, as eight in which igh are not sounded.

In the quotation from Mrs. Barbauld, at the bottom of the alphabetical tables, there is a stroke between the letters *b* and *r* in *February*, and between *t* and *h*, in *there*, to show that these letters are to be sounded together, so as to make one sound. The same is to be observed as to (*ng*) in the word *long*, and also as to the syllable *ing*, which, in the table No. 4, column 4, is directed to be taught as one sound. The mark (.) of obliteration, is put under (*y*) in the word *days*, under *e* final in *there*, and also under one of the *l*'s and the (*w*) in *yellow*, to show that these letters are not to be pronounced. The exceptions to this scheme of articulation are very few; such as occur, are marked, with the number employed in Walker's dictionary, to denote the exception, to which excellent work, the teacher will, of course, refer.

Parents, at the first sight of this new alphabet, will perhaps tremble lest they should be obliged to learn the whole of it before they begin to teach their children: but they may calm their apprehensions, for they need only point out the letters in succession to the child, and sound them as they are sounded in the words annexed to the letters in the table, and the child will soon, by repetition, render the marks of the respective letters familiar to the teacher. We have never found any body complain of difficulty, who has gone on from letter to letter along with the child who was taught.

As soon as our pupil knows the different sounds of (*a*) combined in succession with all the consonants, we may teach him the rest of the vowels joined with all the consonants, which will be a short and easy work. Our readers need not be alarmed at the apparent slowness of this method: six months, at the rate of four or five minutes each day, will render all these combinations perfectly familiar. One of Mrs. Barbauld's lessons for young children, carefully marked in the same manner as the alphabet, should, when they are well acquainted with the sounds of each of the vowels with each of the consonants, be put into our pupil's hands. [7]

The sound of three or four letters together, will immediately become familiar to him; and when any of the less common sounds of the vowels, such as are contained in the second table, and the terminating sounds, *tion*, *ly*, &c. occur, they should be read to the child, and should be added to what he has got by rote from time to time. When all these marks and their corresponding sounds are learnt, the primer should be abandoned, and from that time the child will be able to read slowly the most difficult words in the language. We must observe, that the mark of obliteration is of the greatest service; it is a clue to the whole labyrinth of intricate and uncouth orthography. The word though, by the obliteration of three letters, may be as easily read as *the* or *that*.

It should be observed that all people, before they can read fluently, have acquired a knowledge of the general appearance of most of the words in the language, independently of the syllables of which they are composed. Seven children in the author's family were taught to read in this manner, and three in the common method; the difference of time, labour, and sorrow, between the two modes of learning, appeared so clearly, that we can speak with confidence upon the subject. We think that nine-tenths of the labour and disgust of learning to read, may be saved by this method; and that instead of frowns and tears, the usual harbingers of learning, cheerfulness and smiles may initiate willing pupils in the most difficult of all human attainments.

A and H, at four and five years old, after they had learned the alphabet, without having ever combined the letters into syllables, were set to read one of Mrs. Barbauld's little books. After being employed two or three minutes every day, for a fortnight, in making out the words of this book, a paper with a few raisins well concealed in its folds, was given to each of them, with these words printed on the outside of it, marked according to our alphabet:

"Open this, and eat what you find in it."

In twenty minutes, they read it distinctly without any assistance.

The step from reading with these marks, to reading without them, will be found very easy. Nothing more is necessary, than to give children the same books, without marks, which they can read fluently with them.

Spelling comes next to reading. New trials for the temper; new perils for the understanding; positive rules and arbitrary exceptions; endless examples and contradictions; till at length, out of all patience with the stupid docility of his pupil, the tutor perceives the absolute necessity of making him get by heart, with all convenient speed, every word in the language. The formidable columns in dread succession arise a host of foes; two columns a day, at least, may be conquered. Months and years are devoted to the undertaking; but after going through a whole spelling-book, perhaps a whole dictionary, till we come triumphantly to spell *Zeugma*, we have forgotten to spell *Abbot*, and we must begin again with *Abasement*. Merely the learning to spell so many unconnected words, without any assistance from reason or analogy, is nothing, compared with the difficulty of learning the explanation of them by rote, and the still greater difficulty of understanding the meaning of the explanation. When a child has got by rote,

> "Midnight, the *depth* of night;"
> "Metaphysics, the science which treats of immaterial
> beings, and of forms in general abstracted from matter;"

has he acquired any distinct ideas, either of midnight or of metaphysics? If a boy had eaten rice pudding, till he fancied himself tolerably well acquainted with rice, would he find his knowledge much improved, by learning from his spelling-book, the words

> "Rice, a foreign esculent grain?"

Yet we are surprised to discover, that men have so few accurate ideas, and that so many learned disputes originate in a confused or improper use of words.

"All this is very true," says a candid schoolmaster; "we see the evil, but we cannot new-model the language, or write a perfect philosophical dictionary; and, in the mean time, we are bound to teach children to spell, which we do with the less reluctance, because, though we allow that it is an arduous task, we have found from experience, that it can be accomplished, and that the understandings of many of our pupils, survive all the perils to which you think them exposed during the operation."

The understandings may, and do, survive the operation; but why should they be put in unnecessary danger? and why should we early disgust children with literature, by the pain and difficulty their first lessons? We are convinced, that the business of learning to spell, is made much more laborious to children than it need to be: it may be useful to give them five or six words every day to learn by heart, but more only loads their memory; and we should, at first, select words of which they know the meaning, and which occur most frequently in reading or conversation. The alphabetical list of words in a spelling-book, contains many which are not in common use, and the pupil forgets these as fast as he learns them. We have found it entertaining to children, to ask them to spell any short sentence as it has been accidentally spoken. "Put this book on that table." Ask a child how he would spell these words, if he were obliged to write them down, and you introduce into his mind the idea that he must learn to spell, before he can make his words and thoughts understood in writing. It is a good way to make children write down a few words of their own selection every day, and correct the spelling; and also after they have been reading, whilst the words are yet fresh in their memory, we may ask them to spell some of the words which they have just seen. By these means, and by repeating, at different times in the day, those words which are most frequently wanted, his vocabulary will be pretty well stocked without its having cost him many tears. We should observe that children learn to spell more by the eye than by the ear, and that the more they read and write, the more likely they will be to remember the combination of letters in words which they have continually before their eyes, or which they feel it necessary to represent to others. When young people begin to write, they first feel the use of spelling, and it is then that they will learn it with most ease and precision. Then the greatest care should be taken to look over their writing, and to make them correct every word in which they have made a mistake; because, bad habits of spelling, once contracted, can scarcely be cured: the understanding has nothing to do with the business, and when the memory is puzzled between the rules of spelling right, and the habits of spelling wrong, it becomes a misfortune to the pupil to write even a common letter. The shame which is annexed to bad spelling, excites young people's attention, as soon as they are able to understand, that it is considered as a mark of ignorance and ill breeding. We have often observed, that children listen with anxiety to the remarks that are made upon this subject in their presence, especially when the letters or notes of *grown up people*, are criticised.

Some time ago, a lady, who was reading a newspaper, met with the story of an ignorant magistrate, who gave for his toast, at a public dinner, the two K's, for the King and Constitution. "How very much ashamed the man must have felt, when all the people laughed at him for his mistake! they must all have seen that he did not know how to spell; and what a disgrace for a magistrate too!" said a boy who heard the anecdote. It made a serious impression upon him. A few months afterwards, he was employed by his father in an occupation which was extremely agreeable to him, but in which he continually felt the necessity of spelling correctly. He was employed to send messages by a telegraph; these messages he was obliged to write down hastily, in little journals kept for the purpose; and as these were seen by several people, when the business of the day came to be reviewed, the boy had a considerable motive for orthographical exactness. He became extremely desirous to teach himself, and consequently his success was from that moment certain. As to the rest, we refer to Lady Carlisle's comprehensive maxim, "Spell well if you can."

It is undoubtedly of consequence, to teach the rudiments of literary education early, to get over the first difficulties of reading, writing, and spelling; but much of the anxiety and bustle, and labour of teaching these things, may be advantageously spared. If more attention were turned to the general cultivation of the understanding, and if more pains were taken to make literature agreeable to children, there would be found less difficulty to excite them to mental exertion, or to induce the habits of persevering application.

When we speak of rendering literature agreeable to children, and of the danger of associating pain with the sight of a book, or with the sound of the word *task*, we should at the same time avoid the errour of those who, in their first lessons, accustom their pupils to so much amusement, that they cannot help afterwards feeling disgusted with the sobriety of instruction. It has been the fashion of late to attempt teaching every thing to children in play, and ingenious people have contrived to insinuate much useful knowledge without betraying the design to instruct; but this system cannot be pursued beyond certain bounds without many inconveniences. The habit of being amused not only increases the desire for amusement, but it lessens even the relish for pleasure; so that the mind becomes passive and indolent, and a course of perpetually increasing stimulus is necessary to awaken attention. When dissipated habits are required, the pupil loses power over his own mind, and, instead of vigorous voluntary exertion, which he should be able to command, he shows that wayward imbecility, which can think successfully only by fits and starts: this paralytic state of mind has been found to be one of the greatest calamities attendant on what is called genius; and injudicious education creates or increases this disease. Let us not therefore humour children in this capricious temper, especially if they have quick abilities: let us give rewards proportioned to their exertions with uniform justice, but let us not grant bounties in education, which, however they may appear to succeed in effecting partial and temporary purposes, are not calculated to ensure any consequences permanently beneficial. The truth is, that useful knowledge cannot be obtained without labour; that attention long continued is laborious, but that without this labour nothing excellent can be accomplished. Excite a child to attend in earnest for a short time, his mind will be less fatigued, and his understanding more improved, than if he had exerted but half the energy twice as long: the degree of pain which he may have felt will be amply and properly compensated by his success; this will not be an arbitrary, variable reward, but one within his own power, and that can be ascertained by his own feelings. Here is no deceit practised, no illusion; the same course of conduct may be regularly pursued through the whole of his education, and his confidence in his tutor will progressively increase. On the contrary, if, to entice him to enter the paths of knowledge, we strew them with flowers, how will he feel when he must force his way through thorns and briars!

There is a material difference between teaching children in play, and making learning a task; in the one case we associate factitious pleasure, in the other factitious pain, with the object: both produce pernicious effects upon the temper, and retard the natural progress of the understanding. The advocates in favour of "scholastic badinage" have urged, that it excites an interest in the minds of children similar to that which makes them endure a considerable degree of labour in the pursuit of their amusements. Children, it is said, work hard at play, therefore we should let them play at work. Would not this produce effects the very reverse of what we desire? The whole question must at last depend upon the meaning of the word play: if by play be meant every thing that is not usually called a task, then undoubtedly much may be learned at play: if, on the contrary, we mean by the expression to describe that state of fidgeting idleness, or of boisterous activity, in which the intellectual powers are torpid, or stunned with unmeaning noise, the assertion contradicts itself. At play so defined, children can learn nothing but bodily activity; it is certainly true, that when children are interested about any thing, whether it be about what we call a trifle, or a matter of consequence, they will exert themselves in order to succeed; but from the moment the attention is fixed, no matter on what, children are no longer at idle play, they are at active work.

S— —, a little boy of nine years old, was standing without any book in his hand, and seemingly idle; he was amusing himself with looking at what he called a rainbow upon the floor; he begged his sister M— —to look at it; then he said he wondered what could make it; how it came there. The sun shone bright through the window; the boy moved several things in the room, so as to place them sometimes between the light and the colours which he saw upon the floor, and sometimes in a corner of the room where the sun did not shine. As he moved the things, he said, "This is not it;" "nor this;" "this has'n't any thing to do with it." At last he found, that when he moved a tumbler of water out of the place where it stood, his rainbow vanished. Some violets were in the tumbler; S— — thought they might be the cause of the colours which he saw upon the floor, or, as he expressed it, "Perhaps these may be the thing." He took the violets out of the water; the colours remained upon the floor. He then thought that "it might be the water." He emptied the glass; the colours remained, but they were fainter. S— — immediately observed, that it was the water and glass together that made the rainbow. "But," said he, "there is no glass in the sky, yet there is a rainbow, so that I think the water alone would do, if we could but hold it together without the glass. Oh I know how I can manage." He poured the water slowly out of the tumbler into a basin, which he placed where the sun shone, and he saw the colours on the floor twinkling behind the water as it fell: this delighted him much; but he asked why it would not do when the sun did not shine. The sun went behind a cloud whilst he was trying his experiments: "There was light," said he, "though there was no sunshine." He then said he thought that the different thickness of the glass was the cause of the variety of colours: afterwards he said he thought that the clearness or muddiness of the different drops of water was the cause of the different colours.

A rigid preceptor, who thinks that every boy must be idle who has not a Latin book constantly in his hand, would perhaps have reprimanded S— — for wasting his time *at play*, and would have summoned him from his rainbow to his *task*; but it is very obvious to any person free from prejudices, that this child was not idle whilst he was meditating upon the rainbow on the floor; his attention was fixed; he was reasoning; he was trying experiments. We may call this *play* if we please, and we may say that Descartes was at play, when he first verified Antonio de Dominis bishop of Spalatro's treatise of the rainbow, by an experiment with a glass Globe: [8] and we may say that Buffon was idle, when his pleased attention was first caught with a landscape of green shadows, when one evening at sunset he first observed that the shadows of trees, which fell upon a white wall, were green. He was first delighted with the exact representation of a green arbour, which seemed as if it had been newly painted on the wall. Certainly the boy with his rainbow on the floor was as much amused as the philosopher with his coloured shadows; and, however high sounding the name of Antonio de Dominis, bishop of Spalatro, it does not alter the business in the least; he could have exerted only his *utmost attention* upon the theory of the rainbow, and the child did the same. We do not mean to compare the powers of reasoning, or the abilities of the child and the philosopher; we would only show that the same species of attention was exerted by both.

To fix the attention of children, or, in other words, to interest them about those subjects to which we wish them to apply, must be our first object in the early cultivation of the understanding. This we shall not find a difficult undertaking if we have no false associations, no painful recollections to contend with. We can connect any species of knowledge with those occupations which are immediately agreeable to young people: for instance, if a child is building a house, we may take that opportunity to teach him how bricks are made, how the arches over doors and windows are made, the nature of the keystone and butments of an arch, the manner in which all the different parts of the roof of a house are put together, &c.; whilst he is learning all this he is eagerly and seriously attentive, and we educate his understanding in the best possible method. But if, mistaking the application of the principle, that literature should be made agreeable to children, we should entice a child to learn his letters by a promise of a gilt coach, or by telling him that he would be the cleverest boy in the world if he could but learn the letter *A*, we use false and foolish motives; we may possibly, by such means, effect the immediate purpose, but we shall assuredly have reason to repent of such imprudent deceit. If the child reasons at all, he will be content after his first lesson with being "the cleverest boy in the world," and he will not, on a future occasion, hazard his fame, having much to lose, and nothing to gain; besides, he is now master of a gilt coach, and some new and larger reward must be proffered to excite his industry. Besides the disadvantage of early exhausting our stock of incitements, it is dangerous in teaching to humour pupils with a variety of objects by way of relieving their attention. The pleasure of *thinking*, and much of the profit, must frequently depend upon our preserving the greatest possible connection between our ideas. Those who allow themselves to start from one object to another, acquire such dissipated habits of mind, that they cannot, without extreme difficulty and reluctance, follow any connected train of thought. You cannot teach those who will not follow the chain of your reasons; upon the connection of our ideas, useful memory and reasoning must depend. We will give you an instance: arithmetic is one of the first things that we attempt to teach children. In the following dialogue, which passed between a boy of five years old and his father, we may observe that, till the child followed his father's train of ideas, he could not be taught.

Father. S— —, how many can you take from one?

S— —. None.

Father. None! Think; can you take nothing from one?

S— —. None, except that one.

Father. Except! Then you can take one from one?

S— —. Yes, *that one.*

Father. How many then can you take from one?

S— —. One.

Father. Very true; but now, can you take two from one?

S— —. Yes, if they were figures I could, with a rubber-out. (This child had frequently sums written for him with a black lead pencil, and he used to rub out his figures when they were wrong with Indian rubber, which he had heard called *rubber-out.*)

Father. Yes, you could; but now we will not talk of figures, we will talk of things. There may be one horse or two horses, or one man or two men.

S— —. Yes, or one coat or two coats.

Father. Yes, or one thing or two things, no matter what they are. Now, could you take two things from one thing?

S— —. Yes, if there were three things I could take away two things, and leave one.

His Father took up a cake from the tea-table.

Father. Could I take two cakes from this one cake?

S— —. You could take two pieces.

His Father divided the cake into halves, and held up each half so that the child might distinctly see them.

Father. What would you call these two pieces?

S— —. Two cakes.

Father. No, not two cakes.

S— —. Two biscuits.

Father. Holding up a whole biscuit: What is this?

S — —. A thing to eat.

Father. Yes, but what would you call it?

S — —. A biscuit.

His Father broke it into halves, and showed one half.

Father. What would you call this?

S — —. was silent, and his sister was applied to, who answered, "Half a biscuit."

Father. Very well; that's all at present.

The father prudently stopped here, that he might not confuse his pupil's understanding. Those only who have attempted to teach children can conceive how extremely difficult it is to fix their attention, or to make them seize the connection of ideas, which it appears to us almost impossible to miss. Children are well occupied in examining external objects, but they must also attend to words as well as things. One of the great difficulties in early instruction arises from the want of words: the pupil very often has acquired the necessary ideas, but they are not associated in his mind with the words which his tutor uses; these words are then to him mere sounds, which suggest no correspondent thoughts. Words, as M. Condillac well observes, [9] are essential to our acquisition of knowledge; they are the medium through which one set of beings can convey the result of their experiments and observations to another; they are, in all mental processes, the algebraic signs which assist us in solving the most difficult problems. What agony does a foreigner, knowing himself to be a man of sense, appear to suffer, when, for want of language, he cannot in conversation communicate his knowledge, explain his reasons, enforce his arguments, or make his wit intelligible? In vain he has recourse to the language of action. The language of action, or, as Bacon calls it, of "transitory hieroglyphic," is expressive, but inadequate. As new ideas are collected in the mind, new signs are wanted, and the progress of the understanding would be early and fatally impeded by the want of language. M. de la Condamine tells us that there is a nation who have no sign to express the number three but this word, *poellartarrorincourac*. These people having begun, as Condillac observes, in such an incommodious manner, it is not surprising that they have not advanced further in their knowledge of arithmetic: they have got no further than the number three; their knowledge of arithmetic stops for ever at *poellartarrorincourac*. But even this cumbersome sign is better than none. Those who have the misfortune to be born deaf and dumb, continue for ever in intellectual imbecility. There is an account in the Memoires de l'Academie Royale, p. xxii-xxiii, 1703, of a young man born deaf and dumb,

[10] who recovered his hearing at the age of four-and-twenty, and who, after employing himself in repeating low to himself the words which he heard others pronounce, at length broke silence in company, and declared that he could talk. His conversation was but imperfect; he was examined by several able theologians, who chiefly questioned him on his ideas of God, the soul, and the morality or immorality of actions. It appeared that he had not thought upon any of these subjects; he did not distinctly know what was meant by death, and he never thought of it. He seemed to pass a merely animal life, occupied with sensible, present objects, and with the few ideas which he received by his sense of sight; nor did he seem to have gained as much knowledge as he might have done, by the comparison of these ideas; yet it is said that he did not appear naturally deficient in understanding.

Peter, the wild boy, who is mentioned in Lord Monboddo's Origin of Language, [11] had all his senses in remarkable perfection. He lived at a farm house within half a mile of us in Hertfordshire for some years, and we had frequent opportunities of trying experiments upon him. He could articulate imperfectly a few words, in particular, *King George*, which words he always accompanied with an imitation of the bells, which rang at the coronation of George the Second; he could in a rude manner imitate two or three common tunes, but without words. Though his head, as Mr. Wedgewood and many others had remarked, resembled that of Socrates, he was an idiot: he had acquired a few automatic habits of rationality and industry, but he could never be made to work at any continued occupation: he would shut the door of the farm-yard five hundred times a day, but he would not reap or make hay. Drawing water from a neighbouring river was the only domestic business which he regularly pursued. In 1779 we visited him, and tried the following experiment. He was attended to the river by a person who emptied his buckets repeatedly after Peter had repeatedly filled them. A shilling was put before his face into one of the buckets when it was empty; he took no notice of it, but filled it with water and carried it homeward: his buckets were taken from him before he reached the house and emptied on the ground; the shilling, which had fallen out, was again shown to him, and put into the bucket. Peter returned to the river again, filled his bucket and went home; and when the bucket was emptied by the maid at the house where he lived, he took the shilling and laid it in a place where he was accustomed to deposit the presents that were made to him by curious strangers, and whence the farmer's wife collected the price of his daily exhibition. It appeared that this savage could not be taught to reason for want of language.

Rousseau declaims with eloquence, and often with justice, against what he calls a knowledge of words. Words without correspondent ideas, are worse than useless; they are counterfeit coin, which imposes upon the ignorant and unwary; but words, which really represent ideas, are not only of current use, but of sterling value; they not only show our present store, but they increase our wealth, by keeping it in continual circulation; both the principal and the interest increase together. The importance of signs and words, in our reasonings, has been eloquently explained, since the time of Condillac, by Stewart. We must use the ideas of these excellent writers, because they are just and applicable to the art of education; but whilst we use, it is with proper acknowledgments that we borrow, what we shall never be able to return.

It is a nice and difficult thing in education, to proportion a child's vocabulary exactly to his knowledge, dispositions, or conformation; our management must vary; some will acquire words too quickly, others too slowly. A child who has great facility in pronouncing sounds, will, for that reason, quickly acquire a number of words, whilst those whose organs of speech are not so happily formed, will from that cause alone, be ready in forming a copious vocabulary. Children who have many companions, or who live with people who converse a great deal, have more motive, both from sympathy and emulation, to acquire a variety of words, than those who live with silent people, and who have few companions of their own age. All these circumstances should be considered by parents, before they form their judgment of a child's capacity from his volubility or his taciturnity. Volubility can easily be checked by simply ceasing to attend to it, and taciturnity may be vanquished by the encouragements of praise and affection: we should neither be alarmed at one disposition nor at the other, but steadily pursue the system of conduct which will be most advantageous to both. When a prattling, vivacious child, pours forth a multiplicity of words without understanding their meaning, we may sometimes beg to have an explanation of a few of them, and the child will then be obliged to think, which will prevent him from talking nonsense another time. When a thoughtful boy, who is in the habit of observing every object he sees, is at a loss for words to express his ideas, his countenance usually shows to those who can read the countenance of children, that he is not stupid; therefore, we need not urge him to talk, but assist him judiciously with words "in his utmost need:" at the same time we should observe carefully, whether he grows lazy when we assist him; if his stock of words does not increase in proportion to the assistance we give, we should then stimulate him to exertion, or else he will become habitually indolent in expressing his ideas; though he may *think* in a language of his own, he will not be able to understand our language when we attempt to teach him: this would be a source of daily misery to both parties.

When children begin to read, they seem suddenly to acquire a great variety of words: we should carefully examine whether they annex the proper meaning to these which are so rapidly collected. Instead of giving them lessons and tasks to get by rote, we should cautiously watch over every new phrase and every new word which they learn from books. There are but few books so written that young children can comprehend a single sentence in them without much explanation. It is tiresome to those who hear them read to explain every word; it is not only tiresome, but difficult; besides, the progress of the pupil seems to be retarded; the grand business of reading, of getting through the book, is impeded; and the tutor, more impatient than his pupil, says, "Read on, I cannot stop to explain *that* to you now. You will understand the meaning of the sentence if you will read to the end of the page. You have not read three lines this half hour; we shall never get on at this rate."

A certain dame at a country school, who had never been able to compass the word Nebuchadnezzar, used to desire her pupils to "call it Nazareth, and let it pass."

If they be obliged to pass over words without comprehending them in books, they will probably do the same in conversation; and the difficulty of teaching such pupils, and of understanding what they say, will be equally increased. At the hazard of being tedious, we must dwell a little longer upon this subject, because much of the future capacity of children seems to depend upon the manner in which they first acquire language. If their language be confused, so will be their thoughts; and they will not be able to reason, to invent, or to write, with more precision and accuracy than they speak. The first words that children learn are the names of things; these are easily associated with the objects themselves, and there is little danger of mistake or confusion. We will not enter into the grammatical dispute concerning the right of precedency, amongst pronoun substantives and verbs; we do not know which came first into the mind of man; perhaps, in different minds, and in different circumstances, the precedency must have varied; but this seems to be of little consequence; children see actions performed, and they act themselves; when they want to express their remembrance of these actions, they make use of the sort of words which we call verbs. Let these words be strictly associated with the ideas which they mean to express, and no matter whether children know any thing about the disputes of grammarians, they will understand rational grammar in due time, simply by reflecting upon their own minds. This we shall explain more fully when we speak hereafter of grammar; we just mention the subject here, to warn preceptors against puzzling their pupils too early with grammatical subtleties.

If any person unused to mechanics was to read Dr. Desagulier's description of the manner in which a man walks, the number of a-b-c's, and the travels of the centre of gravity, it would so amaze and confound him, that he would scarcely believe he could ever again perform such a tremendous operation as that of walking. Children, if they were early to hear grammarians talk of the parts of speech, and of syntax, would conclude, that to speak must be one of the most difficult arts in the world; but children, who are not usually so unfortunate as to have grammarians for their preceptors, when they first begin to speak, acquire language, without being aware of the difficulties which would appear so formidable in theory. A child points to, or touches, the table, and when the word table is repeated, at the same instant he learns the name of the thing. The facility with which a number of names are thus learned in infancy is surprising; but we must not imagine that the child, in learning these names, has acquired much knowledge; he has prepared himself to be taught, but he has not yet learnt any thing accurately. When a child sees a guinea and a shilling, and smiling says, "That's a guinea, mama! and that's a shilling!" the mother is pleased and surprised by her son's intelligence, and she gives him credit for more than he really possesses. We have associated with the words guinea and shilling a number of ideas, and when we hear the same words pronounced by a young child, we perhaps have some confused belief that he has acquired the same ideas that we have; hence we are pleased with the mere sound of words of high import from infantine lips.

Children who are delighted in their turn by the expression of pleasure in the countenance of others, repeat the things which they perceive have pleased; and thus their education is begun by those who first smile upon them, and listen to them when they attempt to speak. They who applaud children for knowing the names of things, induce them quickly to learn a number of names by rote; as long as they learn the names of external objects only, which they can see, and smell, and touch, all is well, the names will convey distinct ideas of certain perceptions. A child who learns the name of a taste, or of a colour, who learns that the taste of sugar is called sweet, and that the colour of a red rose is called red, has learned distinct words to express certain perceptions: and we can at any future time recall to his mind the memory of those perceptions by means of their names, and he understands us as well as the most learned philosopher. But, suppose that a boy had learned only the name of gold; that when different metals were shown to him, he could put his finger upon gold, and say, "That is gold;" yet this boy does not know all the properties of gold; he does not know in what it differs from other metals; to what uses it is applied in arts, manufactures, and commerce; the name of gold, in his mind, represents nothing more than a substance of a bright yellow colour, upon which people, he does not precisely know why, set a great value. Now, it is very possible, that a child might, on the contrary, learn all the properties, and the various uses of gold, without having learned its name; his ideas of this metal would be perfectly distinct; but whenever he wished to speak of gold, he would be obliged to use a vast deal of circumlocution to make himself understood; and if he were to enumerate all the properties of the metal every time he wanted to recal the general idea, his conversation would be intolerably tedious to others, and to himself this useless repetition must be extremely laborious. He would certainly be glad to learn that single word *gold*, which would save him so much trouble; his understanding would appear suddenly to have improved, simply from his having acquired a proper sign to represent his ideas. The boy who had learnt the name, without knowing any of the properties of gold, would also appear comparatively ignorant, as soon as it is discovered that he has few ideas annexed to the word. It is, perhaps, for this reason, that some children seem suddenly to shine out with knowledge, which no one suspected they possessed; whilst others, who had appeared to be very quick and clever, come to a dead stop in their education, and appear to be blighted by some unknown cause. The children who suddenly shine out, are those who had acquired a number of ideas, and who, the moment they acquire proper words, can communicate their thoughts to others. Those children who suddenly seem to lose their superiority, are those who had acquired a variety of words, but who had not annexed ideas to them. When their ignorance is detected, we not only despair of them, but they are apt to despair of themselves; they see their companions get before them, and they do not exactly perceive the cause of their sudden incapacity. Where we speak of sensible, visible, tangible objects, we can easily detect and remedy a child's ignorance. It is easy to discover whether he has or has not a complete notion of such a substance as gold; we can enumerate its properties, and readily point out in what his definition is defective. The substance can be easily produced for examination; most of its properties are obvious to the senses; we have nothing to do but to show them to the child, and to associate with each property its usual name; here there can be no danger of puzzling his understanding; but when we come to the explanation of words which do not represent external objects, we shall find the affair more difficult. We can make children understand the meaning of those words which are the names of simple feelings of the mind, such as surprise, joy, grief, pity; because we can either put our pupils in situations where they actually feel these sensations, and then we may associate the name with the feelings; or we may, by the example of other people, who actually suffer pain or enjoy pleasure, point out what we mean by the words joy and grief. But how shall we explain to our young pupils, a number of words which represent neither existing substances nor simple feelings, when we can neither recur to experiment nor to sympathy for assistance? How shall we explain, for instance, the words virtue, justice, benevolence, beauty, taste, &c.? To analyze our own ideas of these, is no easy task; to explain the process to a young child, is scarcely possible. Call upon any man, who has read and reflected, for a definition of virtue, the whole "theory of moral sentiments" rises, perhaps, to his view at once, in all its elegance; the paradoxical acumen of Mandeville, the perspicuous reasoning of Hume, the accurate metaphysics of Condillac, the persuasive eloquence of Stewart; all the various doctrines that have been supported concerning the foundation of morals, such as the fitness of things, the moral sense, the beauty of truth, utility, sympathy, common sense; all that has been said by ancient and modern philosophers, is recalled in transient perplexing succession to his memory. If such be the state of mind of the man who is to define, what must be the condition of the child who is to understand the definition? All that a prudent person will attempt, is to give instances of different virtues; but even these, it will be difficult properly to select for a child. General terms, whether in morals or in natural philosophy, should, we apprehend, be as much as possible avoided in early education. Some people may imagine that children have improved in virtue and wisdom, when they can talk fluently of justice, and charity, and humanity; when they can read with a good emphasis any didactic compositions in verse or prose. But let any person of sober, common sense, be allowed to cross-examine these proficients, and the pretended extent of their knowledge will shrink into a narrow compass; nor will their virtues, which have never seen service, be ready for action.

General terms are, as it were, but the indorsements upon the bundles of our ideas; they are useful to those who have collected a number of ideas, but utterly useless to those who have no collections ready for classification: nor should we be in a hurry to tie up the bundles, till we are sure that the collection is tolerably complete; the trouble, the difficulty, the shame of untying them late in life, is felt even by superior minds. "Sir," said Dr.

Johnson, "I don't like to have any of my opinions attacked. I have made up my faggot, and if you draw out one you weaken the whole bundle."

Preceptors sometimes explain general terms and abstract notions vaguely to their pupils, simply because they are ashamed to make that answer which every sensible person must frequently make to a child's inquiries, "I don't know." [12] Surely it is much better to say at once, "I cannot explain this to you," than to attempt an imperfect or sophistical reply. Fortunately for us, children, if they are not forced to attend to studies for which they have no taste, will not trouble us much with moral and metaphysical questions; their attention will be fully employed upon external objects; intent upon experiments, they will not be very inquisitive about theories. Let us then take care that their simple ideas be accurate, and when these are compounded, their complex notions, their principles, opinions, and tastes, will necessarily be just; their language will then be as accurate as their ideas are distinct; and hence they will be enabled to reason with precision, and to invent with facility. We may observe, that the great difficulty in reasoning is to fix steadily upon our terms; ideas can be readily compared, when the words by which we express them are defined; as in arithmetic and algebra, we can easily solve any problem, when we have precise signs for all the numbers and quantities which are to be considered.

It is not from idleness, it is not from stupidity, it is not from obstinacy, that children frequently show an indisposition to listen to those who attempt to explain things to them. The exertion of attention, which is frequently required from them, is too great for the patience of childhood: the words that are used are so inaccurate in their signification, that they convey to the mind sometimes one idea and sometimes another; we might as well require of them to cast up a sum right whilst we rubbed out and changed the figures every instant, as expect that they should seize a combination of ideas presented to them in variable words. Whoever expects to command the attention of an intelligent child, must be extremely careful in the use of words. If the pupil be paid for the labour of listening by the pleasure of understanding what is said, he will attend, whether it be to his playfellow, or to his tutor, to conversation, or to books. But if he has by fatal experience discovered, that, let him listen ever so intently, he cannot understand, he will spare himself the trouble of fruitless exertion; and, though he may put on a face of attention, his thoughts will wander far from his tutor and his tasks.

"It is impossible to fix the attention of children," exclaims the tutor; "when this boy attends he can do any thing, but he will not attend for a single instant."

Alas! it is in vain to say he *will not* attend; he *cannot*.

[7] Some of these lessons, and others by the authors, will shortly be printed, and marked according to this method.

[8] See Priestley's History of Vision, vol. i. p. 51.

[9] "Art de Penser."

[10] See Condillac's Art de Penser. In the chapter "on the use of signs," this young man is mentioned.

[11] Vol. II.

[12] Rousseau.

CHAPTER III
ON ATTENTION

Pere Bourgeois, one of the missionaries to China, attempted to preach a Chinese sermon to the Chinese. His own account of the business is the best we can give.

"They told me *Chou* signifies a book, so that I thought whenever the word *Chou* was pronounced, a book was the subject of discourse; not at all. Chou, the next time I heard it, I found signified *a tree*. Now I was to recollect Chou was a book, and a tree; but this amounted to nothing. Chou I found also expressed *great heats*. Chou is *to relate*. Chou is *the Aurora*. Chou means *to be accustomed*. Chou expresses the *loss of a wager*, &c. I should never have done were I to enumerate all its meanings******.

"I recited my sermon at least fifty times to my servant before I spoke it in public; and yet I am told, though he continually corrected me, that of the ten parts of the sermon (as the Chinese express themselves) they hardly understood three. Fortunately the Chinese are wonderfully patient."

Children are sometimes in the condition in which the Chinese found themselves at this learned missionary's sermon, and their patience deserves to be equally commended. The difficulty of understanding the Chinese Chou, strikes us immediately, and we sympathise with Pere Bourgeois's perplexity; yet, many words, which are in common use amongst us, may perhaps be as puzzling to children. *Block* (see Johnson's Dictionary) signifies *a heavy piece of timber, a mass of matter.* Block means *the wood on which hats are formed.* Block means *the wood on which criminals are beheaded.* Block is *a sea-term for pulley.* Block is *an obstruction, a stop*; and, finally, Block means *a blockhead.*

There are in our language, ten meanings for *sweet*, ten for *open*, twenty-two for *upon*, and sixty-three for *to fall*. Such are the defects of language! But, whatever they may be, we cannot hope immediately to see them reformed, because common consent, and universal custom, must combine to establish a new vocabulary. None but philosophers could invent, and none but philosophers would adopt, a philosophical language. The new philosophical language of chemistry was received at first with some reluctance, even by chemists, notwithstanding its obvious utility and elegance. Butter of antimony, and liver of sulphur, flowers of zinc, oil of vitriol, and spirit of sulphur by the bell, powder of algaroth, and salt of alembroth, may yet long retain their ancient titles amongst apothecaries. There does not exist in the mineral kingdom either butter or oil, or yet flowers; these treacherous names [13] are given to the most violent poisons, so that there is no analogy to guide the understanding or the memory: but Custom has a prescriptive right to talk nonsense. The barbarous enigmatical jargon of the ancient adepts continued for above a century to be the only chemical language of men of science, notwithstanding the prodigious labour to the memory, and confusion to the understanding, which it occasioned: they have but just now left off calling one of their vessels for distilling, a death's head, and another a helmet. Capricious analogy with difficulty yields to rational arrangement. If such has been the slow progress of a philosophical language amongst the learned, how can we expect to make a general, or even a partial reformation amongst the ignorant? And it may be asked, how can we in education attempt to teach in any but customary terms? There is no occasion to make any sudden or violent alteration in language; but a man who attempts to teach, will find it necessary to select his terms with care, to define them with accuracy, and to abide by them with steadiness; thus he will make a philosophical vocabulary for himself. Persons who want to puzzle and to deceive, always pursue a contrary practice; they use as great a variety of unmeaning, or of ambiguous words, as they possibly can. [14] That state juggler, Oliver Cromwell, excelled in this species of eloquence; his speeches are models in their kind. Count Cagliostro, and the Countess de la Motte, were not his superiors in the power of baffling the understanding. The ancient oracles, and the old books of judicial astrologers, and of alchymists, were contrived upon the same principles; in all these we are confounded by a multiplicity of words which convey a doubtful sense.

Children, who have not the habit of listening to words without understanding them, yawn and writhe with manifest symptoms of disgust, whenever they are compelled to hear sounds which convey no ideas to their minds. All supernumerary words should be avoided in cultivating the power of attention.

The common observation, that we can attend to but one thing at a time, should never be forgotten by those who expect to succeed in the art of teaching. In teaching new terms, or new ideas, we must not produce a number at once. It is prudent to consider, that the actual progress made in our business at one sitting is not of so much consequence, as the desire left in the pupil's mind to sit again. Now a child will be better pleased with himself, and with his tutor, if he acquire one distinct idea from a lesson, than if he retained a confused notion of twenty different things. Some people imagine, that as children appear averse to repetition, variety will amuse them. Variety, to a certain degree, certainly relieves the mind; but then the objects which are varied must not all be entirely new. Novelty and variety, joined, fatigue the mind. Either we remain passive at the show, or else we fatigue ourselves with ineffectual activity.

A few years ago, a gentleman [15] brought two Eskimaux to London—he wished to amuse, and at the same time to astonish, them with the great magnificence of the metropolis. For this purpose, after having equipped them like English gentlemen, he took them out one morning to walk through the streets of London. They walked for several hours in silence; they expressed neither pleasure nor admiration at any thing which they saw. When their walk was ended, they appeared uncommonly melancholy and stupified. As soon as they got home, they sat down with their elbows upon their knees, and hid their faces between their hands. The only words they could be brought to utter, were, "Too much smoke—too much noise—too much houses—too much men—too much every thing!"

Some people who attend public lectures upon natural philosophy, with the expectation of being much amused and instructed, go home with sensations similar to those of the poor Eskimaux; they feel that they have had too much of every thing. The lecturer has not time to explain his terms, or to repeat them till they are distinct in the memory of his audience. [16] To children, every mode of instruction must be hurtful which fatigues attention; therefore, a skilful preceptor will, as much as possible, avoid the manner of teaching, to which the public lecturer is in some degree compelled by his situation. A private preceptor, who undertakes the instruction of several pupils in the same family, will examine with care the different habits and tempers of his pupils; and he will have full leisure to adapt his instructions peculiarly to each.

There are some general observations which apply to all understandings; these we shall first enumerate, and we may afterwards examine what distinctions should be made for pupils of different tempers or dispositions.

Besides distinctness and accuracy in the language which we use, besides care to produce but few ideas or terms that are new in our first lessons, we must exercise attention only during very short periods. In the beginning of every science pupils have much laborious work; we should therefore allow them time; we should repress our own impatience when they appear to be slow in comprehending reasons, or in seizing analogies. We often expect, that those whom we are teaching should know some things intuitively, because these may have been so long known to us that we forget how we learned them. We may from habit learn to pass with extraordinary velocity from one idea to another. "Some often repeated processes of reasoning or invention," says Mr. Stewart, "may be carried on so quickly in the mind, that we may not be conscious of them ourselves." Yet we easily convince ourselves that this rapid facility of thought is purely the result of practice, by observing the comparatively slow progress of our understandings in subjects to which we have not been accustomed: the progress of the mind is there so slow, that we can count every step.

We are disposed to think that those must be naturally slow and stupid, who do not perceive the resemblances between objects which strike us, we say, at the first glance. But what we call the first glance is frequently the fiftieth: we have got the things completely by heart; all the parts are known to us, and we are at leisure to compare and judge. A reasonable preceptor will not expect from his pupils two efforts of attention at the same instant; he will not require them at once to learn terms by heart, and to compare the objects which those terms represent; he will repeat his terms till they are thoroughly fixed in the memory; he will repeat his reasoning till the chain of ideas is completely formed.

Repetition makes all operations easy; even the fatigue of thinking diminishes by habit. That we may not increase the labour of the mind unseasonably, we should watch for the moment when habit has made one lesson easy, and when we may go forward a new step. In teaching the children at the House of Industry at Munich to spin, Count Rumford wisely ordered that they should be made perfect in one motion before any other was shown to them: at first they were allowed only to move the wheel by the treadle with their feet; when, after sufficient practice, the foot became perfect in its lesson, the hands were set to work, and the children were allowed to begin to spin with coarse materials. It is said that these children made remarkable good spinners. Madame de Genlis applied the same principle in teaching Adela to play upon the harp. [17]

In the first attempts to learn any new bodily exercise, as fencing or dancing, persons are not certain what muscles they must use, and what may be left at rest; they generally employ those of which they have the most ready command, but these may not always be the muscles which are really wanted in the new operation. The simplest thing appears difficult, till, by practice, we have associated the various slight motions which ought to be combined. We feel, that from want of use, our motions are not obedient to our will, and to supply this defect, we exert more strength and activity than is requisite. "It does not require strength; you need not use so much force; you need not take so much pains;" we frequently say to those who are making the first painful awkward attempts at some simple operation. Can any thing appear more easy than knitting, when we look at the dexterous, rapid motions of an experienced practitioner? But let a gentleman take up a lady's knitting needles, and knitting appears to him, and to all the spectators, one of the most difficult and laborious operations imaginable. A lady who is learning to work with a tambour needle, puts her head down close to the tambour frame, the colour comes into her face, she strains her eyes, all her faculties are exerted, and perhaps she works at the rate of three links a minute. A week afterwards, probably, practice has made the work perfectly easy; the same lady goes rapidly on with her work; she can talk and laugh, and perhaps even think, whilst she works. She has now discovered that a number of the motions, and a great portion of that attention which she thought necessary to this mighty operation, may be advantageously spared.

In a similar manner, in the exercise of our minds upon subjects that are new to us, we generally exert more attention than is necessary or serviceable, and we consequently soon fatigue ourselves without any advantage. Children, to whom many subjects are new, are often fatigued by these overstrained and misplaced efforts. In these circumstances, a tutor should relieve the attention by introducing indifferent subjects of conversation; he can, by showing no anxiety himself, either in his manner or countenance, relieve his pupil from any apprehension of his displeasure, or of his contempt; he can represent that the object before them is not a matter of life and death; that if the child does not succeed in the first trials, he will not be disgraced in the opinion of any of his friends; that by perseverance he will certainly conquer the difficulty; that it is of little consequence whether he understands the thing in question to-day or to-morrow; these considerations will calm the over-anxious pupil's agitation, and, whether he succeed or not, he will not suffer such a degree of pain as to disgust him in his first attempts.

Besides the command which we, by this prudent management, obtain over the pupil's mind, we shall also prevent him from acquiring any of those awkward gestures and involuntary motions which are sometimes practised to relieve the pain of attention.

Dr. Darwin observes, that when we experience any disagreeable sensations, we endeavour to procure ourselves temporary relief by motions of those muscles and limbs which are most habitually obedient to our will. This observation extends to mental as well as to bodily pain; thus persons in violent grief wring their hands and convulse their countenances; those who are subject to the petty, but acute miseries of false shame, endeavour to relieve themselves by awkward gestures and continual motions. A plough-boy, when he is brought into the presence of those whom he thinks his superiors, endeavours to relieve himself from the uneasy sensations of false shame, by twirling his hat upon his fingers, and by various uncouth gestures. Men who think a great deal, sometimes acquire habitual awkward gestures, to relieve the pain of intense thought.

When attention first becomes irksome to children, they mitigate the mental pain by wrinkling their brows, or they fidget and put themselves into strange attitudes. These odd motions, which at first are voluntary, after they have been frequently associated with certain states of mind, constantly recur involuntarily with those feelings or ideas with which they have been connected. For instance, a boy, who has been used to buckle and unbuckle his shoe, when he repeats his lesson by rote, cannot repeat his lesson without performing this operation; it becomes a sort of artificial memory, which is necessary to prompt his recollective faculty. When children have a *variety* of tricks of this sort, they are of little consequence; but when they have acquired a few constant and habitual motions, whilst they think, or repeat, or listen, these should be attended to, and the habits should be broken, otherwise these young people will appear, when they grow up, awkward and ridiculous in their manners; and, what is worse, perhaps their thoughts and abilities will be too much in the power of external circumstances. Addison represents, with much humour, the case of a poor man who had the habit of twirling a bit of thread round his finger; the thread was accidentally broken, and the orator stood mute.

We once saw a gentleman get up to speak in a public assembly, provided with a paper of notes written in pencil: during the exordium of his speech, he thumbed his notes with incessant agitation; when he looked at the paper, he found that the words were totally obliterated; he was obliged to apologize to his audience; and, after much hesitation, sat down abashed. A father would be sorry to see his son in such a predicament.

To prevent children from acquiring such awkward tricks whilst they are thinking, we should in the first place take care not to make them attend for too long a time together, then the pain of attention will not be so violent as to compel them to use these strange modes of relief. Bodily exercise should immediately follow that entire state of rest, in which our pupils ought to keep themselves whilst they attend. The first symptoms of any awkward trick should be watched; they are easily prevented by early care from becoming habitual. If any such tricks have been acquired, and if the pupil cannot exert his attention in common, unless certain contortions are permitted, we should attempt the cure either by sudden slight bodily pain, or by a total suspension of all the employments with which these bad habits are associated. If a boy could not read without swinging his head like a pendulum, we should rather prohibit him from reading for some time, than suffer him to grow up with this ridiculous habit. But in conversation, whenever opportunities occur of telling him any thing in which he is particularly interested, we should refuse to gratify his curiosity, unless he keeps himself perfectly still. The excitement here would be sufficient to conquer the habit.

Whatever is connected with pain or pleasure commands our attention; but to make this general observation useful in education, we must examine what degrees of stimulus are necessary for different pupils, and in different circumstances. We have formerly observed, [18] that it is not prudent early to use violent or continual stimulus, either of a painful or a pleasurable nature, to excite children to application, because we should by an intemperate use of these, weaken the mind, and because we may with a little patience obtain all we wish without these expedients. Besides these reasons, there is another potent argument against using violent motives to excite attention; such motives frequently disturb and dissipate the very attention which they attempt to fix. If a child be threatened with severe punishment, or flattered with the promise of some delicious reward, in order to induce his performance of any particular task, he desires instantly to perform the task; but this desire will not ensure his success: unless he has previously acquired the habit of voluntary exertion, he will not be able to turn his mind from his ardent wishes, even to the means of accomplishing them. He will be in the situation of Alnaschar in the Arabian tales, who, whilst he dreamt of his future grandeur, forgot his immediate business. The greater his hope or fear, the greater the difficulty of his employing himself.

To teach any new habit or art, we must not employ any alarming excitements: small, certain, regularly recurring motives, which interest, but which do not distract the mind, are evidently the best. The ancient inhabitants of Minorca were said to be the best slingers in the world; when they were children, every morning what they were to eat was slightly suspended from high poles, and they were obliged to throw down their breakfasts with their slings from the places where they were suspended, before they could satisfy their hunger. The motive seems to have been here well proportioned to the effect that was required; it could not be any great misfortune to a boy to go without his breakfast; but as this motive returned every morning, it became sufficiently serious to the hungry slingers.

It is impossible to explain this subject so as to be of use, without descending to minute particulars. When a mother says to her little daughter, as she places on the table before her a bunch of ripe cherries, "Tell me, my dear, how many cherries are there, and I will give them to you?" The child's attention is fixed instantly; there is a sufficient motive, not a motive which excites any violent passions, but which raises just such a degree of hope as is necessary to produce attention. The little girl, if she knows from experience that her mother's promise will be kept, and that her own patience is likely to succeed, counts the cherries carefully, has her reward, and upon the next similar trial she will, from this success, be still more disposed to exert her attention. The pleasure of eating cherries, associated with the pleasure of success, will balance the pain of a few moments prolonged application, and by degrees the cherries may be withdrawn, the association of pleasure will remain. Objects or thoughts, that have been associated with pleasure, retain the power of pleasing; as the needle touched by the loadstone acquires polarity, and retains it long after the loadstone is withdrawn.

Whenever attention is habitually raised by the power of association, we should be careful to withdraw all the excitements that were originally used, because these are now unnecessary; and, as we have formerly observed, the steady rule, with respect to stimulus, should be to give the least possible quantity that will produce the effect we want. Success is a great pleasure; as soon as children become sensible to this pleasure, that is to say, when they have tasted it two or three times, they will exert their attention merely with the hope of succeeding. We have seen a little boy of three years old, frowning with attention for several minutes together, whilst he was trying to clasp and unclasp a lady's bracelet; his whole soul was intent upon the business; he neither saw nor heard any thing else that passed in the room, though several people were talking, and some happened to be looking at him. The pleasure of success, when he clasped the bracelet, was quite sufficient; he looked for no praise, though he was perhaps pleased with the sympathy that was shown in his success. Sympathy is a better reward for young children in such circumstances than praise, because it does not excite vanity, and it is connected with benevolent feelings; besides, it is not so violent a stimulus as applause.

Instead of increasing excitements to produce attention, we may vary them, which will have just the same effect. When sympathy fails, try curiosity; when curiosity fails, try praise; when praise begins to lose its effect, try blame; and when you go back again to sympathy, you will find that, after this interval, it will have recovered all its original power. Doctor Darwin, who has the happy art of illustrating, from the most familiar circumstances in real life, the abstract theories of philosophy, gives us the following picturesque instance of the use of varying motives to prolong exertion.

"A little boy, who was tired of walking, begged of his papa to carry him. "Here," says the reverend doctor, "ride upon my gold headed cane;" and the pleased child, putting it between his legs, galloped away with delight. Here the aid of another sensorial power, that of pleasurable sensation, superadded power to exhausted volition, which could otherwise only have been excited by additional pain, as by the lash of slavery." [19]

Alexander the Great one day saw a poor man carrying upon his shoulders a heavy load of silver for the royal camp: the man tottered under his burden, and was ready to give up the point from fatigue. "Hold on, friend, the rest of the way, and carry it to your own tent, for it is yours," said Alexander.

There are some people, who have the power of exciting others to great mental exertions, not by the promise of specific rewards, or by the threats of any punishment, but by the ardent ambition which they inspire, by the high value which is set upon their love and esteem. When we have formed a high opinion of a friend, his approbation becomes necessary to our own self-complacency, and we think no labour too great to satisfy our attachment. Our exertions are not fatiguing, because they are associated with all the pleasurable sensations of affection, self-complacency, benevolence, and liberty. These feelings, in youth, produce all the virtuous enthusiasm characteristic of great minds; even childhood is capable of it in some degree, as those parents well know, who have never enjoyed the attachment of a grateful affectionate child. Those, who neglect to cultivate the affections of their pupils, will never be able to excite them to "noble ends," by "noble means." Theirs will be the dominion of fear, from which reason will emancipate herself, and from which pride will yet more certainly revolt.

If Henry the Fourth of France had been reduced, like Dionysius the tyrant of Syracuse, to earn his bread as a schoolmaster, what a different preceptor he would probably have made! Dionysius must have been hated by his scholars as much as by his subjects, for it is said, that "he [20] practised upon children that tyranny which he could no longer exercise over men."

The ambassador, who found Henry the Fourth playing upon the carpet with his children, would probably have trusted his own children, if he had any, to the care of such an affectionate tutor.

Henry the Fourth would have attached his pupils whilst he instructed them; they would have exerted themselves because they could not have been happy without his esteem. Henry's courtiers, or rather his friends, for though he was a king he had friends, sometimes expressed surprise at their own disinterestedness: "This king pays us with words," said they, "and yet we are satisfied!" Sully, when he was only Baron de Rosny, and before he had any hopes of being a duke, was once in a passion with the king his master, and half resolved to leave him: "But I don't know how it was," says the honest minister, "with all his faults, there is something about Henry which I found I could not leave; and when I met him again, a few words made me forget all my causes of discontent."

Children are more easily attached than courtiers, and full as easily rewarded. When once this generous desire of affection and esteem is raised in the mind, their exertions seem to be universal and spontaneous: children are then no longer like machines, which require to be wound up regularly to perform certain revolutions; they are animated with a living principle, which directs all that it inspires.

We have endeavoured to point out the general excitements, and the general precautions, to be used in cultivating the power of attention; it may be expected, that we should more particularly apply these to the characters of different pupils. We shall not here examine whether there be any original difference of character or intellect, because this would lead into a wide theoretical discussion; a difference in the temper and talents of children early appears, and some practical remarks may be of service to correct defects, or to improve abilities, whether we suppose them to be natural or acquired. The first differences which a preceptor observes between his pupils, when he begins to teach them, are perhaps scarcely marked so strongly as to strike the careless spectator; but in a few years these varieties are apparent to every eye. This seems to prove, that during the interval the power of education has operated strongly to increase the original propensities. The quick and slow, the timid and presumptuous, should be early instructed so as to correct as much as possible their several defects.

The manner in which children are first instructed must tend either to increase or diminish their timidity, or their confidence in themselves, to encourage them to undertake great things, or to rest content with limited acquirements. Young people, who have found from experience, that they cannot remember or understand one half of what is forced upon their attention, become extremely diffident of their own capacity, and they will not undertake as much even as they are able to perform. With timid tempers, we should therefore begin, by expecting but little from each effort, but whatever is attempted, should be certainly within their attainment; success will encourage the most stupid humility. It should be carefully pointed out to diffident children, that attentive patience can do as much as quickness of intellect. If they perceive that time makes all the difference between the quick and the slow, they will be induced to persevere. The transition of attention from one subject to another is difficult to some children, to others it is easy. If all be expected to do the same things in an equal period of time, the slow will absolutely give up the competition; but, on the contrary, if they are allowed time, they will accomplish their purposes. We have been confirmed in our belief of this doctrine by experiments. The same problems have been frequently given to children of different degrees of quickness, and though some succeeded much more quickly than others, all the individuals in the family have persevered till they have solved the questions; and the timid seem to have been more encouraged by this practical demonstration of the infallibility of persevering attention, than by any other methods which have been tried. When, after a number of small successful trials, they have acquired some share of confidence in themselves, when they are certain of the possibility of their performing any given operations, we may then press them a little as to velocity. When they are well acquainted with any set of ideas, we may urge them to quick transition of attention from one to another; but if we insist upon this rapidity of transition, before they are thoroughly acquainted with each idea in the assemblage, we shall only increase their timidity and hesitation; we shall confound their understandings, and depress their ambition.

It is of consequence to distinguish between slow and sluggish attention. Sometimes children appear stupid and heavy, when they are absolutely exhausted by too great efforts of attention: at other times, they have something like the same dulness of aspect, before they have had any thing to fatigue them, merely from their not having yet awakened themselves to business. We must be certain of our pupil's state of mind before we proceed. If he be incapacitated from fatigue, let him rest; if he be torpid, rouse him with a rattling peal of thunder; but be sure that you have not, as it has been said of Jupiter, [21] recourse to your thunder only when you are in the wrong. Some preceptors scold when they cannot explain, and grow angry in proportion to the fatigue they see expressed in the countenance of their unhappy pupils. If a timid child foresees that an explanation will probably end in a phillipic, he cannot fix his attention; he is anticipating the evil of your anger, instead of listening to your demonstrations; and he says, "Yes, yes, I see, I know, I understand," with trembling eagerness, whilst through the mist and confusion of his fears, he can scarcely see or hear, much less understand, any thing. If you mistake the confusion and fatigue of terror for inattention or indolence, and press your pupil to further exertions, you will confirm, instead of curing, his stupidity. You must diminish his fear before you can increase his attention. With children who are thus, from timid anxiety to please, disposed to exert their faculties too much, it is obvious that no excitation should be used, but every playful, every affectionate means should be employed to dissipate their apprehensions.

It is more difficult to manage with those who have sluggish, than with those who have timid, attention. Indolent children have not usually so lively a taste for pleasure as others have; they do not seem to hear or see so quickly; they are content with a little enjoyment; they have scarcely any ambition; they seem to prefer ease to all sorts of glory; they have little voluntary exertion; and the pain of attention is to them so great, that they would preferably endure the pain of shame, and of all the accumulated punishments which are commonly devised for them by the vengeance of their exasperated tutors. Locke notices this listless, lazy humour in children; he classes it under the head "Sauntering;" and he divides saunterers into two species; those who saunter only at their books and tasks; and those who saunter at play and every thing. The book-saunterers have only an acute, the others have a chronic disease; the one is easily cured, the other disease will cost more time and pains.

If, by some unlucky management, a vivacious child acquires a dislike to literary application, he may appear at his books with all the stupid apathy of a dunce. In this state of literary dereliction, we should not force books and tasks of any sort upon him; we should rather watch him when he is eager at amusements of his own selection, observe to what his attention turns, and cultivate his attention upon that subject, whatever it may be. He may be led to think, and to acquire knowledge upon a variety of subjects, without sitting down to read; and thus he may form habits of attention and application, which will be associated with pleasure. When he returns to books, he will find that he understands a variety of things in them which before appeared incomprehensible; they will "give him back the image of his mind," and he will like them as he likes pictures.

As long as a child shows energy upon any occasion, there is hope. If he "lend his little soul" [22] to whipping a top, there is no danger of his being a dunce. When Alcibiades was a child, he was one day playing at dice with other boys in the street; a loaded waggon came up just as it was his turn to throw. At first he called to the driver to stop, but the waggoner would not stop his horses; all the boys, except Alcibiades, ran away, but Alcibiades threw himself upon his face, directly before the horses, and stretching himself out, bid the waggoner drive on if he pleased. Perhaps, at the time when he showed this energy about a game at dice, Alcibiades might have been a saunterer at his book, and a foolish schoolmaster might have made him a dunce.

Locke advises that children, who are too much addicted to what is called play, should be surfeited with it, that they may return to business with a better appetite. But this advice supposes that play has been previously interdicted, or that it is something pernicious: we have endeavoured to show that play is nothing but a change of employment, and that the attention may be exercised advantageously upon a variety of subjects which are not called Tasks. [23]

With those who show chronic listlessness, Locke advises that we should use every sort of stimulus; praise, amusement, fine clothes, eating; any thing that will make them bestir themselves. He argues, that as there appears a deficiency of vigour, we have no reason to fear excess of appetite for any of these things: nay, further still, where none of these will act, he advises compulsory bodily exercise. If we cannot, he says, make sure of the invisible attention of the mind, we may at least get something done, prevent the habit of total idleness, and perhaps make the children desire to exchange labour of body for labour of mind. These expedients will, we fear, be found rather palliative than effectual; if, by forcing children to bodily exercise, that becomes disagreeable, they may prefer labour of the mind; but, in making this exchange, or bargain, they are sensible that they choose the least of two evils. The evil of application is diminished only by comparison in their estimation; they will avoid it whenever they are at liberty. The love of eating, of fine clothes, &c. if they stimulate a slothful child, must be the ultimate object of his exertions; he will consider the performance of his task merely as a painful condition on his part. Still the association of pain with literature continues; it is then impossible that he should love it. There is no active principle within him, no desire for knowledge excited; his attention is forced, it ceases the moment the external force is withdrawn. He drudges to earn his cream bowl duly set, but he will stretch his lubbar length the moment his task is done.

There is another class of children opposed to saunterers, whom we may denominate volatile geniuses. They show a vast deal of quickness and vivacity; they understand almost before a tutor can put his ideas into words; they observe a variety of objects, but they do not connect their observations, and the very rapidity with which they seize an explanation, prevents them from thoroughly comprehending it; they are easily disturbed by external objects when they are thinking. As they have great sensibility, their associations are strong and various; their thoughts branch off into a thousand beautiful, but useless ramifications. Whilst you are attempting to instruct them upon one subject, they are inventing, perhaps, upon another; or they are following a train of ideas suggested by something you have said, but foreign to your business. They are more pleased with the discovery of resemblances, than with discrimination of difference; the one costs them more time and attention than the other: they are apt to say witty things, and to strike out sparks of invention; but they have not commonly the patience to form exact judgments, or to bring their first inventions to perfection. When they begin the race, every body expects that they should outstrip all competitors; but it is often seen that slower rivals reach the goal before them. The predictions formed of pupils of this temperament, vary much, according to the characters of their tutors. A slow man is provoked by their dissipated vivacity, and, unable to catch or fix their attention, prognosticates that they will never have sufficient application to learn any thing. This prophecy, under certain tuition, would probably be accomplished. The want of sympathy between a slow tutor and a quick child, is a great disadvantage to both; each insists upon going his own pace, and his own way, and these ways are perhaps diametrically opposite. Even in forming a judgment of the child's attention, the tutor, who is not acquainted with the manner in which his pupil goes to work, is liable to frequent mistakes. Children are sometimes suspected of not having listened to what has been said to them, when they cannot exactly repeat the words that they have heard; they often ask questions, and make observations, which seem quite foreign to the present business; but this is not always a proof that their minds are absent, or that their attention is dissipated. Their answers often appear to be far from the point, because they suppress their intermediate ideas, and give only the result of their thoughts. This may be inconvenient to those who teach them; but this habit sufficiently proves that these children are not deficient in attention. To cure them of the fault which they have, we should not accuse them falsely of another. But it may be questioned whether this be a fault; it is absolutely necessary, in many processes of the mind, to suppress a number of intermediate ideas. Life, if this were not practised, would be too short for those who think, and much too short for those who speak. When somebody asked Pyrrhus which of two musicians he liked the best, he answered, "Polysperchon is the best general." This would appear to be the absurd answer of an absent person, or of a fool, if we did not consider the ideas that are implied, as well as those which are expressed.

March 5th, 1796. To-day, at dinner, a lady observed that Nicholson, Williamson, Jackson, &c. were names which originally meant the sons of Nicholas, William, Jack, &c. A boy who was present, H——, added, with a very grave face, as soon as she had finished speaking, "Yes, ma'am, Tydides." His mother asked him what he could mean by this absent speech? H—— calmly repeated, "Ma'am, yes; because I think it is like Tydides." His brother S——eagerly interposed, to supply the intermediate ideas; "Yes, indeed, mother," cried he, "H—— is not absent, because *des*, in Greek, means *the son of* (the race of.) Tydides is the son of Tydeus, as Jackson is the son of Jack." In this instance, H—— was not absent, though he did not make use of a sufficient number of words to explain his ideas.

August, 1796. L——, when he returned home, after some months absence, entertained his brothers and sisters with a new play, which he had learned at Edinburgh. He told them, that when he struck the table with his hand, every person present, was instantaneously to remain fixed in the attitudes in which they should be when the blow was given. The attitudes in which some of the little company were fixed, occasioned much diversion; but in speaking of this new play afterwards, they had no name for it. Whilst they were thinking of a name for it, H— — exclaimed, "The Gorgon!" It was immediately agreed that this was a good name for the play, and H— —, upon this occasion, was perfectly intelligible, without expressing all the intermediate ideas.

Good judges, form an accurate estimate of the abilities of those who converse with them, by what they omit, as well as by what they say. If any one can show that he also has been in Arcadia, he is sure of being well received, without producing minutes of his journey. In the same manner we should judge of children; if they arrive at certain conclusions in reasoning, we may be satisfied that they have taken all the necessary previous steps. We need not question their attention upon subjects where they give proofs of invention; they must have remembered well, or they could not invent; they must have attended well, or they could not have remembered. Nothing wearies a quick child more than to be forced slowly to retrace his own thoughts, and to repeat the words of a discourse to prove that he has listened to it. A tutor, who is slow in understanding the ideas of his vivacious pupil, gives him so much trouble and pain, that he grows silent, from finding it not worth while to speak. It is for this reason, that children appear stupid and silent, with some people, and sprightly and talkative with others. Those who hope to talk to children with any effect, must, as Rousseau observes, be able to hear as well as to speak. M. de Segrais, who was deaf, was much in the right to decline being preceptor to the Duke de Maine. A deaf preceptor would certainly make a child dumb.

To win the attention of vivacious children, we must sometimes follow them in their zigzag course, and even press them to the end of their own train of thought. They will be content when they have obtained a full hearing; then they will have leisure to discover that what they were in such haste to utter, was not so well worth saying as they imagined; that their bright ideas often, when steadily examined by themselves, fade into absurdities.

"Where does this path lead to? Can't we get over this stile? May I *only* go into this wood?" exclaims an active child, when he is taken out to walk. Every path appears more delightful than the straight road; but let him try the paths, they will perhaps end in disappointment, and then his imagination will be corrected. Let him try his own experiments, then he will be ready to try yours; and if yours succeed better than his own, you will secure his confidence. After a child has talked on for some time, till he comes to the end of his ideas, then he will perhaps listen to what you have to say; and if he finds it better than what he has been saying himself, he will voluntarily give you his attention the next time you begin to speak.

Vivacious children are peculiarly susceptible of blame and praise; we have, therefore, great power over their attachment, if we manage these excitements properly. These children should not be praised for their *happy hits*, their first [24] glances should not be extolled; but, on the contrary, they should be rewarded with universal approbation when they give proofs of patient industry, when they bring any thing to perfection. No one can bring any thing to perfection without long continued attention; and industry and perseverance presuppose attention. Proofs of any of these qualities may therefore satisfy us as to the pupil's capacity and habits of attention; we need not stand by to see the attention exercised, the things produced are sufficient evidence. Buffon tells us that he wrote his Epoques de la Nature over eighteen times before he could perfect it to his taste. The high finish of his composition is sufficient evidence to intelligent readers, that he exerted long continued attention upon the work; they do not require to have the eighteen copies produced.

Bacon supposes, that for every disease of the mind, specific remedies might be found in appropriate studies and exercises. Thus, for "bird-witted" children he prescribes the study of mathematics, because, in mathematical studies, the attention must be fixed; the least intermission of thought breaks the whole chain of reasoning, their labour is lost, and they must begin their demonstration again. This principle is excellent; but to apply it advantageously, we should choose moments when a mathematical demonstration is interesting to children, else we have not sufficient motive to excite them to commence the demonstration; they will perceive, that they loose all their labour if their attention is interrupted; but how shall we make them begin to attend? There are a variety of subjects which are interesting to children, to which we may apply Bacon's principle; for instance, a child is eager to hear a story which you are going to tell him; you may exercise his attention by your manner of telling this story; you may employ with advantage the beautiful figure of speech called *suspension*: but you must take care, that the hope which is long deferred be at last gratified. The young critics will look back when your story is finished, and will examine whether their attention has been wasted, or whether all the particulars to which it was directed were essential. Though in amusing stories we recommend the figure called suspension, [25] we do not recommend its use in explanations. Our explanations should be put into as few words as possible: the closer the connection of ideas, the better. When we say, allow time to understand your explanations, we mean, allow time between each idea, do not fill up the interval with words. Never, by way of gaining time, pay in sixpences; this is the last resource of a bankrupt.

We formerly observed that a preceptor, in his first lessons on any new subject, must submit to the drudgery of repeating his terms and his reasoning, until these are sufficiently familiar to his pupils. He must, however, proportion the number of his repetitions to the temper and habits of his pupils, else he will weary, instead of strengthening, the attention. When a thing is clear, let him never try to make it clearer; when a thing is understood, not a word more of exemplification should be added. To mark precisely the moment when the pupil understands what is said, the moment when he is master of the necessary ideas, and, consequently, the moment when repetition should cease, is, perhaps, the most difficult thing in the art of teaching. The countenance, the eye, the voice, and manner of the pupil, mark this instant to an observing preceptor; but a preceptor, who is absorbed in his own ideas, will never think of looking in his pupil's face; he will go on with his routine of explanation, whilst his once lively, attentive pupil, exhibits opposite to him the picture of stupified fatigue. Quick, intelligent children, who have frequently found that lessons are reiterated by a patient but injudicious tutor, will learn a careless mode of listening at intervals; they will say to themselves, "Oh I shall hear this again!" And if any stray thought comes across their minds, they will not scruple to amuse themselves, and will afterwards ask for a repetition of the words or ideas which they missed during this excursion of fancy. When they hear the warning advertisement of "certainly for the last time this season," they will deem it time enough to attend to the performance. To cure them of this presumption in favour of our patience, and of their own superlative quickness, we should press that quickness to its utmost speed. Whenever we call for their attention, let it be on subjects highly interesting or amusing, and let us give them but just sufficient time with their fullest exertion to catch our words and ideas. As these quick gentlemen are proud of their rapidity of apprehension, this method will probably secure their attention, they will dread the disgrace of not understanding what is said, and they will feel that they cannot understand unless they exert prompt, vigorous, unremitted attention.

The Duchess of Kingston used to complain that she could never acquire any knowledge, because she never could meet with any body who could teach her anything "in two words." Her Grace felt the same sort of impatience which was expressed by the tyrant who expected to find a royal road to Geometry.

Those who believe themselves endowed with genius, expect to find a royal road in every science shorter, and less laborious, than the beaten paths of industry. Their expectations are usually in proportion to their ignorance;

they see to the summit only of one hill, and they do not suspect the Alps that will arise as they advance: but as children become less presumptuous, as they acquire more knowledge, we may bear with their juvenile impatience, whilst we take measures to enlarge continually their sphere of information. We should not, however, humour the attention of young people, by teaching them always in the mode which we know suits their temper best. Vivacious pupils should, from time to time, be accustomed to an exact enumeration of particulars; and we should take opportunities to convince them, that an orderly connection of proofs, and a minute observation of apparent trifles, are requisite to produce the lively descriptions, great discoveries, and happy inventions, which pupils of this disposition are ever prone to admire with enthusiasm. They will learn not to pass over *old* things, when they perceive that these may lead to something *new*; and they will even submit to sober attention, when they feel that this is necessary even to the rapidity of genius. In the "Curiosities of Literature," there has been judiciously preserved a curious instance of literary patience; the rough draught of that beautiful passage in Pope's translation of the Iliad which describes the parting of Hector and Andromache. The lines are in Pope's hand-writing, and his numerous corrections appear; the lines which seem to the reader to have been struck off at a single happy stroke, are proved to have been touched and retouched with the indefatigable attention of a great writer. The fragment, with all its climax of corrections, was shown to a young vivacious poet of nine years old, as a practical lesson, to prove the necessity of patience to arrive at perfection. Similar examples, from real life, should be produced to young people at proper times; the testimony of men of acknowledged abilities, of men whom they have admired for genius, will come with peculiar force in favour of application. Parents, well acquainted with literature, cannot be at a loss to find opposite illustrations. The Life of Franklin is an excellent example of persevering industry; the variations in different editions of Voltaire's dramatic poetry, and in Pope's works, are worth examining. All Sir Joshua Reynolds's eloquent academical discourses enforce the doctrine of patience; when he wants to prove to painters the value of continual energetic attention, he quotes from Livy the character of Philopœmen, one of the ablest generals of antiquity. So certain it is, that the same principle pervades all superior minds: whatever may be their pursuits, attention is the avowed primary cause of their success. These examples from the dead, should be well supported by examples from amongst the living. In common life, occurrences can frequently be pointed out, in which attention and application are amply rewarded with success.

It will encourage those who are interested in education, to observe, that two of the most difficult exercises of the mind can, by practice, be rendered familiar, even by persons whom we do not consider as possessed of superior talents. Abstraction and transition—abstraction, the power of withdrawing the attention from all external objects, and concentrating it upon some particular set of ideas, we admire as one of the most difficult exercises of the philosopher. Abstraction was formerly considered as such a difficult and painful operation, that it required perfect silence and solitude; many ancient philosophers quarrelled with their senses, and shut themselves up in caves, to secure their attention from the distraction caused by external objects. But modern [26] philosophers have discovered, that neither caves nor lamps are essential to the full and successful exercise of their mental powers. Persons of ordinary abilities, tradesmen and shop-keepers, in the midst of the tumult of a public city, in the noise of rumbling carts and rattling carriages, amidst the voices of a multitude of people talking upon various subjects, amidst the provoking interruptions of continual questions and answers, and in the broad glare of a hot sun, can command and abstract their attention so far as to calculate yards, ells, and nails, to cast up long sums in addition right to a farthing, and to make out multifarious bills with quick and unerring precision. In almost all the dining houses at Vienna, as a late traveller [27] informs us "a bill of fare containing a vast collection of dishes is written out, and the prices are affixed to each article. As the people of Vienna are fond of variety, the calculation at the conclusion of a repast would appear somewhat embarrassing; this, however, is done by mechanical habit with great speed; the custom is for the party who has dined to name the dishes, and the quantity of bread and wine. The keller who attends on this occasion, follows every article you name with the sum, which this adds to the calculation, and the whole is performed, to whatever amount, without ink or paper. It is curious to hear this ceremony, which is muttered with great gravity, yet performed with accuracy and despatch."

We coolly observe, when we read these things, "Yes, this is all habit; any body who had used himself to it might do the same things." Yet the very same power of abstracting the attention, when employed upon scientific and literary subjects, would excite our astonishment; and we should, perhaps, immediately attribute it to superior original genius. We may surely educate children to this habit of abstracting the attention, which we allow depends entirely upon practice. When we are very much interested upon any subject, we attend to it exclusively, and, without any effort, we surmount all petty interposing interruptions. When we are reading an interesting book, twenty people may converse round about us, without our hearing one word that they say; when we are in a crowded playhouse, the moment we become interested in the play, the audience vanish from our sight, and in the midst of various noises, we hear only the voices of the actors.

In the same manner, children, by their eager looks and their unaffected absence to all external circumstances, show when they are thoroughly interested by any story that is told with eloquence suited to their age. When we would teach them to attend in the midst of noise and interruptions, we should begin by talking to them about things which we are sure will please them; by degrees we may speak on less captivating subjects, when we perceive that their habit of beginning to listen with an expectation of pleasure is formed. Whenever a child happens to be intent upon any favourite amusement, or when he is reading any very entertaining book, we may increase the busy hum around him, we may make what bustle we please, he will probably continue attentive; it is useful therefore to give him such amusements and such books when there is a noise or bustle in the room, because then he will learn to disregard all interruptions; and when this habit is formed, he may even read less amusing books in the same company without being interrupted by the usual noises.

The power of abstracting our attention is universally allowed to be necessary to the successful labour of the understanding; but we may further observe, that this abstraction is characteristic in some cases of heroism as well as of genius. Charles the Twelfth and Archimedes were very different men; yet both, in similar circumstances, gave similar proofs of their uncommon power of abstracting their attention. "What has the bomb to do with what you are writing to Sweden," said the hero to his pale secretary when a bomb burst through the roof of his apartment, and he continued to dictate his letter. Archimedes went on with his demonstration in the midst of a siege, and when a brutal soldier entered with a drawn sword, the philosopher only begged he might solve his problem before he was put to death.

Presence of mind in danger, which is usually supposed to depend upon our quick perception of all the present circumstances, frequently demands a total abstraction of our thoughts. In danger, fear is the motive which excites our exertions; but from all the ideas that fear naturally suggests, we must abstract our attention, or we shall not act with courage or prudence. In proportion to the violence of our terror, our voluntary exertion must be great to withdraw our thoughts from the present danger, and to recollect the means of escape. In some cases, where the danger has been associated with the use of certain methods of escape, we use these without deliberation, and consequently without any effort of attention; as when we see any thing catch fire, we instantly throw water upon the flames to extinguish them. But in new situations, where we have no mechanical courage, we must exert much voluntary, quick, abstract attention, to escape from danger.

When Lee, the poet, was confined in Bedlam, a friend went to visit him; and finding that he could converse reasonably, or at least reasonably for a poet, imagined that Lee was cured of his madness. The poet offered to show him Bedlam. They went over this melancholy, medical prison, Lee moralising philosophically enough all the time to keep his companion perfectly at ease. At length they ascended together to the top of the building; and, as they were both looking down from the perilous height, Lee seized his friend by the arm, "Let us immortalize ourselves!" he exclaimed; "let us take this leap. We'll jump down together this instant." "Any man could jump down," said his friend, coolly; "we should not immortalize ourselves by that leap; but let us go down, and try if we can jump up again." The madman, struck with the idea of a more astonishing leap than that which he had himself proposed, yielded to this new impulse, and his friend rejoiced to see him run down stairs full of a new project for securing immortality.

Lee's friend, upon this occasion, showed rather absence than presence of mind: before he could have invented the happy answer that saved his life, he must have abstracted his mind from the passion of fear; he must have rapidly turned his attention upon a variety of ideas unconnected by any former associations with the exciting motive—falling from a height—fractured skulls—certain death—impossibility of reasoning or wrestling with a madman. This was the train of thoughts which we might naturally expect to arise in such a situation, but from all these the man of presence of mind turned away his attention; he must have directed his thoughts in a contrary line: first, he must have thought of the means of saving himself, of some argument likely to persuade a madman, of some argument peculiarly suited to Lee's imagination, and applicable to his situation; he must at this moment have considered that alarming situation without thinking of his fears; for the interval in which all these ideas passed in his mind, must have been so short that he could not have had leisure to combat fear; if any of the ideas associated with that passion had interrupted his reasonings, he would not have invented his answer in time to have saved his life.

We cannot foresee on what occasions presence of mind may be wanted, but we may, by education, give that general command of abstract attention, which is essential to its exercise in all circumstances.

Transition of thought, the power of turning attention quickly to different subjects or employments, is another of those mental habits, which in some cases we call genius, and which in others we perceive depends entirely upon practice. A number of trials in one newspaper, upon a variety of unconnected subjects, once struck our eye, and we saw the name of a celebrated lawyer [28] as counsel in each cause. We could not help feeling involuntary admiration at that versatility of genius, which could pass from a fractional calculation about a London chaldron of coals, to the Jamaica laws of insurance; from the bargains of a citizen, to the divorce of a fine lady;

from pathos to argument; from arithmetic to wit; from cross examination to eloquence. For a moment we forgot our sober principles, and ascribed all this versatility of mind to natural genius; but upon reflection we recurred to the belief, that this dexterity of intellect was not bestowed by nature. We observe in men who have no pretensions to genius, similar versatility of mind as to their usual employments. The daily occupations of Mr. Elwes's huntsman were as various and incongruous, and required as quick transitions of attention, as any that can well be imagined.

"At [29] four o'clock he milked the cows; then got breakfast for Mr. Elwes and friends; then slipping on a green coat, he hurried into the stable, saddled the horses, got the hounds out of the kennel, and away they went into the field. After the fatigues of hunting, he *refreshed* himself, by rubbing down two or three horses as quickly as he could; then running into the house to lay the cloth, and wait at dinner; then hurrying again into the stable to feed the horses, diversified with an interlude of the cows again to milk, the dogs to feed, and eight hunters to litter down for the night." Mr. Elwes used to call this huntsman an idle dog, who wanted to be paid for doing nothing!

We do not mean to require any such rapid daily transitions in the exercise of attention from our pupils; but we think that much may be done to improve versatility of mind, by a judicious arrangement of their occupations. When we are tired of smelling a rose, we can smell a carnation with pleasure; and when the sense of smell is fatigued, yet we can look at the beautiful colours with delight. When we are tired of thinking upon one subject, we can attend to another; when our memory is fatigued, the exercise of the imagination entertains us; and when we are weary of reasoning, we can amuse ourselves with wit and humour. Men, who have attended much to the cultivation of their mind, seem to have felt all this, and they have kept some subordinate taste as a refreshment after their labours. Descartes went from the system of the world to his flower-garden; Galileo used to read Ariosto; and the metaphysical Dr. Clarke recovered himself from abstraction by jumping over chairs and tables. The learned and indefatigable chancellor d'Aguesseau declared, that change of employment was the only recreation he ever knew. Even Montaigne, who found his recreation in playing with his cat, educated himself better than those are educated who go from intense study to complete idleness. It has been very wisely recommended by Mr. Locke, that young people should early be taught some mechanical employment, or some agreeable art, to which they may recur for relief when they are tired by mental application. [30]

Doctor Darwin supposes that "animal motions, or configurations of the organs of sense, constitute our ideas. [31] The fatigue, he observes, that follows a continued attention of the mind to one object, is relieved by changing the subject of our thoughts, as the continued movement of one limb is relieved by moving another in its stead." Dr. Darwin has further suggested a tempting subject of experiment in his theory of ocular spectra, to which we refer ingenious preceptors. Many useful experiments in education might be tried upon the principles which are there suggested. We dare not here trust ourselves to speculate upon this subject, because we are not at present provided with a sufficient number of facts to apply our theory to practice. If we could exactly discover how to arrange mental employments so as to induce actions in the antagonist faculties of the mind, we might relieve it from fatigue in the same manner as the eye is relieved by change of colour. By pursuing this idea, might we not hope to cultivate the general power of attention to a degree of perfection hitherto unknown?

We have endeavoured to show how, by different arrangements and proper excitations, a preceptor may acquire that command over the attention of his pupils, which is absolutely essential to successful instruction; but we must recollect, that when the years commonly devoted to education are over, when young people are no longer under the care of a preceptor, they will continue to feel the advantages of a command of attention, whenever they mix in the active business of life, or whenever they apply to any profession, to literature, or science. Their attention must now be entirely voluntary; they will have no tutor to excite them to exertion, no nice habitual arrangements to assist them in their daily occupations. It is of consequence, therefore, that we should substitute the power of voluntary, for the habit of associated, attention. With young children we depend upon particular associations of place, time, and manner, upon different sorts of excitement, to produce habits of employment: but as our pupils advance in their education, all these temporary excitements should be withdrawn. Some large, but distant object, some pursuit which is not to be rewarded with immediate praise, but rather with permanent advantage and esteem, should be held out to the ambition of youth. All the arrangements should be left to the pupil himself, all the difficulties should be surmounted by his own industry, and the interest he takes in his own success and improvement, will now probably be a sufficient stimulus; his preceptor will now rather be his partner than his master, he should rather share the labour than attempt to direct it: this species of sympathy in study, diminishes the pain of attention, and gives an agreeable interest even in the most tiresome researches. When a young man perceives that his preceptor becomes in this manner the companion of his exertions, he loses all suspicion that he is compelled to mental labour; it is improper to say *loses*, for in a good education this suspicion need not ever be created: he discovers, we should rather say, that all the habits of attention which he has acquired, are those which are useful to men as well as to children, and he feels the advantage of his cultivated powers on every fresh occasion. He will perceive, that young men who have been ill educated, cannot, by any motive, command their vigorous attention, and he will feel the cause of his own superiority, when he comes to any trial of skill with inattentive *men of genius*.

One of the arguments which Bayle uses, to prove that fortune has a greater influence than prudence in the affairs of men, is founded upon the common observation, that men of the best abilities cannot frequently recollect, in urgent circumstances, what they have said or done; the things occur to them perhaps a moment after they are past. The fact seems to be, that they could not, in the proper moment, command their attention; but this we should attribute to the want of prudence in their early education. Thus, Bayle's argument does not, in this point of view, prove any thing in favour of fortune. Those who can best command their attention, in the greatest variety of circumstances, have the most useful abilities; without this command of mind, men of genius, as they are called, are helpless beings; with it, persons of inferior capacity become valuable. Addison trembled and doubted, and doubted and trembled, when he was to write a common official paper; and it is said, that he was absolutely obliged to resign his place, because he could not decide in time whether he should write a *that* or a *which*. No business could have been transacted by such an imbecile minister.

To substitute voluntary for associated attention, we may withdraw some of the usually associated circumstances, and increase the excitement; and we may afterwards accustom the pupil to act from the hope of distant pleasures. Unless children can be actuated by the view of future distant advantage, they cannot be capable of long continued application. We shall endeavour to explain how the value of distant pleasures can be increased, and made to act with sufficient force upon the mind, when we hereafter speak of judgment and of imagination.

It has been observed, that persons of wit and judgment have perhaps originally the same powers, and that the difference in their characters arises from their habits of attention, and the different class of objects to which they have turned their thoughts. The manner in which we are first taught to observe, and to reason, must in the first years of life decide these habits. There are two methods of teaching; one which ascends from particular facts to general principles, the other which descends from the general principles to particular facts; one which builds up, another which takes to pieces; the synthetic and the analytic method. The words analysis and synthesis are frequently misapplied, and it is difficult to write or to speak long about these methods without confounding them: in learning or in teaching, we often use them alternately. We first observe particulars; then form some general idea of classification; then descend again to new particulars, to observe whether they correspond with our principle.

Children acquire knowledge, and their attention alternates from particular to general ideas, exactly in the same manner. It has been remarked, that men who have begun by forming suppositions, are inclined to adapt and to compress their consequent observations to the measure of their theories; they have been negligent in collecting facts, and have not condescended to try experiments. This disposition of mind, during a long period of time, retarded improvement, and knowledge was confined to a few peremptory maxims and exclusive principles. The necessity of collecting facts, and of trying experiments, was at length perceived; and in all the sciences this mode has lately prevailed: consequently, we have now on many subjects a treasure of accumulated facts. We are, in educating children, to put them in possession of all this knowledge; and a judicious preceptor will wish to know, not only how these facts can be crammed speedily into his pupil's memory, but what order of presenting them will be most advantageous to the understanding; he will desire to cultivate his pupil's faculties, that he may acquire new facts, and make new observations after all the old facts have been arranged in his mind.

By a judicious arrangement of past experiments, and by the rejection of what are useless, an able instructer can show, in a small compass, what it has cost the labour of ages to accumulate; he may teach in a few hours what the most ingenious pupil, left to his own random efforts, could not have learned in many years. It would take up as much time to go over all the steps which have been made in any science, as it originally cost the first discoverers. Simply to repeat all the fruitless experiments which have been made in chemistry, for instance, would probably employ the longest life that ever was devoted to science; nor would the individual have got one step forwarder; he would die, and with him his recapitulated knowledge; neither he nor the world would be the better for it. It is our business to save children all this useless labour, and all this waste of the power of attention. A pupil, who is properly instructed, with the same quantity of attention, learns, perhaps, a hundred times as much in the same time, as he could acquire under the tuition of a learned preceptor ignorant in the art of teaching.

The analytic and synthetic methods of instruction will both be found useful when judiciously employed. Where the enumeration of particulars fatigues the attention, we should, in teaching any science, begin by stating the general principles, and afterwards produce only the facts essential to their illustration and proof. But wherever we have not accumulated a sufficient number of facts to be accurately certain of any general principle, we must, however tedious the task, enumerate all the facts that are known, and warn the pupil of the imperfect state of the science. All the facts must, in this case, be stored up with scrupulous accuracy; we cannot determine which are unimportant, and which may prove essentially useful: this can be decided only by future experiments. By thus stating honestly to our pupils the extent of our ignorance, as well as the extent of our knowledge; by thus directing attention to the imperfections of science, rather than to the study of theories, we shall avoid the just reproaches which have been thrown upon the dogmatic vanity of learned preceptors.

"For as knowledges are now," says Bacon, "there is a kind of contract of errour between the deliverer and receiver; for he that delivereth knowledge, desireth to deliver it in such a form as may be best believed, and not as may be best examined; and he that receiveth knowledge, desireth rather present satisfaction than expectant inquiry; and so rather not to doubt, than not to err; glory making the author not to lay open his weakness, and sloth making the disciple not to know his strength." [32]

[13] V. Preface to Berthollet's Chemical Nomenclature.

[14] V. Condillac's "Art de Penser."

[15] Major Cartwright. See his Journal, &c.

[16] V. Chapter on Mechanics.

[17] V. Adela and Theodore.

[18] Chapter on Tasks.

[19] Zoonomia, vol. i. page 435.

[20] Cicero.

[21] Lucian.

[22] "And lends his little soul at every stroke." *Virg.*

[23] V. Chapter II. on Tasks.

[24] Apercues.

[25] Deinology.

[26] V. Condillac Art de Penser.

[27] Mr. Owen.

[28] Mr. Erskine—The Star.

[29] V. Life of John Elwes, Esq. by T. Topham.

[30] V. Chapter on Toys.

[31] Zoonomia, vol. i. p. 21, 24.

[32] Bacon, vol. i. page 84.

CHAPTER IV
SERVANTS

"Now, master," [33] said a fond nurse to her favourite boy, after having given him sugared bread and butter for supper, "now, master, kiss me; wipe your mouth, dear, and go up to the drawing room to mamma; and when mistress asks you what you have had for supper, you'll say, bread and butter, for you *have had* bread and butter, you know, master." "And sugar," said the boy; "I must say bread and butter and sugar, you know."

How few children would have had the courage to have added, "and sugar!" How dangerous it is to expose them to such temptations! The boy must have immediately perceived the object of his nurse's casuistry. He must guess that she would be blamed for the addition of the sugar, else why should she wish to suppress the word? His gratitude is engaged to his nurse for running this risk to indulge him; his mother, by the force of contrast, appears a severe person, who, for no reason that he can comprehend, would deprive him of the innocent pleasure of eating sugar. As to its making him sick, he has eat it, and he is not sick; as to its spoiling his teeth, he does not care about his teeth, and he sees no immediate change in them: therefore he concludes that his mother's orders are capricious, and that his nurse loves him better because she gives him the most pleasure. His honour and affection towards his nurse, are immediately set in opposition to his duty to his mother. What a hopeful beginning in education! What a number of dangerous ideas may be given by a single word!

The taste for sugared bread and butter is soon over; but servants have it in their power to excite other tastes with premature and factitious enthusiasm. The waiting-maid, a taste for dress; the footman, a taste for gaming; the coachman and groom, for horses and equipage; and the butler, for wine. The simplicity of children is not a defence to them; and though they are totally ignorant of vice, they are exposed to adopt the principles of those with whom they live, even before they can apply them to their own conduct.

The young son of a lady of quality, a boy of six or seven years old, addressed, with great simplicity, the following speech to a lady who visited his mother.

Boy. Miss N— —, I wish you could find somebody, when you go to London, who would keep you. It's a very good thing to be kept.

Lady. What do you mean, my dear?

Boy. Why it's when—you know, when a person's kept, they have every thing found for them; their friend saves them all trouble, you know. They have a *carriage* and *diamonds*, and every thing they want. I wish somebody would keep you.

Lady, laughing. But I'm afraid nobody would. Do you think any body would?

Boy, after a pause. Why yes, I think Sir — —, naming a gentleman whose name had, at this time, been much talked of in a public trial, would be as likely as any body.

The same boy talked familiarly of phætons and gigs, and wished that he was grown up, that he might drive four horses in hand. It is obvious that these ideas were put into the boy's head by the servants with whom he associated.

Without supposing them to be profligate, servants, from their situation, from all that they see of the society of their superiors, and from the early prejudices of their own education, learn to admire that wealth and rank to which they are bound to pay homage. The luxuries and follies of fashionable life they mistake for happiness; they measure the respect they pay to strangers by their external appearance; they value their own masters and mistresses by the same standard; and in their attachment there is a necessary mixture of that sympathy which is sacred to prosperity. Setting aside all interested motives, servants love show and prodigality in their masters; they feel that they partake the triumph, and they wish it to be as magnificent as possible. These dispositions break out naturally in the conversation of servants with one another; if children are suffered to hear them, they will quickly catch the same tastes. But if these ideas break out in their unpremeditated gossiping with one another, how much more strongly will they be expressed when servants wish to ingratiate themselves into a child's affections by flattery! Their method of showing their attachment to a family, is usually to exaggerate in their expressions of admiration of its consequence and grandeur; they depreciate all whom they imagine to be competitors in any respect with their masters, and feed and foster the little jealousies which exist between neighbouring families. The children of these families are thus early set at variance; the children in the same family are often taught, by the imprudence or malice of servants, to dislike and envy each other. In houses where each child has an attendant, the attendants regularly quarrel, and, out of a show of zeal, make their young masters and mistresses parties in their animosity. Three or four maids sometimes produce their little dressed pupils for a few minutes to *the company* in the drawing room, for the express purpose of seeing which shall obtain the greatest share of admiration. This competition, which begins in their nurses' arms, is continued by daily artifices through the whole course of their nursery education. Thus the emulation of children is rendered a torment to them, their ambition is directed to absurd and vile purposes, the understanding is perverted, their temper is spoiled, their simplicity of mind, and their capability of enjoying happiness, materially injured.

The language and manners, the awkward and vulgar tricks which children learn in the society of servants, are immediately perceived, and disgust and shock well-bred parents. This is an evil which is striking and disgraceful; it is more likely to be remedied than those which are more secret and slow in their operation: the habits of cunning, falsehood, envy, which lurk in the temper, are not instantly visible to strangers; they do not appear the moment children are reviewed by parents; they may remain for years without notice or without cure.

All these things have been said a hundred times; and, what is more, they are universally acknowledged to be true. It has passed into a common maxim with all who reflect, and even with all who speak upon the subject of education, that "it is the worst thing in the world to leave children with servants." But, notwithstanding this, each person imagines that he has found some lucky exception to the general rule. There is some favourite maid or phœnix of a footman in each family, who is supposed to be unlike all other servants, and, therefore, qualified for the education of children. But, if their qualifications were scrupulously examined, it is to be feared they would not be found competent to the trust that is reposed in them. They may, nevertheless, be excellent servants, much attached to their masters and mistresses, and sincerely desirous to obey their orders in the management of their pupils; but this is not sufficient. In education it is not enough to obey the laws; it is necessary to understand them, to understand the spirit, as well as the letter of the law. The blind application of general maxims will never succeed; and can that nice discrimination which is necessary to the just use of good principles, be expected from those who have never studied the human mind, who have little motive for the study, whose knowledge is technical, and who have never had any liberal education? Give, or attempt to give, the best waiting-maid in London the general maxim, "That pain should be associated with whatever we wish to make children avoid doing; and pleasure should be associated with whatever we wish that children should love to do;" will the waiting-maid understand this, even if you exchange the word *associated* for *joined*? How will she apply her new principle in practice? She will probably translate it into, "Whip the child when it is troublesome, and give it sweetmeats when it does as it is bid." With this compendious system of tuition she is well satisfied, especially as it contains nothing which is new to her understanding, or foreign to her habits. But if we should expect her to enter into the views of a Locke or a Barbauld, would it not be at once unreasonable and ridiculous?

What has been said of the understanding and dispositions of servants, relates only to servants as they are now educated. Their vices and their ignorance arise from the same causes, the want of education. They are not a separate cast in society, doomed to ignorance, or degraded by inherent vice; they are capable, they are desirous of instruction. Let them be well educated, [34] and the difference in their conduct and understanding will repay society for the trouble of the undertaking. This education must begin as early as possible; let us not imagine that it is practicable to change the habits of servants who are already educated, and to make them suddenly fit companions in a family. They should not, in any degree, be permitted to interfere with the management of children, until their own education has been radically reformed. Let servants be treated with the utmost kindness; let their situations be made as happy as possible; let the reward of their services and attachment be as liberal as possible; but reward with justice, do not sacrifice your children to pay your own debts. Familiarity between servants and children, cannot permanently increase the happiness of either party. Children, who have early lived with servants, as they grow up are notoriously apt to become capricious and tyrannical masters. A boy who has been used to treat a footman as his play-fellow, cannot suddenly command from him that species of deference, which is compounded of habitual respect for the person, and conventional submission to his station; the young master must, therefore, effect a change in his footman's manner of thinking and speaking by violent means; he must extort that tribute of respect which he has neglected so long, and to which, consequently, his right is disputed. [35] He is sensible, that his superiority is merely that of situation, and he, therefore, exerts his dormant prerogatives with jealous insolence. No master is so likely to become the tyrant of his valet-de-chambre, as he who is conscious that he never *can* appear to him a hero. No servant feels the yoke of servitude more galling, than he who has been partially emancipated, who has lost his habits of "proud subordination, and his taste for dignified submission." [36]

No mistaken motive of tenderness to domestics should operate upon the minds of parents; nor should they hesitate, for the general happiness of their families, to insist upon a total separation between those parts of it which will injure each other essentially by their union.

Every body readily disclaims the idea of letting children live with servants; but, besides the exceptions in favour of particular individuals, there is yet another cause of the difference between theory and practice upon this subject. Time is left out of the consideration; people forget that life is made up of days and hours; and they by no means think, that letting children pass several hours every day with servants, has any thing to do with the idea of living with them. We must contract this latitude of expression. If children pass one hour in a day with servants, it will be in vain to attempt their education.

Madame Roland, in one of her letters to De Bosc, says, that her little daughter Eudora had learned to swear; "and yet," continues she, "I leave her but one half hour a day with servants. Admirez la disposition!" Madame Roland could not have been much accustomed to attend to education.

Whilst children are very young, there appears a necessity for their spending at least half an hour a day with servants; until they are four or five years old, they cannot dress or undress themselves, or, if they attempt it, they may learn careless habits, which in girls are particularly to be avoided. If a mother, or a governess, would make it a rule to be present when they are dressing, a maid-servant would not talk to them, and could do them but little injury. It is of consequence, that the maid-servant should herself be perfectly neat both from habit and taste. Children observe exactly the manner in which every thing is done for them, and have the wish, even before they have the power, to imitate what they see; they love order, if they are accustomed to it, and if their first attempts at arrangement are not made irksome by injudicious management. What they see done every day in a particular manner, they learn to think part of the business of the day, and they are uneasy if any of the rites of cleanliness are forgotten; the transition from this uneasiness, to the desire of exerting themselves, is soon made, particularly if they are sometimes left to feel the inconveniences of being helpless. This should, and can, be done, without affectation. A maid cannot be always ready, the instant she is wanted, to attend upon them; they should not be waited upon as being masters and misses, they should be assisted as being helpless. [37] They will not feel their vanity flattered by this attendance; the maid will not be suffered to amuse them, they will be ambitious of independence, and they will soon be proud of doing every thing for themselves.

Another circumstance which keeps children long in subjection to servants, is their not being able to wield a knife, fork, or spoon, with decent dexterity. Such habits are taught to them by the careless maids who feed them, that they cannot for many years be produced even at the side-table without much inconvenience and constant anxiety. If this anxiety in a mother were to begin a little sooner, it need never be intense; patient care in feeding children neatly at first, will save many a bitter reprimand afterwards; their little mouths and hands need not be disgusting at their meals, and their nurses had better take care not to let them touch what is disagreeable, instead of rubbing their lips rudely with a rough napkin, by way of making them love to have their mouths clean. These minutiæ must, in spite of didactic dignity, be noticed, because they lead to things of greater consequence; they are well worth the attention of a prudent mother or governess. If children are early taught to eat with care, they will not, from false shame, desire to dine [38] with the vulgar indulgent nursery-maid, rather than with the fastidious company at their mother's table. Children should first be taught to eat with a spoon what has been neatly cut for them; afterwards they should cut a little meat for themselves towards the end of dinner, when the rage of hunger is appeased; they will then have "leisure to be good." The several operations of learning to eat with a spoon, to cut and to eat with a knife and fork, will become easy and habitual, if sufficient time be allowed.

Several children in a family, who were early attended to in all these little particulars, were produced at table when they were four or five years old; they suffered no constraint, nor were they ever banished to the nursery lest *company* should detect their evil habits. Their eyes and ears were at liberty during the time of dinner; and instead of being absorbed in the contemplation of their plates, and at war with themselves and their neighbours, they could listen to conversation, and were amused even whilst they were eating. Without meaning to assert, with Rousseau, that all children are naturally gluttons or epicures, we must observe, that eating is their first great and natural pleasure; this pleasure should, therefore, be *entirely* at the disposal of those who have the care of their education; it should be associated with the idea of their tutors or governesses. A governess may, perhaps, disdain to use the same means to make herself beloved by a child, as those which are employed by a nursery-maid; nor is it meant that children should be governed by their love of eating. Eating need not be made a reward, nor should we restrain their appetite as a punishment; praise and blame, and a variety of other excitements, must be preferred when we want to act upon their understanding. Upon this subject we shall speak more fully hereafter. All that is here meant to be pointed out, is, that the mere physical pleasure of eating should not be associated in the minds of children with servants; it should not be at the disposal of servants, because they may, in some degree, balance by this pleasure the other motives which a tutor may wish to put in action. "Solid pudding," as well as "empty praise," should be in the gift of the preceptor.

Besides the pleasures of the table, there are many others which usually are associated early with servants. After children have been pent in a close formal drawing-room, motionless and mute, they are frequently dismissed to an apartment where there is no furniture too fine to be touched with impunity, where there is ample space, where they may jump and sing, and make as much noise as can be borne by the much-enduring eardrum of the nursery-maid. Children think this insensibility of ear a most valuable qualification in any person; they have no sympathy with more refined auditory nerves, and they prefer the company of those who are to them the best hearers. A medium between their taste and that of their parents should, in this instance, be struck; parents should not insist upon eternal silence, and children should not be suffered to make mere noise essential to their entertainment. Children should be encouraged to talk at proper times, and should have occupations provided for them when they are required to be still; by these means it will not be a restraint to them to stay in the same room with the rest of the family for some hours in the day. At other times they should have free leave to run about either in rooms where they cannot disturb others, or out of doors; in neither case should they be with servants. Children should never be sent out to walk with servants.

After they have been poring over their lessons, or stiffening under the eye of their preceptors, they are frequently consigned immediately to the ready footman; they cluster round him for their hats, their gloves, their little boots and whips, and all the well known signals of pleasure. The hall door bursts open, and they sally forth under the interregnum of this beloved protector, to enjoy life and liberty; all the natural, and all the factitious ideas of the love of liberty, are connected with this distinct part of the day; the fresh air—the green fields—the busy streets—the gay shops—the variety of objects which the children see and hear—the freedom of their tongues— the joys of bodily exercise, and of mental relaxation, all conspire to make them prefer this period of the day, which they spend with the footman, to any other in the four-and-twenty hours. The footman sees, and is flattered by this; he is therefore assiduous to please, and piques himself upon being more indulgent than the hated preceptor. Servants usually wish to make themselves beloved by children; can it be wondered at if they succeed, when we consider the power that is thrown into their hands?

In towns, children have no gardens, no place where they can take that degree of exercise which is necessary for their health; this tempts their parents to trust them to servants, when they cannot walk with them themselves: but is there no individual in the family, neither tutor, nor governess, nor friend, nor brother, nor sister, who can undertake this daily charge? Cannot parents sacrifice some of their amusements in town, or cannot they live in the country? If none of these things can be done, without hesitation they should prefer a public to a private education. In these circumstances, they cannot educate their children at home; they had much better not attempt it, but send them at once to school.

In the country, arrangements may easily be made, which will preclude all those little dangers which fill a prudent parent's mind with anxiety. Here children want the care of no servant to walk out with them; they can have gardens, and safe places for exercise allotted to them. In rainy weather they can have rooms apart from the rest of the family; they need not be cooped up in an ill-contrived house, where servants are perpetually in their way.

Attention to the arrangement of a house, is of material consequence. Children's rooms should not be passage rooms for servants; they should, on the contrary, be so situated, that servants cannot easily have access to them, and cannot, on any pretence of business, get the habit of frequenting them. Some fixed employment should be provided for children, which will keep them in a different part of the house at those hours when servants must necessarily be in their bed-chambers. There will be a great advantage in teaching children to arrange their own rooms, because this will prevent the necessity of servants being for any length of time in their apartments; their things will not be mislaid; their playthings will not be swept away or broken; no little temptations will arise to ask questions from servants; all necessity, and all opportunity of intercourse, will thus be cut off. Children should never be sent with messages to servants, either on their own business, or on other people's; if they are permitted any times to speak to them, they will not distinguish what times are proper, and what are improper.

Servants have so much the habit of talking to children, and think it such a proof of good nature to be interested about them, that it will be difficult to make them submit to this total silence and separation. The certainty that they shall lose their places, if they break through the regulations of the family, will, however, be a strong motive, provided that their places are agreeable and advantageous; and parents should be absolutely strict in this particular. What is the loss of the service of a good groom, or a good butler, compared with the danger of spoiling a child? It may be feared that some *secret* intercourse should be carried on between children and servants; but this will be lessened by the arrangements in the house, which we have mentioned;

by care in a mother or governess, to know exactly where children are, and what they are doing every hour of the day; this need not be a daily anxiety, for when certain hours have once been fixed for certain occupations, habit is our friend, and we cannot have a safer. There is this great advantage in measures of precaution and prevention, that they diminish all temptation, at the same time that they strengthen the habits of obedience.

Other circumstances will deter servants from running any hazard themselves; they will not be so fond of children who do not live with them; they will consider them as beings moving in a different sphere. Children who are at ease with their parents, and happy in their company, will not seek inferior society; this will be attributed to pride by servants, who will not like them for this reserve. So much the better. Children who are encouraged to converse about every thing that interests them, will naturally tell their mothers if any one talks to them; a servant's speaking to them would be an extraordinary event to be recorded in the history of the day. The idea that it is dishonourable to tell tales, should never be put into their minds; they will never be the spies of servants, nor should they keep their secrets. Thus, as there is no faith expected from the children, the servants will not trust them; they will be certain of detection, and will not transgress the laws.

It may not be impertinent to conclude these minute precepts with assuring parents, that in a numerous family, where they have for above twenty years been steadily observed, success has been the uniform result.

[33] Verbatim from what has been really said to a boy.

[34] Perhaps an institution for the education of attendants upon children, would be of the highest utility.

Mr. — — had once an intention of educating forty children for this purpose; from amongst whom he proposed to select eight or ten as masters for future schools upon the same plan.

[35] V. The comedy of Wild Oats.

[36] Burke.

[37] Rousseau.

[38] V. Sancho Panza.

CHAPTER V
ACQUANTAINCE

"The charming little dears!" exclaims a civil acquaintance, the moment the children are introduced. "Won't you come to me, love?" At this question, perhaps, the bashful child backs towards its nurse, or its mother; but in vain. Rejected at this trying crisis by its natural protectors, it is pushed forward into the middle of the circle, and all prospect of retreat being cut off, the victorious stranger seizes upon her little victim, whom she seats, without a struggle, upon her lap. To win the affections of her captive, the lady begins by a direct appeal to personal vanity: "Who curls this pretty hair of yours, my dear? Won't you let me look at your nice new red shoes? What shall I give you for that fine colour in your cheeks? Let us see what we can find in my pocket!"

Amongst the pocket bribes, the lady never fails to select the most useless trinkets; the child would make a better choice; for, if there should appear a pocket-book, which may be drawn up by a ribbon from its slip case, a screen that would unfold gradually into a green star, a pocket-fan, or a tooth-pick case with a spring lock, the child would seize upon these with delight; but the moment its attention is fixed, it is interrupted by the officious exclamation of, "Oh, let me do that for you, love! Let me open that for you, you'll break your sweet little nails. Ha! there is a looking-glass; whose pretty face is that? but we don't love people for being pretty, you know; (mamma says I must not tell you you are pretty) but we love little girls for being good, and I am sure you look as if you were never naughty. I am sure you don't know what it is to be naughty; will you give me one kiss? and will you hold out your pretty little hand for some sugar-plums? Mamma shakes her head, but mamma will not be angry, though mamma can refuse you nothing, I'll answer for it. Who spoils you? Whose favourite are you? Who do you love best in the world? And will you love me? And will you come and live with me? Shall I carry you away with me in the coach to-night? Oh! but I'm afraid I should eat you up, and then what would mamma say to us both?"

To stop this torrent of nonsense, the child's mother, perhaps, ventures to interfere with, "My dear, I'm afraid you'll be troublesome." But this produces only vehement assertions of the contrary. "The dear little creature can never be troublesome to any body." Wo be to the child who implicitly believes this assertion! frequent rebuffs from his *friends* must be endured before this errour will be thoroughly rectified: this will not tend to make those friends more agreeable, or more beloved. That childish love, which varies from hour to hour, is scarcely worth consideration; it cannot be an object of competition to any reasonable person; but in early education nothing must be thought beneath our attention. A child does not retain much affection, it is true, for every casual visiter by whom he is flattered and caressed. The individuals are here to-day and gone to-morrow; variety prevents the impression from sinking into the mind, it may be said; but the general impression remains, though each particular stroke is not seen. Young children, who are much caressed in company, are less intent than others upon pleasing those they live with, and they are also less independent in their occupations and pleasures. Those who govern such pupils have not sufficient power over them, because they have not the means of giving pleasure; because their praise or blame is frequently counteracted by applause of visiters. That unbroken course of experience, which is necessary for the success of a regular plan of education, cannot be preserved. Every body may have observed the effect, which the extraordinary notice of strangers produces upon children. After the day is over, and the company has left the house, there is a cold blank; a melancholy silence. The children then sink into themselves, and feel the mortifying change in their situation. They look with dislike upon everything around them; yawn with ennui, or fidget with fretfulness, till on the first check which they meet with, their secret discontent bursts forth into a storm. Resistance, caprice, and peevishness, are not borne with patience by a governess, though they are submitted to with smiles by the complaisant visiter. In the same day, the same conduct produces totally different consequences. Experience, it is said, makes fools wise; but such experience as this, makes wise children fools.

Why is this farce of civility, which disgusts all parties, continually repeated between visiters and children? Visiters would willingly be excused from the trouble of flattering and spoiling them; but such is the spell of custom, that no one dares to break it, even when every one feels that it is absurd.

Children, who are thought to be clever, are often produced to entertain company; they fill up the time, and relieve the circle from that embarrassing silence, which proceeds from the having nothing to say. Boys, who are thus brought forward at six or seven years old, and encouraged to say what are called *smart* things, seldom, as they grow up, have really good understandings. Children, who, like the fools in former times, are permitted to say every thing, now and then blurt out those simple truths which politeness conceals: this entertains people, but, in fact, it is a sort of *naivete*, which may exist without any great talent for observation, and without any powers of reasoning. Every thing in our manners, in the customs of the world, is new to children, and the relations of apparently dissimilar things, strike them immediately from their novelty. Children are often witty, without knowing it, or rather without intending it; but as they grow older, the same kind of wit does not please; the same objects do not appear in the same point of view; and boys, who have been the delight of a whole house at seven or eight years old, for the smart things they could say, sink into stupidity and despondency at thirteen or fourteen. "Un nom trop fameaux, est un fardeau tres pesant," said a celebrated wit.

Plain, sober sense, does not entertain common visiters, and children whose minds are occupied, and who are not ambitious of exhibiting themselves for the entertainment of the company, will not in general please. So much the better; they will escape many dangers; not only the dangers of flattery, but also the dangers of nonsense. Few people know how to converse with children; they talk to them of things that are above, or below, their understandings; if they argue with them, they do not reason fairly; they silence them with sentiment, or with authority; or else they baffle them by wit, or by unintelligible terms. They often attempt to try their capacities with quibbles and silly puzzles. Children, who are expert at answering these, have rarely been well educated: the extreme simplicity of sensible children, will surprise those who have not been accustomed to it, and many will be provoked by their inaptitude to understand the common-place wit of conversation.

"How many sticks go to a rook's nest?" said a gentleman to a boy of seven years old; he looked very grave, and having pondered upon the question for some minutes, answered, "I do not know what you mean by the word go." Fortunately for the boy, the gentleman who asked the question, was not a captious querist; he perceived the good sense of this answer; he perceived that the boy had exactly hit upon the ambiguous word which was puzzling to the understanding, and he saw that this showed more capacity than could have been shown by the parrying of a thousand witticisms. We have seen S——, a remarkably intelligent boy of nine years old, stand with the most puzzled face imaginable, considering for a long half hour the common quibble of "There was a carpenter who made a door; he made it too large; he cut it and cut it, and he cut it *too little*; he cut it again, and it fitted." S—— showed very little satisfaction, when he at length discovered the double meaning of the words "too little;" but simply said, "I did not know you meant that the carpenter cut *too little off* the door."

"Which has most legs, a horse or no horse?" "A horse has more legs than no horse," replies the unwary child. "But," continues the witty sophist, "a horse, surely, has but four legs; did you ever see a horse with five legs?" "Never," says the child; "no horse has five legs." "Oh, ho!" exclaims the entrapper, "I have you now! No horse has five legs, you say; then you must acknowledge that *no* horse has more legs than *a* horse. Therefore, when I asked you which has most legs, *a horse* or *no horse*, your answer, you see, should have been, *no horse*."

The famous dilemma of "you have what you have not lost; you have not lost horns; then you have horns;" is much in the same style of reasoning. Children may readily be taught to chop logic, and to parry their adversaries technically in this contest of false wit; but this will not improve their understandings, though it may, to superficial judges, give them the appearance of great quickness of intellect. We should not, *even* in jest, talk of nonsense to children, or suffer them *even* to hear inaccurate language. If confused answers be given to their questions, they will soon be content with a confused notion of things; they will be satisfied with bad reasoning, if they are not taught to distinguish it scrupulously from what is good, and to reject it steadily. Half the expressions current in conversation, have merely a nominal value; they represent no ideas, and they pass merely by common courtesy: but the language of every person of sense has sterling value; it cheats and puzzles nobody; and even when it is addressed to children, it is made intelligible. No common acquaintance, who talks to a child merely for its own amusement, selects his expressions with any care; what becomes of the child afterwards, is no part of his concern; he does not consider the advantage of clear explanations to the understanding, nor would he be at the pains of explaining any thing thoroughly, even if he were able to do so. And how few people are able to explain distinctly, even when they most wish to make themselves understood!

The following conversation passed between a learned doctor (formerly) of the Sorbonne, and a boy of seven years old.

Doctor. So, Sir, I see you are very advanced already in your studies. You are quite expert at Latin. Pray, Sir, allow me to ask you; I suppose you have heard of Tully's Offices?

Boy. Tully's Offices! No, Sir.

Doctor. No matter. You can, I will venture to say, solve me the following question. It is not very difficult, but it has puzzled some abler casuists, I can tell you, though, than you or I; but if you will lend me your attention for a few moments, I flatter myself I shall make myself intelligible to you.

The boy began to stiffen at this exordium, but he fixed himself in an attitude of anxious attention, and the doctor, after having taken two pinches of snuff, proceeded:

"In the Island of Rhodes, there was once, formerly, a great scarcity of provisions, a famine quite; and some merchants fitted out ten ships to relieve the Rhodians; and one of the merchants got into port sooner than the others; and he took advantage of this circumstance to sell his goods at an exorbitant rate, finding himself in possession of the market. The Rhodians did not know that the other ships laden with provisions were to be in the next day; and they, of course, paid this merchant whatsoever price he thought proper to demand. Now the question is, in morality, whether did he act the part of an honest man in this business by the Rhodians? Or should he not rather have informed them of the nine ships which were expected to come with provisions to the market the ensuing day?"

The boy was silent, and did not appear to comprehend the story or the question in the least. In telling his story, the doctor of the Sorbonne unluckily pronounced the words *ship* and *ships* in such a manner, that the child all along mistook them for *sheep* and *sheeps*; and this mistake threw every thing into confusion. Besides this, a number of terms were made use of which were quite new to the boy. Getting into port—being in possession of the market—selling goods at an exorbitant rate; together with the whole mystery of buying and selling, were as new to him, and appeared to him as difficult to be understood, as the most abstract metaphysics. He did not even know what was meant by the ships being expected *in* the next day; and "*acting the part* of an honest man," was to him an unusual mode of expression. The young casuist made no hand of this case of conscience; when at last he attempted an answer, he only exposed himself to the contempt of the learned doctor. When he was desired to repeat the story, he made a strange jumble about some people who wanted to get some *sheep*, and about one man who got in his sheep before the other nine sheep; but he did not know how or why it was wrong in him not to tell of the other sheep. Nor could he imagine why the *Rhodians* could not get sheep without this man. He had never had any idea of a famine. This boy's father, unwilling that he should retire to rest with his intellects in this state of confusion, as soon as the doctor had taken leave, told the story to the child in different words, to try whether it was the words or the ideas that puzzled him.

"In the Ægean sea, which you saw the other day in the map, there is an Island, which is called the Island of Rhodes. In telling my story, I take the opportunity to fix a point in geography in your memory. In the Ægean sea there is an Island which is called the Island of Rhodes. There was once a famine in this Island, that is to say, the people had not food enough to live upon, and they were afraid that they should be starved to death. Now, some merchants, who lived on the continent of Greece, filled ten ships with provisions, and they sailed in these vessels for the Island of Rhodes. It happened that one of these ships got to the Island sooner than any of the others. It was evening, and the captain of this ship knew that the others could not arrive until the morning. Now the people of Rhodes, being extremely hungry, were very eager to buy the provisions which this merchant had brought to sell; and they were ready to give a great deal more money for provisions than they would have done if they had not been almost starved. There was not half a sufficient quantity of food in this one ship, to supply all the people who wanted food; and therefore those who had money, and who knew that the merchant wanted as much money as he could get in exchange for his provisions, offered to give him a large price, the price which he asked for them. Had these people known that nine other ships full of provisions would arrive in the morning, they would not have been ready to give so much money for food, because they would not have been so much afraid of being starved; and they would have known, that, in exchange for their money, they could have a greater quantity of food the next day. The merchant, however, did not tell them that any ships were expected to arrive, and he consequently got a great deal more of their money for his provisions, than he would have done, if he had told them the fact which he knew, and which they did not know. Do you think that he did right or wrong?"

The child, who now had rather more the expression of intelligence in his countenance, than he had when the same question had been put to him after the former statement of the case, immediately answered, that he "thought the merchant had done wrong, that he should have told the people that more ships were to come in the morning." Several different opinions were given afterwards by other children, and grown people who were asked the same question; and what had been an unintelligible story, was rendered, by a little more skill and patience in the art of explanation, an excellent lesson, or rather exercise in reasoning.

It is scarcely possible that a stranger, who sees a child only for a few hours, can guess what he knows, and what he does not know; or that he can perceive the course of his thoughts, which depends upon associations over which he has no command; therefore, when a stranger, let his learning and abilities be what they will, attempts to teach children, he usually puzzles them, and the consequences of the confusion of mind he creates, last sometimes for years: sometimes it influences their moral, sometimes their scientific reasoning. "Every body but my friends," said a little girl of six years old, "tells me I am very pretty." From this contradictory evidence, what must the child have inferred? The perplexity which some young people, almost arrived at the years of discretion, have shown in their first notions of mathematics, has been a matter of astonishment to those who have attempted to teach them: this perplexity has been at length discovered to arise from their having early confounded in their minds the ideas of a triangle, and an angle. In the most common modes of expression there are often strange inaccuracies, which do not strike us, because they are familiar to us; but children, who hear them for the first time, detect their absurdity, and are frequently anxious to have such phrases explained. If they converse much with idle visiters, they will seldom be properly applauded for their precision, and their philosophic curiosity will often be repressed by unmeaning replies. Children, who have the habit of applying to their parents, or to sensible preceptors, in similar difficulties, will be somewhat better received, and will gain rather more accurate information. S—— (nine years old) was in a house where a chimney was on fire; he saw a great bustle, and he heard the servants and people, as they ran backwards and forwards, all exclaim, that "the chimney was on fire." After the fire was put out, and when the bustle was over, S—— said to his father, "What do people mean when they say the *chimney is on fire*? What is it that burns?" At this question a silly acquaintance would probably have laughed in the boy's face; would have expressed astonishment as soon as his visit was over, at such an instance of strange ignorance in a boy of nine years old; or, if civility had prompted any answer, it would perhaps have been, "The chimney's being on fire, my love, means that the chimney's on fire! Every body knows what's meant by 'the chimney's on fire!' There's a great deal of smoke, and sparks, and flame, coming out at the top, you know, when the chimney's on fire. And it's extremely dangerous, and would set a house on fire, or perhaps the whole neighbourhood, if it was not put out immediately. Many dreadful fires, you know, happen in towns, as we hear for ever in the newspaper, by the chimney's taking fire. Did you never hear of a chimney's being on fire before? You are a very happy young gentleman to have lived to your time of life, and to be still at a loss about such a thing. What burns? Why, my dear Sir, the chimney burns; fire burns in the chimney. To be sure fires are sad accidents; many lives are lost by them every day. I had a chimney on fire in my drawing room last year."

Thus would the child's curiosity have been baffled by a number of words without meaning or connection; on the contrary, when he applied to a father, who was interested in his improvement, his sensible question was listened to with approbation. He was told, that the chimney's being on fire, was an inaccurate common expression; that it was the soot in the chimney, not the chimney, that burned; that the soot was sometimes set on fire by sparks of fire, sometimes by flame, which might have been accidentally *drawn up* the chimney. Some of the soot which had been set on fire, was shown to him; the nature of burning in general, the manner in which the chimney *draws*, the meaning of that expression, and many other things connected with the subject, were explained upon this occasion to the inquisitive boy, who was thus encouraged to think and speak accurately, and to apply, in similar difficulties, to the friend who had thus taken the trouble to understand his simple question. A random answer to a child's question, does him a real injury; but can we expect, that those who have no interest in education, should have the patience to correct their whole conversation, and to adapt it precisely to the capacity of children? This would indeed be unreasonable; all we can do, is to keep our pupils out of the way of those who *can* do them no good, and who *may* do them a great deal of harm. We must prefer the permanent advantage of our pupils, to the transient vanity of exhibiting for the amusement of company, their early wit, or "lively nonsense." Children should never be introduced for the amusement of the circle; nor yet should they be condemned to sit stock still, holding up their heads and letting their feet dangle from chairs that are too high for them, merely that they may appear what is called *well* before visiters. Whenever any conversation is going forward which they can understand, they should be kindly summoned to partake of the pleasures of society; its pains and its follies we may spare them. The manners of young people will not be injured by this arrangement; they will be at ease in company, because whenever they are introduced into it, they will make a part of it; they will be interested and happy; they will feel a proper confidence in themselves, and they will not be intent upon their courtesies, their frocks, their manner of holding their hands, or turning out their toes, the proper placing of Sir, Madam, or your Ladyship, with all the other innumerable trifles which embarrass the imagination, and consequently the manners, of those who are taught to think that they are to sit still, and behave in company some way differently from what they behave every day in their own family.

We have hitherto only spoken of acquaintance who do not attempt or desire to interfere in education, but who only caress and talk nonsense to children with the best intentions possible: with these, parents will find it comparatively easy to manage; they can contrive to employ children, or send them out to walk; by cool reserve, they can readily discourage such visiters from flattering their children; and by insisting upon becoming a party in all conversations which are addressed to their pupils, they can, in a great measure, prevent the bad effects of inaccurate or imprudent conversation; they can explain to their pupils what was left unintelligible, and they can counteract false associations, either at the moment they perceive them, or at some well-chosen opportunity. But there is a class of acquaintance with whom it will be more difficult to manage; persons who are, perhaps, on an intimate footing with the family, who are valued for their agreeable talents and estimable qualities; who are, perhaps, persons of general information and good sense, and who may yet never have considered the subject of education; or who, having partially considered it, have formed some peculiar and erroneous opinions. They will feel themselves entitled to talk upon education as well as upon any other topic; they will hazard, and they will support, opinions; they will be eager to prove the truth of their assertions, or the superiority of their favourite theories. Out of pure regard for their friends, they will endeavour to bring them over to their own way of thinking in education; and they will by looks, by hints, by inuendoes, unrestrained by the presence of the children, insinuate their advice and their judgment upon every domestic occurrence. In the heat of debate, people frequently forget that children have eyes and ears, or any portion of understanding; they are not aware of the quickness of that comprehension which is excited by the motives of curiosity and self love. It is dangerous to let children be present at any arguments, in which the management of their minds is concerned, until they can perfectly understand the whole of the subject: they will, if they catch but a few words, or a few ideas, imagine, perhaps, that there is something wrong, some hardships, some injustice, practised against them by their friends; yet they will not distinctly know, nor will they, perhaps, explicitly inquire what it is. They should be sent out of the room before any such arguments are begun; or, if the conversation be abruptly begun before parents can be upon their guard, they may yet, without offending against the common forms of politeness, decline entering into any discussion until their children are withdrawn. As to any direct attempt practically to interfere with the children's education, by blame or praise, by presents, by books, or by conversation; these should, and really must, be resolutely and steadily resisted by parents: this will require some strength of mind. What can be done without it? Many people, who are convinced of the danger of the interference of friends and acquaintance in the education of their children, will yet, from the fear of offending, from the dread of being thought singular, submit to the evil. These persons may be very well received, and very well liked in the world: they must content themselves with this reward; they must not expect to succeed in education, for strength of mind is absolutely necessary to those who would carry a plan of education into effect. Without being tied down to any one exclusive plan, and with universal toleration for different modes of moral and intellectual instruction, it may be safely asserted, that the plan which is most steadily pursued, will probably succeed the best. People who are moved by the advice of all their friends, and who endeavour to adapt their system to every fashionable change in opinion, will inevitably repent of their weak complaisance; they will lose all power over their pupils, and will be forced to abandon the education of their families to chance.

It will be found impossible to educate a child at home, unless all interference from visiters and acquaintance is precluded. But it is of yet more consequence, that the members of the family must entirely agree in their sentiments, or at least in the conduct of the children under their care. Without this there is no hope. Young people perceive very quickly, whether there is unanimity in their government; they make out an alphabet of looks with unerring precision, and decipher with amazing ingenuity, all that is for their interest to understand. When children are blamed or punished, they always know pretty well who pities them, who thinks that they are in the wrong, and who thinks that they are in the right; and thus the influence of public opinion is what ultimately governs. If children find that, when mamma is displeased, grandmamma comforts them, they will console themselves readily under this partial disgrace, and they will suspect others of caprice, instead of ever blaming themselves. They will feel little confidence in their own experience, or in the assertions of others; they will think that there is always some chance of escape amongst the multitude of laws and law-givers. No tutor or preceptor can be answerable, or ought *to undertake to answer for measures which he does not guide.* Le Sage, with an inimitable mixture of humour and good sense, in the short history of the education of the robbers who supped in that cave in which dame Leonardo officiated, has given many excellent lessons in education. Captain Rolando's tutors could never make any thing of him, because, whenever they reprimanded him, he ran to his mother, father, and grandfather, for consolation; and from them constantly received protection in rebellion, and commiseration for the wounds which he had inflicted upon his own hands and face, purposely to excite compassion, and to obtain revenge.

It is obviously impossible, that all the world, the ignorant and the well-informed, the man of genius, the man of fashion, and the man of business, the pedant and the philosopher, should agree in their opinion upon any speculative subject; upon the wide subject of education they will probably differ eternally. It will, therefore, be thought absurd to require this union of opinion amongst the individuals of a family; but, let there be ever so much difference in their private opinions, they can surely discuss any disputed point at leisure, when children are absent, or they can, in these arguments, converse in French, or in some language which their pupils do not understand. The same caution should be observed, as we just now recommended, with respect to acquaintance. It is much better, when any difficulties occur, to send the children at once into any other room, and to tell them that we do so because we have something to say that we do not wish them to hear, than to make false excuses to get rid of their company, or to begin whispering and disputing in their presence.

These precautions are advisable whilst our pupils are young, before they are capable of comprehending arguments of this nature, and whilst their passions are vehemently interested on one side or the other. As young people grow up, the greater variety of opinions they hear upon all subjects, the better; they will then form the habit of judging for themselves: whilst they are very young, they have not the means of forming correct judgments upon abstract subjects, nor are these the subjects upon which their judgment can be properly exercised: upon the subject of education, they cannot be competent judges, because they cannot, till they are nearly educated, have a complete view of the means, or of the end; besides this, no *man* is allowed to be judge in his own case.

Some parents allow their children a vast deal of liberty whilst they are young, and restrain them by absolute authority when their reason is, or ought to be, a sufficient guide for their conduct. The contrary practice will make parents much more beloved, and will make children both wiser and happier. Let no idle visiter, no intrusive, injudicious friend, for one moment interfere to lessen the authority necessary for the purposes of education. Let no weak jealousy, no unseasonable love of command, restrain young people after they are sufficiently reasonable to judge for themselves. In the choice of their friends, their acquaintance, in all the great and small affairs of life, let them have liberty in proportion as they acquire reason. Fathers do not commonly interfere with their sons' amusements, nor with the choice of their acquaintance, so much as in the regulation of their pecuniary affairs: but mothers, who have had any considerable share in the education of boys, are apt to make mistakes as to the proper seasons for indulgence and control. They do not watch the moments when dangerous prejudices and tastes begin to be formed; they do not perceive how the slight conversations of acquaintance operate upon the ever-open ear of childhood; but when the age of passion approaches, and approaches, as it usually does, in storms and tempest, then all their maternal fears are suddenly roused, and their anxiety prompts them to use a thousand injudicious and ineffectual expedients.

A modern princess, who had taken considerable pains in the education of her son, made both herself and him ridiculous by her anxiety upon his introduction into the world. She travelled about with him from place to place, to *make him see* every thing worth seeing; but he was not to stir from her presence; she could not bear to have him out of sight or hearing. In all companies he was *chaperoned* by his mother. Was he invited to a ball, she must be invited also, or he could not accept of the invitation: he must go in the same coach, and return in the same coach with her. "I should like extremely to dance another dance," said he one evening to his partner, "but you see I must go; my mother is putting on her cloak." The tall young man called for some negus, and had the glass at his lips, when his mamma called out in a shrill voice, through a vista of heads, "Eh! My son no drink wine! My son like milk and water!" The son was at this time at years of discretion.

CHAPTER VI
ON TEMPER

We have already, in speaking of the early care of infants, suggested that the temper should be attended to from the moment of their birth. A negligent, a careless, a passionate servant, must necessarily injure the temper of a child. The first language of an infant is intelligible only to its nurse; she can distinguish between the cry of pain and the note of ill humour, or the roar of passion. The cry of pain should be listened to with the utmost care, and every possible means should be used to relieve the child's sufferings; but when it is obvious that he cries from ill humour, a nurse should not sooth him with looks of affection, these she should reserve for the moment when the storm is over. We do not mean that infants should be suffered to cry for a length of time without being regarded; this would give them habits of ill humour: we only wish that the nurse would, as soon as possible, teach the child that what he wants can be obtained without his putting himself in a passion. Great care should be taken to prevent occasions for ill humour; if a nurse neglects her charge, or if she be herself passionate, the child will suffer so much pain, and so many disappointments, that it must be in a continual state of fretfulness. An active, cheerful, good humoured, intelligent nurse, will make a child good humoured by a regular, affectionate attendance; by endeavouring to prevent all unnecessary sufferings, and by quickly comprehending its language of signs. The best humoured woman in the world, if she is stupid, is not fit to have the care of a child; the child will not be able to make her understand any thing less than vociferation. By way of amusing the infant, she will fatigue it with her caresses; without ever discovering the real cause of his wo, she will sing one universal lullaby upon all occasions to pacify her charge.

It requires some ingenuity to discover the cause and cure of those long and loud fits of crying, which frequently arise from imaginary apprehensions. A little boy of two years old, used to cry violently when he awoke in the middle of the night, and saw a candle in the room. It was observed that the shadow of the person who was moving about in the room frightened him, and as soon as the cause of his crying was found out, it was easy to pacify him; his fear of shadows was effectually cured, by playfully showing him, at different times, that shadows had no power to hurt him.

H——, about nine months old, when she first began to observe the hardness of bodies, let her hand fall upon a cat which had crept unperceived upon the table; she was surprised and terrified by the unexpected sensation of softness; she could not touch the cat, or any thing that felt like soft fur, without showing agitation, till she was near four years old, though every gentle means were used to conquer her antipathy; the antipathy was, however, cured at last, by her having a wooden cat covered with fur for a plaything.

A boy, between four and five years old, H——, used to cry bitterly when he was left alone in a room, in which there were some old family pictures. It was found that he was much afraid of these pictures: a maid, who took care of him, had terrified him with the notion that they would come to him, or that they were looking at him, and would be angry with him if he was not *good*. To cure the child of this fear of pictures, a small sized portrait, which was not amongst the number of those that had frightened him, was produced in broad day light. A piece of cake was put upon this picture, which the boy was desired to take; he took it, touched the picture, and was shown the canvas at the back of it, which, as it happened to be torn, he could easily identify with the painting: the picture was then given to him for a plaything; he made use of it as a table, and became very fond of it as soon as he was convinced that it was not alive, and that it could do him no sort of injury.

By patiently endeavouring to discover the causes of terror in children, we may probably prevent their tempers from acquiring many bad habits. It is scarcely possible for any one, who has not constantly lived with a child, and who has not known the whole rise and progress of his little character, to trace the causes of these strange apprehensions; for this reason, a parent has advantages in the education of his child, which no tutor or schoolmaster can have.

A little boy was observed to show signs of fear and dislike at hearing the sound of a drum: to a stranger, such fear must have seemed unaccountable, but those who lived with the child, knew from what it arose. He had been terrified by the sight of a merry-andrew in a mask, who had played upon a drum; this was the first time that he had ever heard the sound of a drum; the sound was associated with fear, and continued to raise apprehensions in the child's mind after he had forgotten the original cause of that apprehension.

We are well aware that we have laid ourselves open to ridicule, by the apparently trifling anecdotes which have just been mentioned; but if we can save one child from an hour's unnecessary misery, or one parent from an hour's anxiety, we shall bear the laugh, we hope, with good humour.

Young children, who have not a great number of ideas, perhaps for that reason associate those which they acquire with tenacity; they cannot reason concerning general causes; they expect that any event, which has once or twice followed another, will always follow in the same order; they do not distinguish between proximate and remote causes, between coincidences and the regular connection of cause and effect: hence children are subject to feel hopes and fears from things which to us appear matters of indifference. Suppose, for instance, that a child is very eager to go out to walk, that his mother puts on her gloves and her cloak; these being the usual signals that she is going out, he instantly expects, if he has been accustomed to accompany her, that he shall have the pleasure of walking out; but if she goes out, and forgets him, he is not only disappointed at that moment, but the disappointment, or, at least, some indistinct apprehension, recurs to him when he is in a similar situation: the putting on of his mother's cloak and gloves, are then circumstances of vast importance to him, and create anxiety, perhaps tears, whilst to every other spectator they are matters of total indifference. Every one, who has had any experience in the education of such children as are apt to form strong associations, must be aware, that many of those fits of crying, which appear to arise solely from ill-humour, are occasioned by association. When these are suffered to become habitual, they are extremely difficult to conquer; it is, therefore, best to conquer them as soon as possible. If a child has, by any accident, been disposed to cry at particular times in the day, without any obvious cause, we should at those hours engage his attention, occupy him, change the room he is in, or by any new circumstance break his habits. It will require some penetration to distinguish between involuntary tears, and tears of caprice; but even when children are really cross, it is not, whilst they are very young, prudent to let them wear out their ill-humour, as some people do, in total neglect. Children, when they are left to weep in solitude, often continue in wo for a considerable length of time, until they quite forget the original cause of complaint, and they continue their convulsive sobs, and whining note of distress, purely from inability to stop themselves.

Thus habits of ill-humour are contracted; it is better, by a little well-timed excitation, to turn the course of a child's thoughts, and to make him forget his trivial miseries. "The tear forgot as soon as shed," is far better than the peevish whine, or sullen lowering brow, which proclaim the unconquered spirit of discontent.

Perhaps, from the anxiety which we have expressed to prevent the petty misfortunes, and unnecessary tears of children, it may be supposed that we are disposed to humour them; far from it—We know too well that a humoured child is one of the most unhappy beings in the world; a burden to himself, and to his friends; capricious, tyrannical, passionate, peevish, sullen, and selfish.

An only child runs a dreadful chance of being spoiled. He is born a person of consequence; he soon discovers his innate merit; every eye is turned upon him the moment he enters the room; his looks, his dress, his appetite, are all matters of daily concern to a whole family; his wishes are divined; his wants are prevented; his witty sayings are repeated in his presence; his smiles are courted; his caresses excite jealousy, and he soon learns how to avail himself of his central situation. His father and mother make him alternately their idol, and their plaything; they do not think of educating, they only think of admiring him; they imagine that he is unlike all other children in the universe, and that his genius and his temper are independent of all cultivation. But when this little paragon of perfection has two or three brothers and sisters, the scene changes; the man of consequence dwindles into an insignificant little boy. We shall hereafter explain more fully the danger of accustoming children to a large share of our sympathy; we hope that the economy of kindness and caresses which we have recommended, [39] will be found to increase domestic affection, and to be essentially serviceable to the temper. In a future chapter, "On Vanity, Pride, and Ambition," some remarks will be found on the use and abuse of the stimuli of praise, emulation, and ambition. The precautions which we have already mentioned with respect to servants, and the methods that have been suggested for inducing habitual and rational obedience, will also, we hope, be considered as serviceable to the temper, as well as to the understanding. Perpetual and contradictory commands and prohibitions, not only make children disobedient, but fretful, peevish, and passionate.

Idleness, amongst children, as amongst men, is the root of all evil, and leads to no evil more certainly than to ill temper. It is said, [40] that the late king of Spain was always so cross during Passion week, when he was obliged to abstain from his favourite amusement of hunting, that none of his courtiers liked to approach his majesty. There is a great similarity between the condition of a prince flattered by his courtiers, and a child humoured by his family; and we may observe, that both the child and prince are most intolerable to their dependants and friends, when any of their daily amusements are interrupted. It is not that the amusements are in themselves delightful, but the pains and penalties of idleness are insupportable. We have endeavoured to provide a variety of occupations, as well as of amusements, for our young pupils, [41] that they may never know the misery of the Spanish monarch. When children are occupied, they are independent of other people, they are not obliged to watch for casual entertainment from those who happen to be unemployed, or who chance to be in a humour to play with them; they have some agreeable object continually in view, and they feel satisfied with themselves. They will not torment every body in the house with incessant requests. "May I have this? Will you give me that? May I go out to see such a thing? When will it be dinner time? When will it be tea time? When will it be time for me to go to supper?" are the impatient questions of a child who is fretful from having nothing to do. Idle children are eternal petitioners, and the refusals they meet with, perpetually irritate their temper. With respect to requests in general, we should either grant immediately what a child desires, or we should give a decided refusal. The state of suspense is not easily borne; the propriety or impropriety of the request should decide us either to grant, or to refuse it; and we should not set the example of caprice, or teach our pupils the arts of courtiers, who watch the humour of tyrants. If we happen to be busy, and a child comes with an eager request about some trifle, it is easy so far to command our temper as to answer, "I am busy, don't talk to me now," instead of driving the petitioner away with harsh looks, and a peremptory refusal, which make as great an impression as harsh words. If we are reasonable, the child will soon learn to apply to us at proper times. By the same steady, gentle conduct, we may teach him to manage his love of talking with discretion, and may prevent those ineffectual exhortations to silence, which irritate the temper of the vivacious pupil. Expostulations, and angry exclamations, will not so effectually command from our pupils temperance of tongue, as their own conviction that they are more likely to gain attention from their friends, if they choose properly their seasons for conversation.

To prevent, we cannot too often repeat it, is better than to punish, without humouring children; that is to say, without yielding to their caprices, or to their *will*, when they express their wishes with impatience, we may prevent many of those little inconveniences which tease and provoke the temper; any continual irritation exhausts our patience; acute pain can be endured with more fortitude.

We have sometimes seen children become fretful from the constant teasing effect of some slight inconveniences in their dress; we have pitied poor little boys, who were continually exhorted to produce their handkerchiefs, and who could scarcely ever get these handkerchiefs out of the tight pockets into which they had been stuffed; into such pockets the hand can never enter, or withdraw itself, without as much difficulty as Trenck had in getting rid of his handcuffs. The torture of tight shoes, of back-boards, collars, and stocks, we hope is nearly abandoned; surely all these are unnecessary trials of fortitude; they exhaust that patience which might be exercised upon things of consequence. Count Rumford tells us, that he observed a striking melioration in the temper of all the mendicants in the establishment at Munich, when they were relieved from the constant torments of rags and vermin.

Some people imagine, that early sufferings, that a number of small inconveniences, habitual severity of reproof, and frequent contradiction and disappointment, inure children to pain, and consequently improve their temper. Early sufferings, which are necessary and inevitable, may improve children in fortitude; but the contradictions and disappointments, which arise immediately from the will of others, have not the same effect. Children, where their own interests are concerned, soon distinguish between these two classes of evils; they submit patiently when they know that it would be in vain to struggle; they murmur and rebel, if they dare, whenever they feel the hand of power press upon them capriciously. We should not invent trials of temper for our pupils; if they can bear with good humour the common course of events, we should be satisfied.

"I tumbled down, and I *bored* it very well," said a little boy of three years old, with a look of great satisfaction. If this little boy had been thrown down on purpose by his parents as a trial of temper, it probably would not have been borne so well. As to inconveniences, in general it is rather a sign of indolence, than a proof of good temper in children, to submit to them quietly; if they can be remedied by exertion, why should they be passively endured? If they cannot be remedied, undoubtedly it is then better to abstract the attention from them as much as possible, because this is the only method of lessening the pain. Children should be assisted in making this distinction, by our applauding their exertions when they struggle against unnecessary evil, by our commending their patience whenever they endure inevitable pain without complaints.

Illness, for instance, is an inevitable evil. To prevent children from becoming peevish, when they are ill, we should give our pity and sympathy with an increased appearance of affection, whenever they bear their illness with patience. No artifice is necessary; we need not affect any increase of pity; patience and good humour in the sufferer, naturally excite the affection and esteem of the spectators. The self-complacency, which the young patient must feel from a sense of his own fortitude, and the perception that he commands the willing hearts of all who attend him, are really alleviations of his bodily sufferings; the only alleviations which, in some cases, can possibly be afforded.

The attention which is thought necessary in learning languages, often becomes extremely painful to the pupils, and the temper is often hurt by ineffectual attempts to improve the understanding. We have endeavoured to explain the methods of managing [42] the attention of children with the least possible degree of pain. Yesterday a little boy of three years old, W— —, was learning his alphabet from his father; after he had looked at one letter for some time with great attention, he raised his eyes, and with a look of much good humour, said to his father, "It makes me tired to stand." His father seated him upon his knee, and told him that he did wisely in telling what tired him: the child, the moment he was seated, fixed his attentive eyes again upon his letters with fresh eagerness, and succeeded. Surely it was not humouring this boy to let him sit down when he was tired. If we teach a child that our assistance is to be purchased by fretful entreaties; if we show him, that we are afraid of a storm, he will make use of our apprehensions to accomplish his purposes. On the contrary, if he perceives that we can steadily resist his tears and ill humour, and especially if we show indifference upon the occasion, he will perceive that he had better dry his tears, suspend his rage, and try how far good humour will prevail. Children, who in every little difficulty are assisted by others, really believe that others are in fault whenever this assistance is not immediately offered. Look at a humoured child, for instance, trying to push a chair along the carpet; if a wrinkle in the carpet stops his progress, he either beats the chair, or instantly turns with an angry appealing look to his mother for assistance; and if she does not get up to help him, he will cry. Another boy, who has not been humoured, will neither beat the chair, nor angrily look round for help; but he will look immediately to see what it is that stops the chair, and when he sees the wrinkle in the carpet, he will either level or surmount the obstacle: during this whole operation, he will not feel in the least inclined to cry. Both these children might have had precisely the same original stock of patience; but by different management, the one would become passionate and peevish, the other both good humoured and persevering. The pleasure of success pays children, as well as men, for long toil and labour. Success is the proper reward of perseverance; but if we sometimes capriciously grant, and sometimes refuse, our help, our pupils cannot learn this important truth, and they imagine that success depends upon the will of others, and not upon their own efforts. A child, educated by a fairy, who sometimes came with magic aid to perform, and who was sometimes deaf to her call, would necessarily become ill humoured.

Several children, who were reading "Evenings at Home," observed that in the story of Juliet and the fairy Order, "it was wrong to make the fairy come whenever Juliet cried, and could not do her task, because that was the way, said the children, to make the little girl ill humoured."

We have formerly observed that children, who live much with companions of their own age, are under but little habitual restraint as to their tempers; they quarrel, fight, and shake hands; they have long and loud altercations, in which the strongest voice often gets the better. It does not improve the temper to be overborne by petulance and clamour: even mild, sensible children, will learn to be positive if they converse with violent dunces. In private families, where children mix in the society of persons of different ages, who encourage them to converse without reserve, they may meet with exact justice; they may see that their respective talents and good qualities are appreciated; they may acquire the habit of arguing without disputing; and they may learn that species of mutual forbearance in trifles, as well as in matters of consequence, which tends so much to domestic happiness. Dr. Franklin, in one of his letters to a young female friend, after answering some questions which she had asked him, apparently referring to an argument which had passed some time before, concludes with this comprehensive compliment: "So, you see, I think you had the best of the *argument*; and, as you give it up in complaisance to the company, I think you had also the best of the *dispute*." When young people perceive that they gain credit by keeping their temper in conversation, they will not be furious for victory, because moderation, during the time of battle, can alone entitle them to the honours of a triumph.

It is particularly necessary for girls to acquire command of temper in arguing, because much of the effect of their powers of reasoning, and of their wit, when they grow up, will depend upon the gentleness and good humour with which they conduct themselves. A woman, who should attempt to thunder like Demosthenes, would not find her eloquence increase her domestic happiness. We by no means wish that women should yield their better judgment to their fathers or husbands; but, without using any of that debasing cunning which Rousseau recommends, they may support the cause of reason with all the graces of female gentleness.

A man, in a furious passion, is terrible to his enemies; but a woman in a passion, is disgusting to her friends; she loses the respect due to her sex, and she has not masculine strength and courage to enforce any other species of respect. These circumstances should be considered by writers who advise that no difference should be made in the education of the two sexes. We cannot help thinking that their happiness is of more consequence than their speculative rights, and we wish to educate women so that they may be happy in the situations in which they are most likely to be placed. So much depends upon the temper of women, that it ought to be most carefully cultivated in early life; girls should be more inured to restraint than boys, because they are likely to meet with more restraint in society. Girls should learn the habit of bearing slight reproofs, without thinking them matters of great consequence; but then they should always be permitted to state their arguments, and they should perceive that justice is shown to them, and that they increase the affection and esteem of their friends by command of temper. Many passionate men are extremely good natured, and make amends for their extravagances by their candour, and their eagerness to please those whom they have injured during their fits of anger. It is said, that the servants of Dean Swift used to throw themselves in his way whenever he was in a passion, because they knew that his generosity would recompense them for standing the full fire of his anger. A woman, who permitted herself to treat her servants with ill humour, and who believed that she could pay them for ill usage, would make a very bad mistress of a family; her husband and her children would suffer from her ill temper, without being recompensed for their misery. We should not let girls imagine that they can balance ill humour by some good quality or accomplishment; because, in fact, there are none which can supply the want of temper in the female sex.

A just idea of the nature of dignity, opposed to what is commonly called *spirit*, should be given early to our female pupils. Many women, who are not disposed to violence of temper, affect a certain degree of petulance, and a certain stubbornness of opinion, merely because they imagine that to be gentle, is to be mean; and that to listen to reason, is to be deficient in spirit.

Enlarging the understanding of young women, will prevent them from the trifling vexations which irritate those who have none but trifling objects. We have observed that concerted trials of temper are not advantageous for very young children. Those trials which are sometimes prepared for pupils at a more advanced period of education, are not always more happy in their consequences. We make trifles appear important; and then we are surprised that they are thought so.

Lord Kames tells us that he was acquainted with a gentleman, who, though otherwise a man of good understanding, did not show his good sense in the education of his daughters temper. "He had," says Lord Kames, "three comely daughters, between twelve and sixteen, and to inure them to bear disappointments, he would propose to make a visit which he knew would delight them. The coach was bespoke, and the young ladies, completely armed for conquest, were ready to take their seats. But, behold! their father had changed his mind. This, indeed, was a disappointment; but as it appeared to proceed from whim, or caprice, it might sour their temper, instead of improving it." [43]

But why should a visit be made a matter of such mighty consequence to girls? Why should it be a disappointment to stay at home? And why should Lord Kames advise that disappointments should *be made to appear* the effects of chance? This method of making things appear to be what they are not, we cannot too often reprobate; it will not have better success in the education of the temper, than in the management of the understanding; it would ruin the one or the other, or both: even when promises are made with perfect good faith to young people, the state of suspense which they create, is not serviceable to the temper, and it is extremely difficult to promise proper rewards. [44] The celebrated Serena surely established her reputation for good temper, without any very severe trials. Our standard of female excellence, is evidently changed since the days of Griselda; but we are inclined to think, that even in these degenerate days, public amusements would not fill the female imagination, if they were not early represented as such charming things, such great rewards to girls, by their imprudent friends.

The temper depends much upon the understanding; and whenever we give our pupils, whether male or female, false ideas of pleasure, we prepare for them innumerable causes of discontent. "You ought to be above such things! You ought not to let yourself be vexed by such trifles!" are common expressions, which do not immediately change the irritated person's feelings. You must alter the habits of thinking; you must change the view of the object, before you can alter the feelings. Suppose a girl has, from the conversation of all her acquaintance, learned to imagine that there is some vast pleasure in going to a masquerade; it is in vain to tell her, in the moment that she is disappointed about her masquerade dress, that "it is a trifle, and she ought to be above trifles." She cannot be above them at a moment's warning: but if she had never been inspired with a violent desire to go to a masquerade, the disappointment would really appear trifling. We may calculate the probability of any person's mortification, by observing the vehemence of their hopes; thus we are led to observe, that the imagination influences the temper. Upon this subject we shall speak more fully when we treat of Imagination and Judgment.

To measure the degree of indulgence which may be safe for any given pupils, we must attend to the effect produced by pleasure upon their imagination and temper. If a small diminution of their usual enjoyments disturbs them, they have been rendered not too happy, but too susceptible. Happy people, who have resources in their own power, do not feel every slight variation in external circumstances. We may safely allow children to be as happy as they possibly can be without sacrificing the future to the present. Such prosperity will not enervate their minds.

We make this assertion with some confidence, because experience has in many instances confirmed our opinion. Amongst a large family of children, who have never been tormented with artificial trials of temper, and who have been made as happy as it was in the power of their parents to make them, there is not one ill tempered child. We have examples every day before us of different ages from three years old to fifteen.

Before parents adopt either Epicurean or Stoical doctrines in the education of the temper, it may be prudent to calculate the probabilities of the good and evil, which their pupils are likely to meet with in life. The Sybarite, whose night's rest was disturbed by a doubled rose leaf, deserves to be pitied almost as much as the young man who, when he was benighted in the snow, was reproached by his severe father for having collected a heap of snow to make himself a pillow. Unless we could for ever ensure the bed of roses to our pupils, we should do very imprudently to make it early necessary to their repose: unless the pillow of snow is likely to be their lot, we need not inure them to it from their infancy.

[39] V. Chapter on Sympathy and Sensibility.

[40] By Mr. Townsend, in his Travels into Spain.

[41] V. Chapter on Toys.

[42] V. Chapter on Attention.

[43] Lord Kames, p. 109.

[44] V. Chapter on Rewards and Punishments.

CHAPTER VII
ON OBEDIENCE

Obedience has been often called the virtue of childhood. How far it is entitled to the name of virtue, we need not at present stop to examine. Obedience is expected from children long before they can reason upon the justice of our commands; consequently it must be taught as a habit. By associating pleasure with those things which we first desire children to do, we should make them necessarily like to obey; on the contrary, if we begin by ordering them to do what is difficult and disagreeable to them, they must dislike obedience. The poet seems to understand this subject when he says,

"Or bid her wear your necklace rowed with pearl,
You'll find your Fanny an obedient girl." [45]

The taste for a necklace rowed with pearl, is not the *first* taste, even in girls, that we should wish to cultivate; but the poet's *principle* is good, notwithstanding. Bid your child do things that are agreeable to him, and you may be sure of his obedience. Bid a hungry boy eat apple pye; order a shivering urchin to warm himself at a good fire; desire him to go to bed when you see him yawn with fatigue, and by such seasonable commands you will soon form associations of pleasure in his mind, with the voice and tone of authority. This tone should never be threatening, or alarming; it should be gentle, but decided. Whenever it becomes necessary that a child should do what he feels disagreeable, it is better to make him submit at once to necessity, than to create any doubt and struggle in his mind, by leaving him a possibility of resistance. Suppose a little boy wishes to sit up later than the hour at which you think proper that he should go to bed; it is most prudent to take him to bed at the appointed time, without saying one word to him, either in the way of entreaty or command. If you entreat, you give the child an idea that he has it in his power to refuse you: if you command, and he does not instantly obey, you hazard your authority, and you teach him that he can successfully set his will in opposition to yours. The boy wishes to sit up; he sees no reason, in the moral fitness of things, why he should go to bed at one hour more than at another; all he perceives is, that such is your will. What does he gain by obeying you? Nothing: he loses the pleasure of sitting up half an hour longer. How can you then expect that he should, in consequence of these reasonings, give up his obvious immediate interest, and march off to bed heroically at the word of command? Let him not be put to the trial; when he has for some time been regularly taken to bed at a fixed hour, he will acquire the habit of thinking that he must go at that hour: association will make him expect it; and if his experience has been uniform, he will, without knowing why, think it necessary that he should do as he has been used to do. When the habit of obedience to customary necessity is thus formed, we may, without much risk, engraft upon it obedience to the voice of authority. For instance, when the boy hears the clock strike, the usual signal for his departure, you may, if you see that he is habitually ready to obey this signal, associate your commands with that to which he has already learned to pay attention. "Go; it is time that you should go to bed now," will only seem to the child a confirmation of the sentence already pronounced by the clock: by degrees, your commands, after they have been regularly repeated, when the child feels no hope of evading them, will, even in new circumstances, have from association the power of compelling obedience.

Whenever we desire a child to do any thing, we should be perfectly certain, not only that it is a thing which he is capable of doing, but also, that it is something we can, in case it comes to that ultimate argument, force him to do. You cannot oblige a child to stand up, if he has a mind to sit down; or to walk, if he does not choose to exert his muscles for that purpose: but you can absolutely prevent him from touching whatever you desire him not to meddle with, by your superior strength. It is best, then, to begin with prohibitions; with such prohibitions as you can, and will, steadily persevere to enforce: if you are not exact in requiring obedience, you will never obtain it either by persuasion or authority. As it will require a considerable portion of time and unremitting attention, to enforce the punctual observance of a variety of prohibitions, it will, for your own sake, be most prudent to issue as few edicts as possible, and to be sparing in the use of the imperative mood. It will, if you calculate the trouble you must take day after day to watch your pupil, cost you less to begin by arranging every circumstance in your power, so as to prevent the necessity of trusting to laws what ought to be guarded against by precaution. Do you, for instance, wish to prevent your son from breaking a beautiful china jar in your drawing room; instead of forbidding him to touch it, put it out of his reach.—Would you prevent your son from talking to servants; let your house, in the first place, be so arranged, that he shall never be obliged to pass through any rooms where he is likely to meet with servants; let all his wants be gratified without their interference; let him be able to get at his hat without asking the footman to reach it for him, from its inaccessible height. [46] The simple expedient of hanging the hat in a place where the boy can reach it, will save you the trouble of continually repeating, "Don't ask William, child, to reach your hat; can't you come and ask me?" Yes, the boy can come and ask you; but if you are busy, you will not like to go in quest of the hat; your reluctance will possibly appear in your countenance, and the child, who understands the language of looks better than that of words, will clearly comprehend, that you are displeased with him at the very instant that he is fulfilling the letter of the law.

A lady, who was fond of having her house well arranged, discovered, to the amazement of her acquaintance, the art of making all her servants keep every thing in its place. Even in the kitchen, from the most minute article to the most unwieldy, every thing was invariably to be found in its allotted station; the servants were thought miracles of obedience; but, in fact, they obeyed because it was the easiest thing they could possibly do. Order was made more convenient to them than disorder, and, with their utmost ingenuity to save themselves trouble, they could not invent places for every thing more appropriate than those which had been assigned by their mistress's legislative economy. In the same manner we may secure the *orderly* obedience of children, without exhausting their patience or our own. Rousseau advises, that children should be governed solely by the necessity of circumstances; but there are *one and twenty* excellent objections to this system; the first being, that it is impossible: of this Rousseau must have been sensible in the trials which he made as a preceptor. When he had the management of a refractory child, he found himself obliged to invent and arrange a whole drama, by artificial experience, to convince his little pupil, that he had better not walk out in the streets of Paris alone; and that, therefore, he should wait until his pupil could conveniently accompany him. Rousseau had prepared the neighbours on each side of the street to make proper speeches as his pupil passed by their doors, which alarmed and piqued the boy effectually. At length the child was met at a proper time, by a friend who had been appointed to watch him; and thus he was brought home submissive. This scene, as Rousseau observes, was admirably well performed; [47] but what occasion could there be for so much contrivance and deceit? If his pupil had not been uncommonly deficient in penetration, he would soon have discovered his preceptor in some of his artifices; then adieu both to obedience and confidence. A false idea of the pleasures of liberty misled Rousseau. Children have not our abstract ideas of the pleasures of liberty; they do not, until they have suffered from ill judged restraints, feel any strong desire to exercise what we call free will; liberty is, with them, the liberty of doing certain specific things which they have found to be agreeable; liberty is not the general idea of pleasure, in doing whatever they WILL to do. Rousseau desires, that *we should not let our pupil know, that in doing our will he is obedient to us.* But why? Why should we not let a child know the truth? If we attempt to conceal it, we shall only get into endless absurdities and difficulties. Lord Kames tells us, that he was acquainted with a couple, who, in the education of their family, pursued as much as possible Rousseau's plan. One evening, as the father was playing at chess with a friend, one of his children, a boy of about four years old, took a piece from the board, and ran away to play with it. The father, whose principles would not permit him to assert his right to his own chessman, began to bargain for his property with his son. "Harry," said he, "let us have back the man, and there's an apple for you." The apple was soon devoured, and the child returned to the chess board, and kidnapped another chessman. What this man's ransom might be, we are not yet informed; but Lord Kames tells us, that the father was obliged to suspend his game at chess until his son was led away to his supper. Does it seem just, that parents should become slaves to the liberties of their children? If one set of beings or another should sacrifice a portion of happiness, surely those who are the most useful, and the most capable of increasing the knowledge and the pleasures of life, have some claim to a preference; and when the power is entirely in their own hands, it is most probable that they will defend their own interests. We shall not, like many who have spoken of Rousseau, steal from him after having abused him. His remarks upon the absurd and tyrannical restraints which are continually imposed upon children by the folly of nurses and servants, or by the imprudent anxiety of parents and preceptors, are excellent. Whenever Rousseau is in the right, his eloquence is irresistible.

To determine what degree of obedience it is just to require from children, we must always consider what degree of reason they possess: whenever we can use reason, we should never use force; it is only whilst children are too young to comprehend reason, that we should expect from them implicit submission. The means which have been pointed out for teaching the habit of obedience, must not be depended upon for teaching any thing more than the mere habit. When children begin to reason, they do not act merely from habit; they will not be obedient at this age, unless their understanding is convinced that it is for their advantage to be so. Wherever we can explain the reasons for any of our requests, we should attempt it; but whenever these cannot be fully explained, it is better not to give a partial explanation; it will be best to say steadily, "You cannot understand this now, you will, perhaps, understand it some time hence." Whenever we tell children, that we forbid them to do such and such things for any particular reason, we must take care that the reason assigned is adequate, and that it will in all cases hold good. For instance, if we forbid a boy to eat unripe fruit, *because it will make him ill,* and if afterwards the boy eat some unripe gooseberries without feeling ill in consequence of his disobedience, he will doubt the truth of the person who prohibited unripe fruit; he will rather trust his own partial experience than any assertions. The idea of *hurting his health,* is a general idea, which he does not yet comprehend. It is more prudent to keep him out of the way of unripe gooseberries, than to hazard at once his obedience and his integrity. We need not expatiate further; the instance we have given, may be readily applied to all cases in which children have it in their power to disobey with *immediate* impunity, and, what is still more dangerous, with the certainty of obtaining immediate pleasure. The gratification of their senses, and the desire of bodily exercise, ought never to be unnecessarily restrained. Our pupils should distinctly perceive, that we wish to make them happy, and every instance, in which they discover that obedience has really made them happier, will be more in our favour, than all the lectures we could preach. From the past, they will judge of the future. Children, who have for many years experienced, that their parents have exacted obedience only to such commands as proved to be ultimately wise and beneficial, will surely be disposed from habit, from gratitude, and yet more from prudence, to consult their parents in all the material actions of their lives.

We may observe, that the spirit of contradiction, which sometimes breaks out in young people the moment they are able to act for themselves, arises frequently from slight causes in their early education. Children, who have experienced, that submission to the will of others has constantly made them unhappy, will necessarily, by reasoning inversely, imagine, that felicity consists in following their own free will.

The French poet Boileau was made very unhappy by neglect and restraint during his education: when he grew up, he would never agree with those who talked to him of the pleasures of childhood. [49] "Peut on," disoit ce poëte amoureux de l'indépendance, "ne pas regarder comme un grand malheur, le chagrin continuel et particulier à cet age, de ne jamais faire sa volonté?" It was in vain, continues his biographer, to boast to him of the advantages of this happy constraint, which saves youth from so many follies. "What signifies our knowing the value of our chains when we have shaken them off, if we feel nothing but their weight whilst we wear them?" the galled poet used to reply. Nor did Boileau enjoy his freedom, though he thought with such horror of his slavery. He declared, that if he had it in his choice, either to be born again upon the hard conditions of again going through his childhood, or not to exist, he would rather not exist: but he was not happy during any period of his existence; he quarrelled with all the seasons of life; "all seemed to him equally disagreeable; youth, manhood, and old age, are each subject, he observed, to impetuous passions, to care, and to infirmities." Hence we may conclude, that the severity of his education had not succeeded in teaching him to submit philosophically to necessity, or yet in giving him much enjoyment from that *liberty* which he so much coveted. Thus it too often happens, that an imaginary value is set upon the exercise of the free will by those who, during their childhood, have suffered under injudicious restrictions. Sometimes the love of free will is so uncontrollably excited, even during childhood, that it breaks out, unfortunately both for the pupils and the preceptors, in the formidable shape of obstinacy.

Of all the faults to which children are subject, there is none which is more difficult to cure, or more easy to prevent, than obstinacy. As it is early observed by those who are engaged in education, it is sometimes supposed to be inherent in the temper; but, so far from being naturally obstinate, infants show those strong propensities to sympathy and imitation, which prepare them for an opposite character. The folly of the nurse, however, makes an intemperate use of these happy propensities. She perpetually torments the child to exert himself for her amusement; all his senses and all his muscles she commands. He must see, hear, talk, or be silent, move or be still, when she thinks proper; and often with the desire of amusing her charge, or of showing him off to the company, she disgusts him with voluntary exertion. Before young children have completely acquired the use of their limbs, they cannot perform feats of activity or of dexterity at a moment's warning. Their muscles do not instantaneously obey their will; the efforts they make are painful to themselves; the awkwardness of their attempts is painful to others; the delay of the body is often mistaken for the reluctance of the mind; and the impatient tutor pronounces the child to be obstinate, whilst all the time he may be doing his utmost to obey. Instead of growing angry with the helpless child, it would be surely more wise to assist his feeble and inexperienced efforts. If we press him to make unsuccessful attempts, we shall associate pain both with voluntary exertion and with obedience.

Little W—— (a boy of three years old) was one day asked by his father to jump. The boy stood stock still. Perhaps he did not know the meaning of the word jump. The father, instead of pressing him further, asked several other children who happened to be in the room to jump, and he jumped along with them: all this was done playfully. The little boy looked on silently for a short time, and seemed much pleased. "Papa jumps!" he exclaimed. His brother L—— lifted him up two or three times; and he then tried to jump, and succeeded: from sympathy he learned the command of the muscles which were necessary to his jumping, and to his obedience. If this boy had been importuned, or forced to exert himself, he might have been thus taught obstinacy, merely from the imprudent impatience of the spectators. The reluctance to stop when a child is once in motion, is often mistaken for obstinacy: when he is running, singing, laughing, or talking, if you suddenly command him to stop, he cannot instantly obey you. If we reflect upon our own minds, we may perceive that we cannot, without considerable effort, turn our thoughts suddenly from any subject on which we have been long intent. If we have been long in a carriage, the noise of the wheels sounds in our ear, and we seem to be yet going on after the carriage has stopped. We do not pretend to found any accurate reasoning upon analogy; but we may observe, the difficulty with which our minds are stopped or put in motion, resembles the vis-inertiæ of the body.

W— — (three years old) had for some minutes vociferated two or three words of a song, until the noise could be no longer patiently endured; his father called to him, and desired that he would not make so much noise. W— — paused for a moment, but then went on singing the same words. His brother said, Hush! W— — paused for another second or two; but then went on with his roundelay. In his countenance there was not the slightest appearance of ill humour. One of his sisters put him upon a board which was lying on the floor, and which was a little unsteady; as he walked cautiously along this board, his attention was occupied, and he forgot his song.

This inability suddenly to desist from any occupation, may easily grow into obstinacy, because the pain of checking themselves will be great in children, and this pain will be associated with the commands of those who govern them; it is better to stop them by presenting new objects to their attention, than by the stimulus of a peremptory voice. Children should never be accused of obstinacy; the accusation cannot cure, but may superinduce the disease. If, unfortunately, they have been suffered to contract a disposition to this fault, it may be cured by a little patience and good temper. We have mentioned how example and sympathy may be advantageously used; praise and looks of affection, which naturally express our feeling when children do right, encourage the slightest efforts to obey; but we must carefully avoid showing any triumph in our victory over yielding stubbornness.

"Aye, I knew that you would do what we desired at last, you might as well have done it at first," is a common nursery-maid's speech, which is well calculated to pique the pride of a half-subdued penitent. When children are made ashamed of submission, they will become intrepid, probably unconquerable, rebels.

Neither rewards nor punishments will then avail; the pupil perceives, that both the wit and the strength of his master are set in competition with his: at the expense of a certain degree of pain, he has the power to resist as long as he thinks proper; and there is scarcely any degree of pain that a tutor dares to inflict, which an obstinate hero is not able to endure. With the spirit of a martyr, he sustains reproaches and torture. If, at length, the master changes his tone, and tries to soften and win the child to his purpose, his rewards are considered as bribes: if the boy really thinks that he is in the right to rebel, he must yield his sense of honour to the force of temptation when he obeys. If he has formed no such idea of honour, he perhaps considers the reward as the price of his submission; and, upon a future occasion, he will know how to raise that price by prolonging his show of resistance. Where the child has formed a false idea of honour, his obstinacy is only mistaken resolution; we should address ourselves to his understanding, and endeavour to convince him of his errour. Where the understanding is convinced, and the *habit* of opposition still continues, we should carefully avoid calling his false associations into action; we should not ask him to do any thing for which he has acquired an habitual aversion; we should alter our manner of speaking to him, that neither the tones of our voice, the words, or the looks, which have been his customary signals for resistance, may recall the same feelings to his mind: placed in new circumstances, he may acquire new habits, and his old associates will in time be forgotten. Sufficient time must, however, be allowed; we may judge when it is prudent to try him on any old dangerous subjects, by many symptoms: by observing the degree of alacrity with which he obeys on indifferent occasions; by observing what degree of command he has acquired over himself in general; by observing in what manner he judges of the conduct and temper of other children in similar circumstances; by observing whether the consciousness of his former self continues in full force. Children often completely forget what they have been.

Where obstinacy arises from principle, if we may use the expression, it cannot be cured by the same means which are taken to cure that species of the disease which depends merely upon habit. The same courage and fortitude which in one case we reprobate, and try to conquer with all our might, in the other we admire and extol. This should be pointed out to children; and if they act from a love of glory, as soon as they perceive it, they will follow that course which will secure to them the prize.

Charles XII. whom the Turks, when incensed by his disobedience to the grand seignior, called Demirbash, or *head of iron*, showed early symptoms of this headstrong nature; yet in his childhood, if his preceptor [50] named but glory, any thing could be obtained from Charles. Charles had a great aversion to learning Latin; but when he was told that the kings of Poland and Denmark understood it, he began to study it in good earnest. We do not mean to infer, that emulation with the kings of Poland and Denmark, was the best possible motive which Charles the Twelfth's preceptor could have used, to make the young prince conquer his aversion to Latin; but we would point out, that where the love of glory is connected with obstinate temper, the passion is more than a match for the temper. Let us but enlighten this love of glory, and we produce magnanimity in the place of obstinacy. Examples, in conversation and in books, of great characters, who have not been ashamed to change their opinions, and to acknowledge that they have been mistaken, will probably make a great impression upon young people; they will from these learn to admire candour, and will be taught, that it is *mean* to persist in the wrong. Examples from books must, however, be also uniformly supported by examples in real life; preceptors and parents must practise the virtues which they preach. It is said, that the amiable Fenelon acquired the most permanent influence over his pupil, by the candour with which he always treated him. Fenelon did not think that he could lessen his dignity by confessing himself to be in the wrong.

Young people who have quick abilities, and who happen to live with those who are inferiour to them either in knowledge or incapacity, are apt to become positive and self-willed; they measure all the world by the individuals with whom they have measured themselves; and, as they have been convinced that they have been in the right in many cases, they take it for granted that their judgment must be always infallible. This disease may be easily cured; it is only necessary to place the patient amongst his superiors in intellect, his own experience will work his cure: he liked to follow his will, because his judgment had taught him that he might trust more securely to the *tact* of his own understanding, than to the decision of others. As soon as he discovers more sense in the arguments of his companions, he will listen to them, and if he finds their reason superior to his own, he will submit. A preceptor, who wishes to gain ascendency over a clever positive boy, must reason with all possible precision, and must always show that he is willing to be decided by the strongest arguments which can be produced. If he ever prophesies, he sets his judgment at stake; therefore he should not prophesy about matters of chance, but rather in affairs where he can calculate with certainty. If his prophecies are frequently accomplished, his pupil's confidence in him will rapidly increase; and if he desires that confidence to be permanent, he will not affect mystery, but he will honestly explain the circumstances by which he formed his opinions. Young people who are accustomed to hear and to give reasons for their opinions, will not be violent and positive in assertions; they will not think that the truth of any assertion can be manifested by repeating over the same words a thousand times; they will not ask how many people are of this or that opinion, but rather what arguments are produced on each side. There is very little danger that any people, whether young or old, should continue to be positive, who are in the habit of exercising their reasoning faculty.

It has been often observed that extremely good humoured, complaisant children, when they grow up, become ill tempered; and young men who are generally liked in society as pleasant companions, become surly, tyrannical masters in their own families, positive about mere trifles, and anxious to subjugate the *wills* of all who are any wise dependent upon them. This character has been nicely touched by de Boissy, in his comedy called "Dehors trompeurs."

We must observe, that whilst young people are in company, and under the immediate influence of the excitements of novelty, numbers and dissipation, it is scarcely possible to form a just estimate of the goodness of their temper. Young men who are the most ready to yield their inclinations to the humour of their companions, are not therefore to be considered as of really compliant dispositions; the idle or indolent, who have no resources in their own minds, and no independent occupations, are victims to the yawning demon of ennui the moment they are left in solitude. They consequently dread so heartily to be left alone, that they readily give up a portion of their liberty to purchase the pleasures and mental support which society affords. When they give up their wishes, and follow the lead of the company, they in fact give up but very little; their object is amusement; and this obtained, their time is sacrificed without regret. On the contrary, those who are engaged in literary or professional pursuits, set a great value upon their time, and feel considerable reluctance to part with it without some adequate compensation; they must consequently be less complaisant companions, and by the generality of superficial observers, would be thought, perhaps, less complying in their tempers, than the idle and dissipated. But when the idle man has past the common season for dissipation, and is settled in domestic life, his spirits flag from the want of his usual excitements; and, as he has no amusements in his own family, to purchase by the polite sacrifice of his opinion or his will, he is not inclined to complaisance. The pleasures of exercising his free will, becomes important in his eyes; he has few pleasures, and of those few he is tenacious. He has been accustomed to submit to others in society; he is proud to be master at home; he has few emotions, and the emotion caused by the exertion of command, becomes agreeable and necessary to him. Thus many of the same causes which make a young man a pleasant companion abroad, tend naturally to make him a tyrant at home. This perversity and positiveness of temper, ultimately arise from the want of occupation, and from deficient energy of mind. We may guard against these evils by education: when we see a playful, active child, we have little fear of his temper. "Oh, he will certainly be good tempered, he is the most obedient, complying creature in the world, he'll do any thing you ask him." But let us cultivate his understanding, and give him tastes which shall occupy and interest him agreeably through life, or else this sweet, complying temper will not last till he is thirty.

An ill cured obstinacy of temper, when it breaks out after young people have arrived at years of discretion, is terrible. Those who attempt to conquer obstinacy in children by bodily pain, or by severe punishments of any kind, often appear to succeed, and to have entirely eradicated, when they have merely suppressed, the disease for a time. As soon as the child that is intimidated by force or fear, is relieved from restraint, he will resume his former habits; he may change the mode of showing it, but the disposition will continue the same. It will appear in various parts of the conduct, as the limbs of the giant appeared unexpectedly at different periods, and in different parts of the Castle of Otranto.

[45] Elegy on an old Beauty. Parnell.

[46] Rousseau.

[47] Emilius, vol. i. page 23.

[49] Histoire des Membres de l'Académie, par M. d'Alembert. Tome troisieme, p. 24.

[50] Voltaire's Hist. Charles XII. page 13.

CHAPTER VIII
ON TRUTH

It is not necessary here to pronounce a panegyric upon truth; its use and value is thoroughly understood by all the world; but we shall endeavour to give some practical advice, which may be of service in educating children, not only to the love, but to the habits, of integrity. These are not always found, as they ought to be, inseparable.

Rousseau's eloquence, and Locke's reasoning, have sufficiently reprobated, and it is to be hoped have exploded, the system of lecturing children upon morality; of giving them precepts and general maxims which they do not understand, and which they cannot apply. We shall not produce long quotations from books which are in every body's hands. [51] There is one particular in which Rousseau especially, and most other authors who have written upon education, have given very dangerous counsel; they have counselled parents to teach truth by falsehood. The privilege of using contrivance, and ingenious deceptions, has been uniformly reserved for preceptors; and the pupils, by moral delusions, and the theatric effect of circumstances treacherously arranged, are to be duped, surprised, and cheated, into virtue. The dialogue between the gardener and Emilius about the Maltese melon-seed, is an instance of this method of instruction. Honest Robert, the gardener, in concert with the tutor, tells poor Emilius a series of lies, prepares a garden, "choice Maltese melon-seed," and "worthless beans," all to cheat the boy into just notions of the rights of property, and the nature of exchange and barter.

Part of the *artificial course of experience* in that excellent work on education, Adele and Theodore, is defective upon the same principle. There should be no moral delusions; no *artificial* course of experience; no plots laid by parents to make out the truth; no listening fathers, mothers, or governesses; no pretended confidence, or perfidious friends; in one word, no falsehood should be practised: that magic which cheats the senses, at the same time confounds the understanding. The spells of Prospero, the strangenesses of the isle, perplex and confound the senses and understanding of all who are subjected to his magic, till at length, worked by force of wonders into credulity, his captives declare that they will believe any thing; "that there are men dewlapt like bulls; and what else does want credit," says the Duke Anthonio, "come to me, and I'll be sworn 'tis true."

Children, whose simplicity has been practised upon by the fabling morality of their preceptors, begin by feeling something like the implicit credulity of Anthonio; but the arts of the preceptors are quickly suspected by their subjects, and the charm is for ever reversed. When once a child detects you in falsehood, you lose his confidence; his incredulity will then be as extravagant as his former belief was gratuitous. It is in vain to expect, by the most eloquent manifestoes, or by the most secret leagues offensive and defensive, to conceal your real views, sentiments, and actions, from children. Their interest keeps their attention continually awake; not a word, not a look, in which they are concerned, escapes them; they see, hear, and combine, with sagacious rapidity; if falsehood be in the wind, detection hunts her to discovery.

Honesty is the best policy, must be the maxim in education, as well as in all the other affairs of life. We must not only be exact in speaking truth to our pupils, but to every body else; to acquaintance, to servants, to friends, to enemies. It is not here meant to enter any overstrained protest against the common phrases and forms of politeness; the current coin may not be pure; but when once its alloy has been ascertained, and its value appreciated, there is no fraud, though there may be some folly, in continuing to trade upon equal terms with our neighbours, with money of high nominal, and scarcely any real, value. No fraud is committed by a gentleman's saying he is *not at home*, because no deception is intended; the words are silly, but they mean, and are understood to mean, nothing more than that the person in question does not choose to see the visiters who knock at his door. "I am, sir, your obedient and humble servant," at the end of a letter, does not mean that the person who signs the letter is a servant, or humble, or obedient, but it simply expresses that he knows how to conclude his letter according to the usual form of civility. Change this absurd phrase, and welcome; but do not let us, in the spirit of Draco, make no distinction between errours and crimes. The foibles of fashion or folly, are not to be treated with the detestation due to hypocrisy and falsehood; if small faults are to incur such grievous punishments, there can, indeed, be none found sufficiently severe for great crimes; great crimes, consequently, for want of adequate punishment, will increase, and the little faults, that have met with disproportionate persecution, will become amiable and innocent in the eyes of commiserating human nature. It is not difficult to explain to young people the real meaning, or rather the nonsense, of a few complimentary phrases; their integrity will not be increased or diminished by either saying, or omitting to say, "I am much obliged to you," or "I shall be very happy to see you at dinner," &c. We do not mean to include in the harmless list of compliments, any expressions which are meant to deceive; the common custom of the country, and of the society in which we live, sufficiently regulates the style of complimentary language; and there are few so ignorant of the world as seriously to misunderstand this, or to mistake civility for friendship.

There is a story told of a Chinese mandarin, who paid a visit to a friend at Paris, at the time when Paris was the seat of politeness. His well-bred host, on the first evening of his arrival, gave him a handsome supper, lodged him in the best bed-chamber, and when he wished him a good night, amongst other civil things, said he hoped the mandarin would, during his stay at Paris, consider that house as his own. Early the next morning, the polite Parisian was awakened by the sound of loud hammering in the mandarin's bed-chamber; on entering the room, he found the mandarin and some masons hard at work, throwing down the walls of the house. "You rascals, are you mad?" exclaimed the Frenchman to the masons. "Not at all, my dear friend," said the Chinese man, soberly, "I set the poor fellows to work; this room is too small for my taste; you see I have lost no time in availing myself of your goodness. Did not you desire me to use this house as if it were my own, during my stay at Paris?" "Assuredly, my dear friend, and so I hope you will," replied the French gentleman, "the only misfortune here is, that I did not understand Chinese, and that I had no interpreter." They found an interpreter, or a Chinese dictionary, and when the Parisian phrase was properly translated, the mandarin, who was an honest man, begged his polite host's pardon for having pulled down the partition. It was rebuilt; the mandarin learned French, and the two friends continued upon the best terms with each other, during the remainder of the visit.

The Chesterfieldian system of endeavouring to please by dissimulation, is obviously distinguishable by any common capacity, from the usual forms of civility. There is no hope of educating young people to a love of integrity in any family, where this practice is adopted. If children observe that their parents deceive common acquaintance, by pretending to like the company, and to esteem the characters, of those whom they really think disagreeable and contemptible, how can they learn to respect truth? How can children believe in the praise of their parents, if they detect them in continual flattery towards indifferent people? It may be thought, by latitudinarians in politeness, that we are too rigid in expecting this strict adherence to truth from people who live in society; it may be said, that in Practical Education, no such Utopian ideas of perfection should be suggested. If we thought them Utopian, we certainly should not waste our time upon them; but we do not here speak theoretically of what may be done, we speak of what has been done. Without the affectation of using a more sanctified language than other people; without departing from the common forms of society; without any painful, awkward efforts, we believe that parents may, in all their conversation in private and in public, set their children the uniform example of truth and integrity.

We do not mean that the example of parents can alone produce this effect; a number of other circumstances must be combined. Servants must have no communication with children, if you wish to teach them the habit of speaking truth. The education, and custom, and situation of servants, are at present such, that it is morally impossible to depend upon their veracity in their intercourse with children. Servants think it good natured to try to excuse and conceal all the little faults of children; to give them secret indulgences, and even positively to deny facts, in order to save them from blame or punishment. Even when they are not fond of the children, their example must be dangerous, because servants do not scruple to falsify for their own advantage; if they break any thing, what a multitude of equivocations! If they neglect any thing, what a variety of excuses! What evasions in actions, or in words, do they continually invent!

It may be said, that as the Spartans taught their children to detest drunkenness, by showing them intoxicated Helots, we can make falsehood odious and contemptible to our pupils, by the daily example of its mean deformity. But if children, before they can perceive the general advantage of integrity, and before they can understand the utility of truth, see the partial immediate success of falsehood, how can they avoid believing in their own experience? If they see that servants escape blame, and screen themselves from punishment, by telling falsehoods, they not only learn that falsehood preserves from pain, but they feel obliged to those who practise it for their sakes; thus it is connected with the feelings of affection and of gratitude in their hearts, as well as with a sense of pleasure and safety. When servants have exacted promises from their *protégés*, those promises cannot be broken without treachery; thus deceit brings on deceit, and the ideas of truth and falsehood, become confused and contradictory. In the chapter upon servants, we have expatiated upon this subject, and have endeavoured to point out how all communication between children and servants may be most effectually prevented. To that chapter, without further repetition, we refer. And now that we have adjusted the preliminaries concerning parents and servants, we may proceed with confidence.

When young children first begin to speak, from not having a sufficient number of words to express their ideas, or from not having annexed precise ideas to the words which they are taught to use, they frequently make mistakes, which are attributed to the desire of deceiving. We should not precipitately suspect them of falsehood; it is some time before they perfectly understand what we mean by truth. Small deviations should not be marked with too much rigour; but whenever a child relates *exactly* any thing which he has seen, heard, or felt, we should listen with attention and pleasure, and we should not show the least doubt of his veracity. Rousseau is perfectly right in advising, that children should never be questioned in any circumstances upon which it can be their interest to deceive. We should, at least, treat children with the same degree of wise lenity, which the English law extends to all who have arrived at years of discretion. No criminal is bound to accuse himself. If any mischief has been committed, we should never, when we are uncertain by whom it has been done, either directly accuse, or betray injurious suspicions. We should neither say to the child, "I believe you have done this," nor, "I believe you have not done this;" we should say nothing; the mischief is done, we cannot repair it: because a glass is broken, we need not spoil a child; we may put glasses out of his reach in future. If it should, however, happen, that a child voluntarily comes to us with a history of an accident, may no love of goods or chattels, of windows, of china, or even of looking-glasses, come in competition with our love of truth? An angry word, an angry look, may intimidate the child, who has summoned all his little courage to make this confession. It is not requisite that parents should pretend to be pleased and gratified with the destruction of their furniture, but they may, it is to be hoped, without dissimulation, show that they set more value upon the integrity of their children, than upon a looking-glass, and they will "keep their temper still, though china fall."

H— —, one day when his father and mother were absent from home, broke a looking-glass. As soon as he heard the sound of the returning carriage, he ran and posted himself at the hall door. His father, the moment he got out of the carriage, beheld his erect figure, and pale, but intrepid countenance. "Father," said the boy, "I have *broke* the best looking-glass in your house!" His father assured him, that he would rather all the looking-glasses in his house should be broken, than that one of his children should attempt to make an excuse. H— — was most agreeably relieved from his anxiety by the kindness of his father's voice and manner, and still more so, perhaps, by perceiving that he rose in his esteem. When the glass was examined, it appeared that the boy had neglected to produce all the circumstances in his own favour. Before he had begun to play at ball, he had had the precaution to turn the back of the looking-glass towards him; his ball, however, accidentally struck against the wooden back, and broke the glass. H— — did not make out this favourable state of the case for himself at first; he told it simply after the business was settled, seeming much more interested about the fate of the glass, than eager to exculpate himself.

There is no great danger of teaching children to do mischief by this indulgence to their accidental misfortunes. When they break, or waste any thing, from pure carelesness, let them, even when they speak the truth about it, suffer the natural consequences of their carelesness; but at the same time praise their integrity, and let them distinctly feel the difference between the slight inconvenience to which they expose themselves by speaking the truth, and the great disgrace to which falsehood would subject them. The pleasure of being esteemed, and trusted, is early felt, and the consciousness of deserving confidence is delightful to children; but their young fortitude and courage should never be exposed to severe temptations. It is not sufficient to excite an admiration of truth by example, by eloquent praise, or by the just rewards of esteem and affection; we must take care to form the habits at the same time that we inspire the love of this virtue. Many children admire truth, and feel all the shame of telling falsehoods, who yet, either from habit or from fear, continue to tell lies. We must observe, that though the taste for praise is strong in childhood, yet it is not a match for any of the bodily appetites, when they are strongly excited. Those children, who are restrained as to the choice, or the quantity, of their food, usually think that eating is a matter of vast consequence, and they are strongly tempted to be dishonest to gratify their appetites. Children do not understand the prudential maxims concerning health, upon which these restraints are founded; and if they can, "by any indirection," obtain things which gratify their palate, they will. On the contrary, young people who are regularly let to eat and drink as much as they please, can have no temptation from hunger and thirst, to deceive; if they partake of the usual family meals, and if there are no whimsical distinctions between wholesome and unwholesome dishes, or epicurean distinctions between rarities and plain food, the imagination and the pride of children will not be roused about eating. Their pride is piqued, if they perceive that they are prohibited from touching what *grown up people* are privileged to eat; their imagination is set to work by seeing any extraordinary difference made by judges of eating between one species of food and another. In families where a regularly good table is kept, children accustomed to the sight and taste of all kinds of food, are seldom delicate, capricious, or disposed to exceed; but in houses where entertainments are made from time to time with great bustle and anxiety, fine clothes, and company-manners, and company-faces, and all that politeness can do to give the appearance of festivity, deceive children at least, and make them imagine that there is some extraordinary joy in seeing a greater number of dishes than usual upon the table. Upon these occasions, indeed, the pleasure is to them substantial; they eat more, they eat a greater variety, and of things that please them better than usual; the pleasure of eating is associated with unusual cheerfulness, and thus the imagination, and the reality, conspire to make them epicures. To these children, the temptations to deceive about sweetmeats and dainties are beyond measure great, especially as ill-bred strangers commonly show their affection for them by pressing them to eat what they are not allowed to say *"if you please"* to. Rousseau thinks all children are gluttons. All children may be rendered gluttons; but few, who are properly treated with respect to food, and who have any literary tastes, can be in danger of continuing to be fond of eating. We therefore, without hesitation, recommend it to parents never to hazard the truth and honour of their pupils by prohibitions, which seldom produce any of the effects that are expected.

Children are sometimes injudiciously restrained with regard to exercise; they are required to promise to keep within certain boundaries when they are sent out to play; these promises are often broken with impunity, and thus the children learn habits of successful deceit. Instead of circumscribing their play grounds, as they are sometimes called, by narrow inconvenient limits, we should allow them as much space as we can with convenience, and at all events exact no promises. We should absolutely make it impossible for them to go without detection into any place which we forbid. It requires some patience and activity in preceptors to take all the necessary precautions in issuing orders, but these precautions will be more useful in preserving the integrity of their pupils, than the most severe punishments that can be devised. We are not so unreasonable as to expect, with some theoretic writers on education, that tutors and parents should sacrifice the whole of their time to the convenience, amusement, and education of their pupils. This would be putting one set of beings *"sadly over the head of another:"* but if parents would, as much as possible, mix their occupations and recreations with those of their children, besides many other advantages which have been elsewhere pointed out with respect to the improvement of the understanding, they would secure them from many temptations to falsehood. They should be encouraged to talk freely of all their amusements to their parents, and to ask them for whatever they want to complete their little inventions. Instead of banishing all the freedom of wit and humour, by the austerity of his presence, a preceptor, with superior talents, and all the resources of property in his favour, might easily become the *arbiter deliciarum* of his pupils.

When young people begin to taste the pleasures of praise, and to feel the strong excitations of emulation and ambition, their integrity is exposed to a new species of temptation. They are tempted, not only by the hope of obtaining "well-earned praise," but by the desire to obtain praise without the labour of earning it. In large schools, where boys assist each other in their literary exercises, and in all private families where masters are allowed to show off the accomplishments of young gentlemen and ladies, there are so many temptations to fraudulent exhibitions, that we despair of guarding against their consequences. The best possible method is to inspire children with a generous contempt for flattery, and to teach them to judge impartially of their own merits. If we are exact in the measure of approbation which we bestow, they will hence form a scale by which they can estimate the sincerity of other people. It is said [52] that the preceptor of the duke of Burgundy succeeded so well in inspiring him with disdain for unmerited praise, that when the duke was only nine years old, he one day called his tutor to account for having concealed some of his childish faults; and when this promising boy, and singular prince, was asked "why he disliked one of his courtiers," he answered, "Because he flatters me." Anecdotes like these will make a useful impression upon children. The life of Cyrus, in the Cyropædia; several passages in Plutarch's Lives; and the lively, interesting picture which Sully draws of his noble-hearted master's love of truth, will strongly command the admiration of young people, if they read them at a proper time of life. We must, however, wait for this proper time; for if these things are read too early, they lose all their effect. Without any lectures upon the beauty of truth, we may, now and then in conversation, when occurrences in real life naturally lead to the subject, express with energy our esteem for integrity. The approbation which we bestow upon those who give proofs of integrity, should be quite in a different tone, in a much higher style of praise, than any commendations for trifling accomplishments; hence children will become more ambitious to obtain a reputation for truth, than for any other less honourable and less honoured qualification.

We will venture to give two or three slight instances of the unaffected truth and simplicity of mind, which we have seen in children educated upon these principles. No good-natured reader will suspect, that they are produced from ostentation: whenever the children, who are mentioned, see this in print, it is ten to one that they will not be surprised at their own good deeds. They will be a little surprised, probably, that it should have been thought worth while to record things, which are only what they see and feel every day. It is this character of every-day goodness which we wish to represent; not any fine thoughts, fine sentiments, or fine actions, which come out for holyday admiration. We wish that parents, in reading any of these little anecdotes, may never exclaim, "Oh that's charming, that's surprising *for a child*!" but we wish that they may sometimes smile, and say

"That's very natural; I am sure *that* is perfectly true; my little boy, or my little girl, say and do just such things continually."

March, 1792. We were at Clifton; the river Avon ran close under the windows of our house in Prince's Place, and the children used to be much amused with looking at the vessels which came up the river. One night a ship, that was sailing by the windows, fired some of her guns; the children, who were looking out of the windows, were asked "why the light was seen when the guns were fired, before the noise was heard?" C——, who at this time was nine years old, answered, "Because light comes quicker to the eye, than sound to the ear." Her father was extremely pleased with this answer; but just as he was going to kiss her, the little girl said, "Father, the reason of my knowing it, was, that L—— (her elder brother) just before had told it to me."

There is, it is usually found, most temptation for children to deceive when they are put in competition with each other, when their ambition is excited by the same object; but if the transient glory of excelling in quickness, or abilities of any sort, be much inferiour to the permanent honour which is secured by integrity, there is, even in competition, no danger of unfair play.

March, 1792. One evening —— called the children round the tea-table, and told them the following story, which he had just met with in "The Curiosities of Literature."

When the queen of Sheba went to visit king Solomon, she one day presented herself before his throne with a wreath of real flowers in one hand, and a wreath of artificial flowers in the other hand; the artificial flowers were made so exactly to resemble nature, that at the distance at which they were held from Solomon, it was scarcely possible that his eye could distinguish any difference between them and the natural flowers; nor could he, at the distance at which they were held from him, know them asunder by their smell. "Which of these two wreaths," demanded the queen of Sheba, "is the work of nature?" Solomon reflected for some minutes; and how did he discover which was real? S—— (five years old) *replied*, "Perhaps he went out of the room very *softly*, and if the woman stood near the door, as he went near her, he might *see better*."

Father. But Solomon was not to move from his place.

S——.. Then he might wait till the woman was tired of holding them, and then perhaps she might lay them down on the table, and then perhaps he might see better.

Father. Well, C——, what do you say?

C——. I think he might have looked at the stalks, and have seen which looked stiff like wire, and which were bent down by the weight of the natural flowers.

Father. Well, H——?

H——. (ten years old.) I think he might send for a great pair of bellows, and blow, blow, till the real leaves dropped off.

Father. But would it not have been somewhat uncivil of Solomon to *blow, blow,* with his great pair of bellows, full in the queen of Sheba's face?

H——. (doubting.) Yes, yes. Well, then he might have sent for a telescope, or a magnifying glass, and looked through it; and then he could have seen which were the real flowers, and which were artificial.

Father. Well, B——, and what do you say?

B——. (eleven years old.) He might have waited till the queen moved the flowers, and then, if he listened, he might hear the rustling of the artificial ones.

Father. S——, have you any thing more to say?

S—— repeated the same thing that B—— had said; his attention was dissipated by hearing the other children speak. During this pause, whilst S—— was trying to collect his thoughts, Mrs. E—— whispered to somebody near her, and accidentally said the word *animals* loud enough to be overheard.

Father. Well, H——, you look as if you had something to say?

H——. Father, I heard my mother say something, and *that* made me think of the rest.

Mrs. E—— shook hands with H——, and praised him for this instance of integrity. H—— then said that "he supposed Solomon thought of some *animal* which would feed upon flowers, and sent it to the two nosegays; and then the animal would stay upon the real flowers."

Father. What animal?

H——. A fly.

Father. Think again.

H——. A bee.

Father. Yes.

The story says that Solomon, seeing some bees hover about the window, ordered the window to be thrown open, and watched upon which wreath of flowers the bee settled.

August 1st, 1796. S— — (nine years old) when he was reading in Ovid the fable of Perseus and Andromeda, said that he wondered that Perseus fought with the monster; he wondered that Perseus did not turn him into stone at once with his Gorgon shield. We believe that S— — saw that his father was pleased with this observation. A few days afterwards somebody in the family recollected Mr. E— —'s having said, that when he was a boy he thought Perseus a simpleton for not making use of the Gorgon's head to turn the monster into stone. We were not sure whether S— — had heard Mr. E— — say this or not; Mr. E— — asked him whether he recollected to have heard any such thing. S— — answered, without hesitation, that he did remember it.

When children have formed habits of speaking truth, and when we see that these habits are grown quite easy to them, we may venture to question them about their thoughts and feelings; this must, however, be done with great caution, but without the appearance of anxiety or suspicion. Children are alarmed if they see that you are very anxious and impatient for their answer; they think that they hazard much by their reply; they hesitate, and look eagerly in your face, to discover by your countenance what they ought to think and feel, and what sort of answer you expect. All who are governed by any species of fear are disposed to equivocation. Amongst the lower class of Irish labourers, and *under-tenants*, a class of people who are much oppressed, you can scarcely meet with any man who will give you a direct answer to the most indifferent question; their whole ingenuity, and they have a great deal of ingenuity, is upon the *qui vive* with you the instant you begin to speak; they either pretend not to hear, that they may gain time to think, whilst you repeat your question, or they reply to you with a fresh question, to draw out your remote meaning; for they, judging by their own habits, always think you have a remote meaning, and they never can believe that your words have no intention to ensnare. Simplicity puzzles them much more than wit: for instance, if you were to ask the most direct and harmless question, as, "Did it rain yesterday?" the first answer would probably be, "Is it yesterday you mean?" "Yes." "Yesterday! No, please your honour, I was not at the bog at all yesterday. Wasn't I after setting my potatoes? Sure I did not know your honour wanted me at all yesterday. Upon my conscience, there's not a man in the country, let alone all Ireland, I'd sooner serve than your honour any day in the year, and they have belied me that went behind my back to tell your honour the contrary. If your honour sent after me, sure I never *got the word*, I'll take my affidavit, or I'd been at the bog." "My good friend, I don't know what you mean about the bog; I only ask you whether it rained yesterday." "Please your honour, I couldn't get a car and horse any way, to draw home my little straw, or I'd have had the house thatched long ago." "Cannot you give me a plain answer to this plain question? Did it rain yesterday?" "Oh sure, I wouldn't go to tell your honour a lie about the matter. Sarrah much it rained yesterday after twelve o'clock, barring a few showers; but in the night there was a great fall of rain any how; and that was the reason prevented my going to Dublin yesterday, for fear the mistress's band-box should get wet upon my cars. But, please your honour, if your honour's displeased about it, I'll not be waiting for a loading; I'll take my car and go to Dublin to-morrow for the slates, if that be what your honour means. Oh, sure I would not tell a lie for the entire price of the slates; I know very well it didn't rain to call rain yesterday. But after twelve o'clock, I don't say I noticed one way or other."

In this perverse and ludicrous method of beating about the bush, the man would persist till he had fairly exhausted your patience; and all this he would do, partly from cunning, and partly from that apprehension of injustice which he has been taught to feel by hard experience. The effects of the example of their parents is early and most strikingly visible in the children of this class of people in Ireland. The children, who are remarkably quick and intelligent, are universally addicted to lying. We do not here scruple or hesitate in the choice of our terms, because we are convinced that this unqualified assertion would not shock the feelings of the parties concerned. These poor children are not brought up to think falsehood a disgrace; they are praised for the ingenuity with which they escape from the cross examination of their superiors; and their capacities are admired in proportion to the *acuteness*, or, as their parents pronounce it, '*cuteness*, of their equivocating replies. Sometimes (the *garçon* [53]) the little boy of the family is despatched by his mother to the landlord's neighbouring bog or turf rick, to *bring home*, in their phraseology, in ours to *steal*, a few turf; if, upon this expedition, the little Spartan be detected, he is tolerably certain of being whipped by his mother, or some of his friends, upon his return home. "Ah, ye little brat! and what made ye tell the gentleman when he met ye, ye rogue, that ye were going to the rick? And what business had ye to go and belie me to his honour, ye unnatural piece of goods! I'll teach ye to make mischief through the country! So I will. Have ye got no better sense and manners at this time o'day, than to behave, when one trusts ye abroad, so like an innocent?" An innocent in Ireland, as formerly in England, (witness the Rape of the Lock) is synonymous with a fool. "And fools and innocents shall still believe."

The associations of pleasure, of pride and gayety, are so strong in the minds of these well educated children, that they sometimes expect the very people who suffer by their dishonesty, should sympathise in the self-complacency they feel from roguery. A gentleman riding near his own house in Ireland, saw a cow's head and fore feet appear at the *top of a ditch*, through a gap in the hedge by the road's side, at the same time he heard a voice alternately threatening and encouraging the cow; the gentleman rode up closer to the scene of action, and he saw a boy's head appear behind the cow. "My good boy," said he, "that's a fine cow." "Oh, faith, that she is," replied the boy, "and I'm teaching her to get her own living, please your honour." The gentleman did not precisely understand the meaning of the expression, and had he directly asked for an explanation, would probably have died in ignorance; but the boy, proud of his cow, encouraged an exhibition of her talents: she was made to jump across the ditch several times, and this adroitness in breaking through fences, was termed "getting her own living." As soon as the cow's education is finished, she may be sent loose into the world to provide for herself; turned to graze in the poorest pasture, she will be able and willing to live upon the fat of the land.

It is curious to observe how regularly the same moral causes produce the same temper and character. We talk of climate, and frequently attribute to climate the different dispositions of different nations: the climate of Ireland, and that of the West Indies, are not precisely similar, yet the following description, which Mr. Edwards, in his history of the West Indies, gives of the propensity to falsehood amongst the negro slaves, might stand word for word for a character of that class of the Irish people who, until very lately, actually, not metaphorically, called themselves *slaves*.

"If a negro is asked even an indifferent question by his master, he seldom gives an immediate reply; but affecting not to understand what is said, compels a repetition of the question, that he may have time to consider, not what is the true answer, but what is the most politic one for him to give."

Mr. Edwards assures us, that many of these unfortunate negroes learn cowardice and falsehood after they become slaves. When they first come from Africa, many of them show "a frank and fearless temper;" [54] but all distinction of character amongst the native Africans, is soon lost under the levelling influence of slavery. Oppression and terror necessarily produce meanness and deceit in all climates, and in all ages; and wherever fear is the governing motive in education, we must expect to find in children a propensity to dissimulation, if not confirmed habits of falsehood. Look at the true born Briton under the government of a tyrannical pedagogue, and listen to the language of *in-born* truth; in the whining tone, in the pitiful evasions, in the stubborn falsehoods which you hear from the school-boy, can you discover any of that innate dignity of soul which is the boasted national characteristic? Look again; look at the same boy in the company of those who inspire no terror; in the company of his school-fellows, of his friends, of his parents; would you know him to be the same being? his countenance is open; his attitude erect; his voice firm; his language free and fluent; his thoughts are upon his lips; he speaks truth without effort, without fear. Where individuals are oppressed, or where they believe that they are oppressed, they combine against their oppressors, and oppose cunning and falsehood to power and force; they think themselves released from the compact of truth with their masters, and bind themselves in a strict league with each other; thus school-boys hold no faith with their schoolmaster, though they would think it shameful to be dishonourable amongst one another. We do not think that these maxims are the peculiar growth of schools; in private families the same feelings are to be found under the same species of culture: if preceptors or parents are unjust or tyrannical, their pupils will contrive to conceal from them their actions and their thoughts. On the contrary, in families where sincerity has been encouraged by the voice of praise and affection, a generous freedom of conversation and countenance appears, and the young people talk to each other, and to their parents, without distinction or reserve; without any distinction but such as superior esteem and respect dictate. These are feelings totally distinct from servile fear: these feelings inspire the love of truth, the ambition to acquire and to preserve character.

The value of a character for truth, should be distinctly felt by children in their own family: whilst they were very young, we advised that their integrity should not be tempted; as they grow up, trust should by degrees be put in them, and we should distinctly explain to them, that our confidence is to be deserved before it can be given. Our belief in any person's truth, is not a matter of affection, but of experience and necessity; we cannot doubt the assertions of any person whom we have found to speak uniformly the truth; we cannot believe any person, let us wish to do it ever so much, if we have detected him in falsehoods. Before we have had experience of a person's integrity, we may hope, or take it for granted, that he is perfectly sincere and honest; but we cannot feel more than *belief upon trust,* until we have actually seen his integrity tried. We should not pretend that we have faith in our pupils before we have tried them; we may hope from their habits, from the examples they have seen, and from the advantageous manner in which truth has always been represented to them, that they will act honourably; this hope is natural and just, but confidence is another feeling of the mind. The first time we trust a child, we should not say, "I am sure you will not deceive me; I can trust you with any thing in the world." This is flattery or folly; it is paying beforehand, which is not the way to get business done; why cannot we, especially as we are teaching truth, say the thing that is—"I *hope* you will not deceive me. If I find that you may be trusted, you know I shall be able to trust you another time: this must depend upon you, not entirely upon me." We must make ourselves certain upon these occasions, how the child conducts himself; nor is it necessary to use any artifice, or to affect, from false delicacy, any security that we do not feel; it is better openly to say, "You see, I do you the justice to examine carefully, how you have conducted yourself; I wish to be able to trust you another time."

It may be said, that this method of strict inquiry reduces a trust to no trust at all, and that it betrays suspicion. If you examine evidently with the belief that a child has deceived you, certainly you betray injurious suspicion, and you educate the child very ill; but if you feel and express a strong desire to find that your pupil has conducted himself honourably, he will be glad and proud of the strictest scrutiny; he will feel that he has earned your future confidence, and this confidence, which he clearly knows how he has obtained, will be more valuable to him than all the belief upon trust which you could affect to feel. By degrees, after your pupil has taught you to depend upon him, your confidence will prevent the necessity of any examination into his conduct. This is the just and delightful reward of integrity: children know how to feel and understand it thoroughly: besides the many restraints from which our confidence will naturally relieve them, they feel the pride for being trusted; the honour of having a character for integrity: nor can it be too strongly impressed upon their minds, that this character must be preserved, as it was obtained, by their own conduct. If one link in the chain of confidence be broken, the whole is destroyed. Indeed, where habits of truth are early formed, we may safely depend upon them. A young person, who has never deceived, would see, that the first step in falsehood costs too much to be hazarded. Let this appear in the form of calculation, rather than of sentiment. To habit, to enthusiasm, we owe much of all our virtues—to reason more; and the more of them we owe to reason, the better. Habit and enthusiasm are subject to sudden or gradual changes—but reason continues for ever the same. As the understanding unfolds, we should fortify all our pupil's habits; and virtuous enthusiasm, by the conviction of their utility, of their being essential to the happiness of society in general, and conducive immediately to the happiness of every individual. Possessed of this conviction, and provided with substantial arguments in its support, young people will not be exposed to danger, either from sophistry or ridicule.

Ridicule certainly is not the test of truth; but it is a test which truth sometimes finds it difficult to stand. Vice never "bolts her arguments" with more success, than when she assumes the air of raillery, and the tone of gayety. All vivacious young people are fond of wit; we do not mean children, for they do not understand it. Those who have the best capacities, and the strictest habits of veracity, often appear to common observers absolutely stupid, from their aversion to any play upon words, and from the literal simplicity with which they believe every thing that is asserted. A remarkably intelligent little girl of four years old, but who had never in her own family been used to the common phrases which sometimes pass for humour, happened to hear a gentleman say, as he looked out of the window one rainy morning, "It rains cats and dogs to-day." The child, with a surprised, but believing look, immediately went to look out of the window to see the phenomenon. This extreme simplicity in childhood, is sometimes succeeded in youth by a strong taste for wit and humour. Young people are, in the first place, proud to show that they understand them; and they are gratified by the perception of a new intellectual pleasure. At this period of their education, great attention must be paid to them, lest their admiration for wit and frolic should diminish their reverence and their love for sober truth. In many engaging characters in society, and in many entertaining books, deceit and dishonesty are associated with superior abilities, with ease and gayety of manners, and with a certain air of frank carelessness, which can scarcely fail to please. Gil Blas, [55] Tom Jones, Lovelace, Count Fathom, are all of this class of characters. They should not be introduced to our pupils till their habits of integrity are thoroughly formed; and till they are sufficiently skilful in analysing their own feelings, to distinguish whence their approbation and pleasure in reading of these characters arise. In books, we do not actually suffer by the tricks of rogues, or by the lies they tell. Hence their truth is to us a quality of no value; but their wit, humour, and the ingenuity of their contrivances, are of great value to us, because they afford us entertainment. The most honest man in the universe may not have had half so many adventures as the greatest rogue; in a romance, the history upon oath of all the honest man's bargains and sales, law-suits and losses; nay, even a complete view of his ledger and day-book, together with the regular balancings of his accounts, would probably not afford quite so much entertainment, even to a reader of the most unblemished integrity and phlegmatic temper, as the adventures of Gil Blas, and Jonathan Wild, adorned with all the wit of Le Sage, and humour of Fielding. When Gil Blas lays open his whole heart to us, and tells us all his sins, unwhipt of justice, we give him credit for making us his confidant, and we forget that this sincerity, and these liberal confessions, are not characteristic of the hero's disposition, but essential only to the novel. The novel writer could not tell us all he had to say without this dying confession, and inconsistent openness, from his accomplished villain. The reader is ready enough to forgive, having never been duped. When young people can make all these reflections for themselves, they may read Gil Blas with as much safety as the Life of Franklin, or any other the most moral performance. "Tout est sain aux sains," [56] as Madame de Sevigne very judiciously observes, in one of her letters upon the choice of books for her grand-daughter. We refer for more detailed observations upon this subject to the chapter upon Books. But we cannot help here reiterating our advice to preceptors, not to force the detestable characters, which are sometimes held up to admiration in ancient and modern history, upon the common sense, or, if they please, the moral feelings, of their pupils. The bad actions of *great* characters, should not be palliated by eloquence, and fraud and villainy should never be explained away by the hero's or warrior's code; a code which confounds all just ideas of right and wrong. Boys, in reading the classics, must read of a variety of crimes; but that is no reason that they should approve of them, or that their tutors should undertake to vindicate the cause of falsehood and treachery. A gentleman, who has taught his sons Latin, has uniformly pursued the practice of abandoning to the just and prompt indignation of his young pupils all the ancient heroes who are deficient in moral honesty: his sons, in reading Cornelius Nepos, could not absolutely comprehend, that the treachery of Themistocles or of Alcibiades could be applauded by a wise and polished nation. Xenophon has made an eloquent attempt to explain the nature of military good faith. Cambyses tells his son, that, in taking advantage of an enemy, a man must be "crafty, deceitful, a dissembler, a thief, and a robber." Oh Jupiter! exclaims the young Cyrus, what a man, my father, you say I must be! And he very sensibly asks his father, why, if it be necessary in some cases to ensnare and deceive men, he had not in his childhood been taught by his preceptors the art of doing harm to his fellow-creatures, as well as of doing them good. "And why," says Cyrus, "have I always been punished whenever I have been discovered in practising deceit?" The answers of Cambyses are by no means satisfactory upon this subject; nor do we think that the conversation between the old general and Mr. Williams, [57] could have made the matter perfectly intelligible to the young gentleman, whose scrupulous integrity made him object to the military profession.

It is certain, that many persons of strict honour and honesty in some points, on others are utterly inconsistent in their principles. Thus it is said, that private integrity and public corruption frequently meet in the same character: thus some gentlemen are jockies, and they have a convenient latitude of conscience as jockies, whilst they would not for the universe cheat a man of a guinea in any way but in the sale of a horse: others in gambling, others in love, others in war, think all stratagems fair. We endeavour to think that these are all honourable men; but we hope, that we are not obliged to lay down rules for the formation of such moral prodigies in a system of practical education.

We are aware, that with children [58] who are educated at public schools, truth and integrity cannot be taught precisely in the same manner as in private families; because ushers and schoolmasters cannot pay the same hourly attention to each of their pupils, nor have they the command of all the necessary circumstances.—There are, however, some advantages attending the early commerce which numbers of children at public seminaries have with each other; they find that no society can subsist without truth; they feel the utility of this virtue, and, however they may deal with their masters, they learn to speak truth towards each other.—This partial species of honesty, or rather of honour, is not the very best of its kind, but it may easily be improved into a more rational principle of action. It is illiberal to assert, that any virtue is to be taught only by one process of education: many different methods of education may produce the same effects. Men of integrity and honour have been formed both by private and public education; neither system should be exclusively supported by those who really wish well to the improvement of mankind. All the errours of each system should be impartially pointed out, and such remedies as may most easily be adopted with any hope of success, should be proposed. We think, that if parents paid sufficient attention to the habits of their children, from the age of three to seven years old, they would be properly prepared for public education; they would not then bring with them to public schools all that they have learned of vice and falsehood in the company of servants. [59] We have purposely repeated all this, in hopes of impressing it strongly. May we suggest to the masters of these important seminaries, that Greek and Latin, and all the elegance of classical literature, are matters but of secondary consequence, compared with those habits of truth, which are essential to the character and happiness of their pupils? By rewarding the moral virtues more highly than the mere display of talents, a generous emulation to excel in these virtues may with certainty be excited.

Many preceptors and parents will readily agree, that Bacon, in his "general distribution of human knowledge," was perfectly right not to omit that branch of philosophy, which his lordship terms *"The doctrine of rising in the world."* To this art, integrity at length becomes necessary; for talents, whether for business or for oratory, are now become so cheap, that they cannot alone ensure pre-eminence to their possessors. — The public opinion, which in England bestows celebrity, and necessarily leads to honour, is intimately connected with the public confidence. Public confidence is not the same thing as popularity; the one may be won, the other must be earned. There is amongst all parties, who at present aim at political power, an unsatisfied demand for honest men. Those who speculate in this line for their children, will do wisely to keep this fact in their remembrance during their whole education.

We have delayed, from a full consciousness of the difficulty of the undertaking, to speak of the method of curing either the habits or the propensity to falsehood. Physicians, for mental as well as bodily diseases, can give long histories of maladies; but are surprisingly concise when they come to treat of the method of cure. With patients of different ages, and different temperaments, to speak with due medical solemnity, we should advise different remedies. With young children, we should be most anxious to break the habits; with children at a more advanced period of their education, we should be most careful to rectify the principles. Children, before they reason, act merely from habit, and without having acquired command over themselves, they have no power to break their own habits; but when young people reflect and deliberate, their principles are of much more importance than their habits, because their principles, in fact, in most cases, govern their habits. It is in consequence of their deliberations and reflections that they act; and, before we can change their way of acting, we must change their way of thinking.

To break *habits* of falsehood in young children, let us begin by removing the temptation, whatever it may be. For instance, if the child has the habit of denying that he has seen, heard, or done things which he has seen, heard, and done, we must not, upon any account, ever question him about any of these particulars, but we should forbear to give him any pleasure which he might hope to obtain by our faith in his assertions. Without entering into any explanations, we should absolutely [60] disregard what he says, and with looks of cool contempt, turn away without listening to his falsities. A total change of occupations, new objects, especially such as excite and employ the senses, will be found highly advantageous. Sudden pleasure, from strong expressions of affection, or eloquent praise, whenever the child speaks truth, will operate powerfully in breaking his habits of equivocation. We do not advise parents to try sudden pain with children at this early age, neither do we advise bodily correction, or lasting *penitences*, meant to excite shame, because these depress and enfeeble the mind, and a propensity to falsehood ultimately arises from weakness and timidity. Strengthen the body and mind by all means; try to give the pupils command over themselves upon occasions where they have no opportunities of deceiving: the same command of mind and courage, proceeding from the consciousness of strength and fortitude, may, when once acquired, be exerted in any manner we direct. A boy who tells a falsehood to avoid some trifling pain, or to procure some trifling gratification, would perhaps dare to speak the truth, if he were certain that he could bear the pain, or do without the gratification. Without talking to him about truth or falsehood, we should begin by exercising him in the art of bearing and forbearing. The slightest trials are best for beginners, such as their fortitude can bear, for success is necessary to increase their courage.

Madame de Genlis, in her Adele and Theodore, gives Theodore, when he is about seven years old, a box of sugar-plums to take care of, to teach him to command his passions. Theodore produces the untouched treasure to her mother, from time to time, with great self-complacency. We think this a good practical lesson. Some years ago the experiment was tried, with complete success, upon a little boy between five and six years old. This boy kept raisins and almonds in a little box in his pocket, day after day, without ever thinking of touching them. His only difficulty was to remember at the appointed time, at the week's end, to produce them. The raisins were regularly counted from time to time, and were, when found to be right, sometimes given to the child, but not always. When, for several weeks, the boy had faithfully executed his trust, the time was extended for which he was to keep the raisins, and every body in the family expressed that they were now certain, before they counted the raisins, that they should find the number exact. This confidence, which was not pretended confidence, pleased the child, but the rest he considered as a matter of course. We think such little trials as these might be made with children of five or six years old, to give them early habits of exactness. The boy we have just mentioned, has grown up with a more unblemished reputation for truth, than any child with whom we were ever acquainted. This is the same boy who broke the looking-glass.

When a patient, far advanced in his childhood, is yet to be cured of a propensity to deceive, the business becomes formidable. It is dangerous to set our vigilance in direct opposition to his cunning, and it is yet more dangerous to trust and give him opportunities of fresh deceit. If the pupil's temper is timid, fear has probably been his chief inducement to dissimulation. If his temper is sanguine, hope and success, and perhaps the pleasure of inventing schemes, or of outwitting his superiors, have been his motives. In one case we should prove to the patient, that he has nothing to fear from speaking the truth to us; in the other case we should demonstrate to him, that he has nothing to hope from telling us falsehoods. Those who are pleased with the ingenuity of cunning, should have opportunities of showing their ingenuity in honourable employments, and the highest praise should be given to their successful abilities whenever they are thus exerted. They will compare their feelings when they are the objects of esteem, and of contempt, and they will be led permanently to pursue what most tends to their happiness. We should never deprive them of the hope of establishing a character for integrity; on the contrary, we should explain distinctly to them, that this is absolutely in their own power. Examples from real life will strike the mind of a young person just entering into the world, much more than any fictitious characters, or moral stories; and strong indignation, expressed incidentally, will have more effect than any lectures prepared for the purpose. We do not mean, that any artifice should be used to make our lessons impressive; but there is no artifice in seizing opportunities, which must occur in real life, to exemplify the advantages of a good character. The opinions which young people hear expressed of actions in which they have no share, and of characters with whom they are not connected, make a great impression upon them. The horror which is shown to falsehood, the shame which overwhelms the culprit, they have then leisure to contemplate; they see the effects of the storm at a distance; they dread to be exposed to its violence, and they will prepare for their own security. When any such strong impression has been made upon the mind, we should seize that moment to connect new principles with new habits of action: we should try the pupil in some situation in which he has never been tried before, and where he consequently may feel hope of obtaining reputation, if he deserves it, by integrity. All reproaches upon his former conduct should now be forborne, and he should be allowed to feel, in full security, the pleasures and the honours of his new character.

We cannot better conclude a chapter upon Truth, than by honestly referring the reader to a charming piece of eloquence, with which Mr. Godwin concludes his essay upon Deception and Frankness. [61] We are sensible how much we shall lose by the comparison: we had written this chapter before we saw his essay.

[51] We refer to Locke's Thoughts concerning Education, and Rousseau's Emilius, vol. i.

[52] V. The Life of the Duke of Burgundy in Madame de la Fite's agreeable and instructive work for children, "Contes, Drames et Entretiens, &c."

[53] Pronounced gossoon.

[54] Edwards's History West Indies, vol. ii.

[55] See Mrs. Macaulay's Letters on Education.

[56] Every thing is healthful to the healthy.

[57] See Mr. Williams's Lectures on Education, where Xenophon is quoted, page 16, &c. vol. ii.—also, page 31.

[58] Vide Williams.

[59] V. Servants and "Public and Private Education."

[60] Rousseau and Williams.

CHAPTER IX
ON REWARDS AND PUNISHMENTS

To avoid, in education, all unnecessary severity, and all dangerous indulgence, we must form just ideas of the nature and use of rewards and punishments. Let us begin with considering the nature of punishment, since it is best to get the most disagreeable part of our business done the first.

Several benevolent and enlightened authors [62] have endeavoured to explain the use of penal laws, and to correct the ideas which formerly prevailed concerning public justice. Punishment is no longer considered, except by the ignorant and sanguinary, as vengeance from the injured, or expiation from the guilty. We now distinctly understand, that the greatest possible happiness of the whole society must be the ultimate object of all just legislation; that the partial evil of punishment is consequently to be tolerated by the wise and humane legislator, only so far as it is proved to be necessary for the general good. When a crime has been committed, it cannot be undone by all the art, or all the power of man; by vengeance the most sanguinary, or remorse the most painful. The past is irrevocable; all that remains, is to provide for the future. It would be absurd, after an offence has already been committed, to increase the sum of misery in the world, by inflicting pain upon the offender, unless that pain were afterwards to be productive of happiness to society, either by preventing the criminal from repeating his offence, or by deterring others from similar enormities. With this double view of restraining individuals, by the recollection of past sufferings, from future crimes, and of teaching others, by public examples, to expect, and to fear, certain evils as the necessary consequences of certain actions hurtful to society, all wise laws are framed, and all just punishments are inflicted. It is only by the conviction that certain punishments are essential to the general security and happiness, that a person of humanity can, or ought, to fortify his mind against the natural feelings of compassion. These feelings are the most painful, and the most difficult to resist, when, as it sometimes unavoidably happens, public justice requires the total sacrifice of the happiness, liberty, or perhaps the life, of a fellow-creature, whose ignorance precluded him from virtue, and whose neglected or depraved education prepared him, by inevitable degrees, for vice and all its miseries. How exquisitely painful must be the feelings of a humane judge, in pronouncing sentence upon such a devoted being! But the law permits of no refined metaphysical disquisitions. It would be vain to plead the necessitarian's doctrine of an unavoidable connection between the past and the future, in all human actions; the same necessity compels the punishment that compels the crime; nor could, nor ought, the most eloquent advocate, in a court of justice, to obtain a criminal's acquittal by entering into a minute history of the errours of his education.

It is the business of education to prevent crimes, and to prevent all those habitual propensities which necessarily lead to their commission. The legislator can consider only the large interests of society; the preceptor's view is fixed upon the individual interests of his pupil. Fortunately both must ultimately agree. To secure for his pupil the greatest possible quantity of happiness, taking in the whole of life, must be the wish of the preceptor: this includes every thing. We immediately perceive the connection between that happiness, and obedience to all the laws on which the prosperity of society depends.—We yet further perceive, that the probability of our pupil's yielding not only an implicit, but an habitual, rational, voluntary, happy obedience, to such laws, must arise from the connection which *he* believes, and feels, that there exists between his social duties and his social happiness. How to induce this important belief, is the question.

It is obvious, that we cannot explain to the comprehension of a child of three or four years old, all the truths of morality; nor can we demonstrate to him the justice of punishments, by showing him that we give present pain to ensure future advantage. But, though we cannot demonstrate to the child that we are just, we may satisfy ourselves upon this subject, and we may conduct ourselves, during his non-age of understanding, with the scrupulous integrity of a guardian. Before we can govern by reason, we can, by associating pain or pleasure with certain actions, give habits, and these habits will be either beneficial or hurtful to the pupil: we must, if they be hurtful habits, conquer them by fresh punishments, and thus we make the helpless child suffer for our negligence and mistakes. Formerly in Scotland there existed a law, which obliged every farrier who, through ignorance or drunkenness, pricked a horse's foot in shoeing him, to deposit the price of the horse until he was sound, to furnish the owner with another, and in case the horse could not be cured, the farrier was doomed to indemnify the injured owner. At the same rate of punishment, what indemnification should be demanded from a careless or ignorant preceptor?

When a young child puts his finger too near the fire, he burns himself; the pain immediately follows the action; they are associated together in the child's memory; if he repeat the experiment often, and constantly with the same result, the association will be so strongly formed, that the child will ever afterwards expect these two things to happen together: whenever he puts his finger into fire, he will expect to feel pain; he will learn yet further, as these things regularly follow one another, to think one the cause, and the other the effect. He may not have words to express these ideas; nor can we explain how the belief that events, which have happened together, will again happen together, is by experience induced in the mind. This is a fact, which no metaphysicians pretend to dispute; but it has not yet, that we know of, been accounted for by any. It would be rash to assert, that it will not in future be explained, but at present we are totally in the dark upon the subject. It is sufficient for our purpose to observe, that this association of facts, or of ideas, affects the actions of all rational beings, and of many animals who are called irrational. Would you teach a dog or a horse to obey you; do you not associate pleasure, or pain, with the things you wish that they should practise, or avoid? The impatient and ignorant give infinitely more pain than is necessary to the animals they educate. If the pain, which we would associate with any action, do not *immediately* follow it, the child does not understand us; if several events happen nearly at the same time, it is impossible that a child can at first distinguish which are causes, and which are effects. Suppose, that a mother would teach her little son, that he must not put his dirty shoes upon her clean sofa: if she frowns upon him, or speaks to him in an angry tone, at the instant that he sets his foot and shoe upon the sofa, he desists; but he has only learned, that putting a foot upon the sofa, and his mother's frown, follow each other; his mother's frown, from former associations, gives him perhaps, some pain, or the expectation of some pain, and consequently he avoids repeating the action which immediately preceded the frown. If, a short time afterwards, the little boy, forgetting the frown, accidentally gets upon the sofa *without his shoes*, no evil follows; but it is not probable, that he can, by this single experiment, discover that his shoes have made all the difference in the two cases. Children are frequently so much puzzled by their confused experience of impunity and punishment, that they are quite at a loss how to conduct themselves. Whenever our punishments are not made intelligible, they are cruel; they give pain, without producing any future advantage. To make punishment intelligible to children, it must be not only *immediately*, but *repeatedly* and *uniformly*, associated with the actions which we wish them to avoid.

When children begin to reason, punishment affects them in a different manner from what it did whilst they were governed, like irrational animals, merely by the direct associations of pleasure and pain. They distinguish, in many instances, between coincidence and causation; they discover, that the will of others is the immediate cause, frequently, of the pain they suffer;

they learn by experience, that the *will* is not an unchangeable cause, that it is influenced by circumstances, by passions, by persuasion, by caprice. It must be, however, by slow degrees, that they acquire any ideas of justice. They cannot know our views relative to their future happiness; their first ideas of the justice of the punishments we inflict, cannot, therefore, be accurate. They regulate these first judgments by the simple idea, that our punishments ought to be exactly the same always in the same circumstances; when they understand words, they learn to expect that our words and actions should precisely agree, that we should keep our promises, and *fulfil* our threats. They next learn, that as they are punished for voluntary faults, they cannot justly be punished until it has been distinctly explained to them what is *wrong* or *forbidden*, and what is *right* or *permitted*. The words *right* or *wrong*, and *permitted* or *forbidden*, are synonymous at first in the apprehensions of children; and obedience and disobedience are their only ideas of virtue and vice. Whatever we command to be done, or rather whatever we associate with pleasure, they imagine to be right; whatever we prohibit, provided we have uniformly associated it with pain, they believe to be wrong. This implicit submission to our authority, and these confined ideas of right and wrong, are convenient, or apparently convenient, to indolent or tyrannical governours; and they sometimes endeavour to prolong the reign of ignorance, with the hope of establishing in the mind an opinion of their own infallibility. But this is a dangerous, as well as an unjust, system. By comparison with the conduct and opinions of others, children learn to judge of their parents and preceptors; by reading and by conversation, they acquire more enlarged notions of right and wrong; and their obedience, unless it then arise from the conviction of their understandings, depends but on a very precarious foundation. The mere association of pleasure and pain, in the form of reward and punishment, with any given action, will not govern them; they will now examine whether there is any moral or physical *necessary* connection between the action and punishment; nor will they believe the punishment they suffer to be a consequence of the action they have committed, but rather a consequence of their being obliged to submit to the will of those who are stronger or more powerful than they are themselves. Unjust punishments do not effect their intended purpose, because the pain is not associated with the action which we would prohibit; but, on the contrary, it is associated with the idea of our tyranny; it consequently excites the sentiment of hatred towards us, instead of aversion to the forbidden action. When once, by reasoning, children acquire even a vague idea that those who educate them are unjust, it is in vain either to punish or reward them; if they submit, or if they rebel, their education is equally spoiled; in the one case they become cowardly, in the other, headstrong. To avoid these evils, there is but one method; we must early secure reason for our friend, else she will become our unconquerable enemy. As soon as children are able, in any instance, to understand the meaning and nature of punishment, it should, in that instance, be explained to them. Just punishment is pain, inflicted with the reasonable hope of preventing greater pain in future. In a family, where there are several children educated together, or in public schools, punishments may be inflicted with justice for the sake of example, but still the reformation and future good of the sufferer is always a principal object; and of this he should be made sensible. If our practice upon all occasions correspond with our theory, and if children really perceive, that we do not punish them to gratify our own spleen or passion, we shall not become, even when we give them pain, objects of their hatred. The pain will not be associated with us, but, as it ought to be, with the fault which was the real cause of it. As much as possible we should let children feel the natural consequences of their own conduct. The natural consequence of speaking truth, is the being believed; the natural consequence of falsehood, is the loss of trust and confidence; the natural consequence of all the useful virtues, is esteem; of all the amiable virtues, love; of each of the prudential virtues, some peculiar advantage to their possessor. But plum-pudding is not the appropriate reward of truth, nor is the loss of it the natural or necessary consequence of falsehood. Prudence is not to be rewarded with the affection due to humanity, nor is humanity to be recompensed with the esteem claimed by prudence. Let each good and bad quality have its proper share of praise and blame, and let the consequences of each follow as constantly as possible. That young people may form a steady judgment of the danger of any vice, they must uniformly perceive, that certain painful consequences result from its practice. It is in vain that we inflict punishments, unless all the precepts and all the examples which they see, confirm them in the same belief.

In the unfortunate son of Peter the Great, we have a striking instance of the effects of a disagreement between precept and example, [63] which, in a less elevated situation, might have escaped our notice. It seems as if the different parts and stages of his education had been purposely contrived to counteract each other. Till he was eleven years old, he was committed to the care of women, and of ignorant bigotted priests, who were continually inveighing against his father for the abolition of certain barbarous customs. Then came baron Huysen for his governour, a sensible man, who had just begun to make something of his pupil, when prince Menzikof insisted upon having the sole management of the unfortunate Alexey. Prince Menzikof abandoned him to the company of the lowest wretches, who encouraged him in continual ebriety, and in a taste for every thing mean and profligate. At length came Euphrosyne, his Finlandish mistress, who, upon his trial for rebellion, deposed to every angry expression which, in his most unguarded moments, the wretched son had uttered against the tyrannical father. Amidst such scenes of contradictory experience, can we be surprised, that Alexey Petrovitch became feeble, ignorant, and profligate; that he rebelled against the father whom he had early been taught to fear and hate; that he listened to the pernicious counsels of the companions who had, by pretended sympathy and flattery, obtained that place in his confidence which no parental kindness had ever secured? Those historians who are zealous for the glory of Peter the Great, have eagerly refuted, as a most atrocious calumny, the report of his having had any part in the mysterious death of his son. But how will they apologize for the Czar's neglect of that son's education, from which all the misfortunes of his life arose?

But all this is past for ever; the only advantage we can gain from recalling these circumstances, is a confirmation of this important principle in education; that, when precept and example counteract one another, there is no hope of success. Nor can the utmost severity effect any useful purpose, whilst the daily experience of the pupil contradicts his preceptor's lessons. In fact, severity is seldom necessary in a well conducted education. The smallest possible degree of pain, which can, in any case, produce the required effect, is indisputably the just measure of the punishment which ought to be inflicted in any given case. This simple axiom will lead us to a number of truths, which immediately depend upon, or result from it. We must attend to every circumstance which can diminish the quantity of pain, without lessening the efficacy of punishment. Now it has been found from experience, that there are several circumstances which operate uniformly to this purpose. We formerly observed, that the effect of punishment upon the minds of children, before they reason, depends much upon its *immediately* succeeding the fault, and also upon its being certainly repeated whenever the same fault is committed. After children acquire the power of reasoning, from a variety of new motives, these laws, with respect to punishment, derive additional force. A trifling degree of pain will answer the purpose, if it be made inevitable; whilst the fear of an enormous proportion of uncertain punishment, will not be found sufficient to govern the imagination. The contemplation of a distant punishment, however severe, does not affect the imagination with much terror, because there is still a secret hope of escape in the mind. Hence it is found from experience, that the most sanguinary penal laws have always been ineffectual to restrain from crimes. [64] Even if detection be inevitable, and consequent punishment equally inevitable, if punishment be not inflicted as soon as the criminal is convicted, it has been found that it has not, either as a preventative, or a public example, the same power upon the human mind. Not only should the punishment be immediate after conviction, but detection should follow the offence as speedily as possible. Without entering at large into the intricate arguments concerning identity and consciousness, we may observe, that the consciousness of having committed the offence for which he suffers, ought, at the time of suffering, to be strong in the offender's mind. Though proofs of his identity may have been legally established in a court of justice; and though, as far as it relates to public justice, it matters not whether the offence for which he is punished has been committed yesterday or a year ago; yet, as to the effect which the punishment produces on the culprit's own mind, there must be a material difference.

"I desire you to judge of me, not by what I was, but by what I am," said a philosopher, when he was reproached for some of his past transgressions. If the interval between an offence and its punishment be long, it is possible that, during this interval, a complete change may be made in the views and habits of the offender; such a change as shall absolutely preclude all probability of his repeating his offence. His punishment must then be purely for the sake of example to others. He suffers pain at the time, perhaps, when he is in the best social dispositions possible; and thus we punish the present good man for the faults of the former offender. We readily excuse the violence which a man in a passion may have committed, when, upon his return to his sober senses, he expresses contrition and surprise at his own excesses; he assures us, and we believe him, that he is now a perfectly different person. If we do not feel any material ill consequences from his late anger, we are willing, and even desirous, that the passionate man should not, in his sober state, be punished for his madness; all that we can desire, is to have some security against his falling into any fresh fit of anger. Could his habits of temper be instantly changed, and could we have a moral certainty that his frenzy would never more do us any injury, would it not be malevolent and unjust to punish him for his old insanity? If we think and act upon these principles with respect to men, how much more indulgent should we be to children? Indulgence is perhaps an improper word—but in other words, how careful should we be never to chain children to their dead faults! [65] Children, during their education, must be in a continual state of progression; they are not the same to-day that they were yesterday; they have little reflection; their consciousness of the present occupies them; and it would be extremely difficult from day to day, or from hour to hour, to identify their minds. Far from wishing that they should distinctly remember all their past thoughts, and that they should value themselves upon their continuing the same, we must frequently desire that they should forget their former errours, and absolutely change their manner of thinking. They should feel no interest in adhering to former bad habits or false opinions; therefore, their pride should not be roused to defend these by our making them a part of their standing character. The character of children is *to be* formed—we should never speak of it as positively fixed. Man has been defined to be a bundle of habits; till the bundle is made up, we may continually increase or diminish it. Children who are zealous in defence of their own perfections, are of all others most likely to become stationary in their intellectual progress, and disingenuous in their temper. It would be in vain to repeat to them this sensible and elegant observation—"To confess that you have been in the wrong, is only saying, in other words, that you are wiser to-day than you were yesterday." This remark will rather pique, than comfort, the pride of those who are anxious to prove that they have been equally wise and immaculate in every day of their existence.

It may be said, that children cannot too early be made sensible of the value of reputation, and they must be taught to connect the ideas of their past and present *selves*, otherwise they cannot perceive, for instance, why confidence should be placed in them in proportion to their past integrity; or why falsehood should lead to distrust. The force of this argument must be admitted; yet still we must consider the age and strength of mind in children in applying it to practice. Truth is not instinctive in the mind, and the ideas of integrity, and of the advantages of reputation, must be very cautiously introduced, lest, by giving children too perfect a theory of morality, before they have sufficient strength of mind to adhere to it in practice, we may make them hypocrites, or else give them a fatal distrust of themselves, founded upon too early an experience of their own weakness, and too great sensibility to shame.

Shame, when it once becomes familiar to the mind, loses its effect; it should not, therefore, be used as a common punishment for slight faults. Nor should we trust very early in education to the delicate secret influence of conscience; but we should take every precaution to prevent the necessity of having recourse to the punishment of disgrace; and we must, if we mean to preserve the power of conscience, take care that it be never disregarded with impunity. We must avoid opposing it to strong temptation; nor should we ever try the integrity of children, except in situations where we can be perfectly certain of the result of the experiment. We must neither run the risk of injuring them by unjust suspicions, nor unmerited confidence. By prudent arrangements, and by unremitted daily attention, we should absolutely prevent the possibility of deceit. By giving few commands, or prohibitions, we may avoid the danger of either secret or open disobedience. By diminishing temptations to do wrong, we act more humanely than by multiplying restraints and punishments.

It has been found, that no restraints or punishments have proved adequate to ensure obedience to laws, whenever strong temptations, and many probabilities of evasion, combine in opposition to conscience or fear. The terrors of the law have been for years ineffectually directed against a race of beings called smugglers: yet smuggling is still an extensive, lucrative, and not universally discreditable, profession. Let any person look into the history of the excise laws, [66] and he will be astonished at the accumulation of penal statutes, which the active, but ineffectual, ingenuity of prohibitory legislators has devised in the course of about thirty years. Open war was declared against all illegal distillers; yet the temptation to illegal distilling continually increased, in proportion to the heavy duties laid upon the fair trader. It came at length to a trial of skill between revenue officers and distillers, which could cheat, or which could detect, the fastest. The distiller had the strongest interest in the business, and he usually came off victorious. *Coursing officers*, and *watching officers* (once ten *watching officers* were set upon one distiller) and *surveyors* and *supervisors*, multiplied without end: the land in their fiscal maps was portioned out into *divisions* and *districts*, and each gauger had the charge of all the distillers in his division: the watching officer went first, and the coursing officer went after him, and after him the supervisor; and they had *table-books*, and *gauging-rods*, and *dockets*, and *permits*; permits for sellers, and permits for buyers, and permits for foreign spirits, printed in red ink, and permits for British spirits, in black ink; and they went about night and day with their hydrometers, to ascertain the strength of spirits; and with their gauging-rods, to measure *wash*. But the pertinacious distiller was still flourishing; permits were forged; concealed pipes were fabricated; and the proportion between the *wash* and *spirits* was seldom legal. The commisioners complained, and the legislators went to work again. Under a penalty of one hundred pounds, distillers were ordered to paint the words *distiller, dealer in spirits*, over their doors; and it was further enacted, that all the distillers should furnish, at their own expense, any kind of locks, and fastenings, which the revenue officers should require for locking up the doors of their own furnaces, the heads of their own stills, pumps, pipes, &c. First, suspicions fell upon the public distiller for exportation; then his utensils were locked up; afterwards the private distiller was suspected, and he was locked up: then they set him and his furnaces at liberty, and went back in a passion to the public distiller. The legislature condescended to interfere, and with a new lock and key, precisely described in an act of parliament, it was hoped all would be made secure. Any person being a distiller, who should lock up his furnace or pipes with a key constructed differently from that which the act described, or any person making such illegal key for said distiller, was subject to the forfeiture of one hundred pounds. The padlock was never fixed upon the mind, and even the lock and key, prescribed by act of parliament, were found inefficacious. Any common blacksmith, with a picklock in his possession, laughed at the combined skill of the two houses of parliament.

This digression from the rewards and punishments of children, to the distillery laws, may, it is hoped, be pardoned, if the useful moral can be drawn from it, that, where there are great temptations to fraud, and continual opportunities of evasion, no laws, however ingenious, no punishments, however exorbitant, can avail. The history of coiners, venders, and utterers, of his majesty's coin, as lately detailed to us by respectable authority, [67] may afford further illustration of this principle.

There is no imminent danger of children's becoming either coiners or fraudulent distillers; but an ingenious preceptor will not be much puzzled in applying the remarks that have been made, to the subject of education. For the anticlimax, in descending from the legislation of men to the government of children, no apology is attempted.

The fewer the laws we make for children, the better. Whatever they may be, they should be distinctly expressed; the letter and spirit should both agree, and the words should bear but one signification, clear to all the parties concerned. They should never be subject to the ex post facto interpretation of an angry preceptor, or a cunning pupil; no loose general terms should permit tyranny, or encourage quibbling. There is said [68] to be a Chinese law, which decrees, that whoever does not show *proper respect* to the sovereign, is to be punished with death. What is meant by the words *proper respect*, is not defined. Two persons made a mistake in some account of an insignificant affair, in one of their court gazettes. It was declared, that *to lie* in a court gazette, is to be wanting in *proper respect* to the court. Both the careless scribes were put to death. One of the princes of the blood inadvertently put some mark upon a memorial, which had been signed by the emperor Bogdo Chan. This was construed to be a want of *proper respect* to Bogdo Chan the emperor, and a horrible persecution hence arose against the scrawling prince and his whole family. May no schoolmasters, ushers, or others, ever (even as far as they are able) imitate Bogdo Chan, and may they always define to their subjects, what they mean by *proper respect*!

There is a sort of mistaken mercy sometimes shown to children, which is, in reality, the greatest cruelty. People, who are too angry to refrain from threats, are often too indolent, or too compassionate, to put their threats in execution. Between their words and actions there is hence a manifest contradiction; their pupils learn from experience, either totally to disregard these threats, or else to calculate, from the various degrees of anger which appear in the threatener's countenance, what real probability there is of his being as good or as bad as his word. Far from perceiving that punishment, in this case, is *pain given with the reasonable hope of making him wiser or happier*, the pupil is convinced, that his master punishes him only to gratify the passion of anger, to which he is unfortunately subject. Even supposing that threateners are exact in fulfilling their threats, and that they are not passionate, but simply wish to avoid giving pain; they endeavour to excite the fears of their pupils as the means of governing them with the least possible pain. But with fear they excite all the passions and habits which are connected with that mean principle of action, and they extinguish that vigorous spirit, that independent energy of soul, which is essential to all the active and manly virtues. Young people, who find that their daily pleasures depend not so much upon their own exertions as upon the humour and caprice of others, become absolute courtiers; they practise all the arts of persuasion, and all the crouching hypocrisy which can deprecate wrath, or propitiate favour. Their notions of right and wrong cannot be enlarged; their recollection of the rewards and punishments of their childhood, is always connected with the ideas of tyranny and slavery; and when they break their own chains, they are impatient to impose similar bonds upon their inferiors.

An argument has been used to prove, that in some cases anger is part of the *justice* of punishment, because "mere *reproof*, without sufficient marks of *displeasure* and *emotion*, affects a child very little, and is soon forgotten." [69] It cannot be doubted, that the expression of indignation is a just consequence of certain faults, and the general indignation with which these are spoken of before young people, must make a strong and useful impression upon their minds. They reflect upon the actions of others; they see the effects which these produce upon the human mind; they put themselves in the situation alternately of the person who expresses indignation, and of him who suffers shame; they measure the fault and its consequences, and they resolve to conduct themselves so as to avoid that just indignation of which they dread to be the object. These are the general conclusions which children draw when they are *impartial spectators*; but where they are themselves concerned, their feelings and their reasonings are very different. If they have done any thing which they know to be wrong, they expect, and are sensible that they deserve, displeasure and indignation; but if any precise penalty is annexed to the fault, the person who is to inflict it, appears to them in the character of a judge, who is bound to repress his own feelings, and coolly to execute justice. If the judge both reproaches and punishes, he doubles the punishment. Whenever indignation is expressed, no vulgar trivial penalties should accompany it; the pupil should feel that it is indignation against his fault, and not against himself; and that it is not excited in his preceptor's mind by any petty personal considerations. A child distinguishes between anger and indignation very exactly; the one commands his respect, the other raises his contempt as soon as his fears subside. Dr. Priestley seems to think that, "it is not possible to express displeasure with sufficient *force*, especially to a child, when a man is perfectly cool." May we not reply to this, that it is scarcely possible to express displeasure with sufficient *propriety*, especially to a child, when a man is in a passion? The propriety is, in this case, of at least as much consequence as the force of the reprimand. — The effect which the preceptor's displeasure will produce, must be, in some proportion, to the esteem which his pupil feels for him. If he cannot command his irascible passions, his pupil cannot continue to esteem him; and there is an end of all that fear of his disapprobation, which was founded upon esteem, and which can never be founded upon a stronger or a better basis. We should further consider, that the opinions of all the bystanders, especially if they be any of them of the pupil's own age, have great influence upon his mind. It is not to be expected that they should all sympathize equally with the angry preceptor; and we know, that whenever the indignation expressed against any fault, appears, in the least, to pass the bound of exact justice, the sympathy of the spectators immediately revolts in favour of the culprit; the fault is forgotten or excused, and all join in spontaneous compassion. In public schools, this happens so frequently, that the master's displeasure seldom affects the little community with any sorrow; combined together, they make each other amends for public punishments, by private pity or encouragement. In families, which are not well regulated, that is to say, in which the interests of all the individuals do not coalesce, the same evils are to be dreaded. Neither indignation nor *shame* can affect children in such schools, or such families; the laws and manners, public precept and private opinion, contradict one another.

In a variety of instances in society, we may observe, that the best laws and the best principles are not sufficient to resist the combination of numbers. Never attempt to affix infamy to a number of people at once, says a philosophic legislator. [70] This advice showed that he perfectly understood the nature of the passion of shame. Numbers keep one another in countenance; they form a society for themselves; and sometimes by peculiar phrases, and an appropriate language, confound the established opinions of virtue and vice, and enjoy a species of self-complacency independent of public opinion, and often in direct opposition to their former *conscience*. Whenever any set of men want to get rid of the shame annexed to particular actions, they begin by changing the names and epithets which have been generally used to express them, and which they know are associated with the feelings of shame: these feelings are not awakened by the new language, and by degrees they are forgotten, or they are supposed to have been merely prejudices and habits, which *former methods of speaking* taught people to reverence. Thus the most disgraceful combinations of men, who live by violating and evading the laws of society, have all a peculiar phraseology amongst themselves, by which jocular ideas are associated with the most disreputable actions.

Those who live by depredation on the river Thames, do not call themselves thieves, but *lumpers* and *mudlarks*. Coiners give regular mercantile names to the different branches of their trade, and to the various kinds of false money which they circulate: such as *flats*, or *figs*, or *fig-things*. Unlicensed lottery wheels, are called *little goes*; and the men who are sent about to public houses to entice poor people into illegal lottery insurances, are called *Morocco-men*: a set of villains, hired by these fraudulent lottery keepers, to resist the civil power during the drawing of the lottery, call themselves *bludgeon-men*; and in the language of robbers, a receiver of stolen goods is said to be *staunch*, when it is believed that he will go all lengths rather than betray the secrets of a gang of highwaymen. [71]

Since words have such power in their turn over ideas, we must, in education, attend to the language of children as a means of judging of the state of their minds; and whenever we find, that in their conversation with one another, they have any slang, which turns moral ideas into ridicule, we may be certain that this must have arisen from some defect in their education. The power of shame must then be tried in some new shape, to break this false association of ideas. Shame, in a new shape, affects the mind with surprising force, in the same manner as danger in a new form alarms the courage of veterans. An extraordinary instance of this, may be observed in the management of Gloucester jail: a blue and yellow jacket has been found to have a most powerful effect upon men supposed to be dead to shame. The keeper of the prison told us, that the most unruly offenders could be kept in awe by the dread of a dress which exposed them to the ridicule of their companions, no new term having been yet invented to counteract the terrors of the yellow jacket. To prevent the mind from becoming insensible to shame, it must be very sparingly used; and the hope and possibility of recovering esteem, must always be kept alive. Those who are excluded from hope, are necessarily excluded from virtue; the loss of reputation, we see, is almost always followed by total depravity. The cruel prejudices which are harboured against particular classes of people, usually tend to make the individuals who are the best disposed amongst these sects, despair of obtaining esteem; and, consequently, careless about deserving it. There can be nothing inherent in the knavish propensity of Jews; but the prevailing opinion, that avarice, dishonesty and extortion, are the characteristics of a Jew, has probably induced many of the tribe to justify the antipathy which they could not conquer. Children are frequently confirmed in faults, by the imprudent and cruel custom which some parents have of settling early in life, that such a thing is natural; that such and such dispositions are not to be cured; that cunning, perhaps, is the characteristic of one child, and caprice of another. This general odium oppresses and dispirits: such children think it is in vain to struggle against nature, especially as they do not clearly understand what is meant by nature. They submit to our imputations, without knowing how to refute them. On the contrary, if we treat them with more good sense and benevolence, if we explain to them the nature of the human mind, and if we lay open to them the history of their own, they will assist us in endeavouring to cure their faults, and they will not be debilitated by indistinct, superstitious fears. At ten or eleven years old, children are capable of understanding some of the general principles of rational morality, and these they can apply to their own conduct in many instances, which, however trivial they may appear, are not beneath our notice.

June 16, 1796. S— — (nine years old) had lost his pencil; his father said to him, "I wish to give you another pencil, but I am afraid I should do you harm if I did; you would not take care of your things if you did not feel some inconvenience when you lose them." The boy's lips moved as if he were saying to himself, "I understand this; it is just." His father guessed that these were the thoughts that were passing in his mind, and asked whether he interpreted rightly the motion of the lips. "Yes," said S— —, "that was exactly what I was thinking." "Then," said his father, "I will give you a bit of my own pencil this instant: all I want is to make the necessary impression upon your mind; that is all the use of punishment; you know we do not want to torment you."

As young people grow up, and perceive the consequences of their own actions, and the advantages of credit and character, they become extremely solicitous to preserve the good opinion of those whom they love and esteem. They are now capable of taking the future into their view as well as the present; and at this period of their education, the hand of authority should never be hastily used; the voice of reason will never fail to make herself heard, especially if reason speak with the tone of affection. During the first years of childhood, it did not seem prudent to make any punishment lasting, because young children quickly forget their faults; and having little experience, cannot feel how their past conduct is likely to affect their future happiness: but as soon as they have more enlarged experience, the nature of their punishments should alter; if we have any reason to esteem or love them less, our contempt and displeasure should not lightly be dissipated. Those who reflect, are more influenced by the idea of the duration, than of the intensity of any mental pain. In those calculations which are constantly made before we determine upon action or forbearance, some tempers estimate any evil which is likely to be but of short duration, infinitely below its real importance. Young men, of sanguine and courageous dispositions, hence frequently act imprudently; the consequences of their temerity will, they think, soon be over, and they feel that they are able to support evil for a short time, however great it may be. Anger, they know, is a short-lived passion, and they do not scruple running the hazard of exciting anger in the hearts of those they love the best in the world. The experience of lasting, sober disapprobation, is intolerably irksome to them; any inconvenience which continues for a length of time, wearies them excessively. After they have endured, as the consequence of any actions, this species of punishment, they will long remember their sufferings, and will carefully avoid incurring, in future, similar penalties. Sudden and transient pain appears to be most effectual with persons of an opposite temperament.

Young people, of a torpid, indolent temperament, are much under the dominion of habit; if they happen to have contracted any disagreeable or bad habits, they have seldom sufficient energy to break them. The stimulus of sudden pain is necessary in this case. The pupil may be perfectly convinced, that such a habit ought to be broken, and may wish to break it most sincerely; but may yet be incapable of the voluntary exertion requisite to obtain success. It would be dangerous to let the habit, however insignificant, continue victorious, because the child would hence be discouraged from all future attempts to battle with himself. Either we should not attempt the conquest of the habit, or we should persist till we have vanquished. The confidence, which this sense of success will give the pupil, will probably, in his own opinion, be thought well worthy the price. Neither his reason nor his will was in fault; all he wanted, was strength to break the diminutive chains of habit; chains which, it seems, have power to enfeeble their captives exactly in proportion to the length of time they are worn.

Every body has probably found, from their own experience, how difficult it is to alter little habits in manners, pronunciation, &c. Children are often teased with frequent admonitions about their habits of sitting, standing, walking, talking, eating, speaking, &c. Parents are early aware of the importance of agreeable, graceful manners; every body who sees children, can judge, or think that they can judge, of their manners; and from anxiety that children should appear to advantage in company, parents solicitously watch all their gestures, and correct all their attitudes according to that image of the "*beau ideal*," which happens to be most fashionable. The most convenient and natural attitudes are not always the most approved. The constraint which children suffer from their obedience, obliges them at length to rest their tortured muscles, and to throw themselves, for relief, into attitudes the very reverse of those which they have practised with so much pain. Hence they acquire opposite habits in their manners, and there is a continual struggle between these. They find it impossible to correct, instantaneously, the awkward tricks which they have acquired, and they learn *ineffectually* to attempt a conquest over themselves; or else, which is most commonly the catastrophe, they learn to hear the exhortations and rebukes of all around them, without being stimulated to any degree of exertion. [72] The same voices which lose their power on these trifling occasions, lose, at the same time, much of their general influence. More *power* is wasted upon trifling defects in the manners of children, than can be imagined by any who have not particularly attended to this subject. If it be thought indispensably necessary to speak to children eternally about their manners, this irritating and disagreeable office should devolve upon somebody whose influence over the children we are not anxious to preserve undiminished. A little ingenuity in contriving the dress, writing desks, reading desks, &c. of children, who are any way defective in their shape, might spare much of the anxiety which is felt by their parents, and much of the bodily and mental pain which they alternately endure themselves. For these patients, would it not be rather more safe to consult the philosophic physician, [73] than the dancing master who is not bound to understand either anatomy or metaphysics?

Every preventative which is discovered for any defect, either in manners, temper, or understanding, diminishes the necessity for punishment. Punishments are *the abrupt, brutal resource of ignorance, frequently*, [74] to cure the effects of former negligence. With children who have been reasonably and affectionately educated, scarcely any punishments are requisite. This is not an assertion hazarded without experience; the happy experience of several years, and of several children of different ages and tempers, justifies this assertion. As for corporeal punishments, they may be necessary where boys are to be *drilled* in a given time into scholars; but the language of blows need seldom be used to reasonable creatures. The idea that it is disgraceful to be governed by force, should be kept alive in the minds of children; the dread of shame is a more powerful motive than the fear of bodily pain. To prove the truth of this, we may recollect that few people have ever been known to destroy themselves in order to escape from bodily pain; but numbers, to avoid shame, have put an end to their existence. It has been a question, whether mankind are most governed by hope or by fear, by rewards or by punishments? This question, like many others which have occasioned tedious debates, turns chiefly upon words. Hope and fear are sometimes used to denote mixed, and sometimes unmixed, passions. Those who speak of them as unmixed passions, cannot have accurately examined their own feelings. [75] The probability of good, produces hope; the probability of evil, excites fear; and as this probability appears less or greater, more remote or nearer to us, the mind fluctuates between the opposite passions. When the probability increases on either side, so does the corresponding passion. Since these passions seldom exist in absolute separation from one another, it appears that we cannot philosophically speak of either as an independent motive: to the question, therefore, "which governs mankind the most, hope or fear?" we cannot give an explicit answer.

When we would determine upon the probability of any good or evil, we are insensibly influenced, not only by the view of the circumstances before us, but also by our previous habits; we judge not only by the general laws of human events, but also by our own individual experience. If we have been usually successful, we are inclined to hope; have we been accustomed to misfortunes, we are hence disposed to fear. "Cæsar and his fortune are on board," exclaimed the confident hero to the mariners. Hope excites the mind to exertion; fear represses all activity. As a preventative from vice, you may employ fear; to restrain the excesses of all the furious passions, it is useful and necessary: but would you rouse the energies of virtue, you must inspire and invigorate the soul with hope. Courage, generosity, industry, perseverance, all the magic of talents, all the powers of genius, all the virtues that appear spontaneous in great minds, spring from hope. But how different is the hope of a great and of a little mind; not only are the objects of this hope different, but the passion itself is raised and supported in a different manner. A feeble person, if he presumes to hope, hopes as superstitiously as he fears; he keeps his attention sedulously fixed upon all the probabilities in his favour; he will not listen to any arguments in opposition to his wishes; he knows he is unreasonable, he persists in continuing so; he does not connect any idea of exertion with hope; his hope usually rests upon the exertions of others, or upon some fortuitous circumstances. A man of a strong mind, reasons before he hopes; he takes in, at one quick, comprehensive glance, all that is to be seen both for and against him; he is, from experience, disposed to depend much upon his own exertions, if they can turn the balance in his favour; he hopes, he acts, he succeeds. Poets, in all ages, have celebrated the charms of hope; without her propitious influence, life, they tell us, would be worse than death; without her smiles, nature would smile in vain; without her promises, treacherous though they often prove, reality would have nothing to give worthy of our acceptance. We are not bound, however, to understand literally, the rhetoric of poets. Hope is to them a beautiful and useful allegorical personage: sometimes leaning upon an anchor; sometimes "waving her golden hair;"

always young, smiling, enchanting, furnished with a rich assortment of epithets suited to the ode, the sonnet, the madrigal, with a traditionary number of images and allusions; what more can a poet desire? Men, except when they are poets, do not value hope as the first of terrestrial blessings. The action and energies which hope produces, are to many more agreeable than the passion itself; that feverish state of suspense, which prevents settled thought or vigorous exertion, far from being agreeable, is highly painful to a well regulated mind; the continued repetition of the same ideas and the same calculations, fatigues the mind, which, in reasoning, has been accustomed to arrive at some certain conclusion, or to advance, at least, a step at every effort. The exercise of the mind, in changing the views of its object, which is supposed to be a great part of the pleasure of hope, is soon over to an active imagination, which quickly runs through all the possible changes; or is this exercise, even while it lasts, so delightful to a man who has a variety of intellectual occupations, as it frequently appears to him who knows scarcely any other species of mental activity? The vacillating state of mind, peculiar to hope and fear, is by no means favourable to industry; half our time is generally consumed in speculating upon the reward, instead of earning it, whenever the value of that reward is not *precisely ascertainable.* In all occupations, where judgment or accurate observation is essential, if the reward of our labour is brought suddenly to excite our hope, there is an immediate interruption of all effectual labour; the thoughts take a new direction; the mind becomes tremulous, and nothing decisive can be done, till the emotions of hope and fear either subside or are vanquished.

M. l'Abbé Chappe, who was sent by the king of France, at the desire of the French Academy, to Siberia, to observe the transit of Venus, gives us a striking picture of the state of his own mind when the moment of this famous observation approached. In the description of his own feelings, this traveller may be admitted as good authority. A few hours before the observation, a black cloud appeared in the sky; the idea of returning to Paris, after such a long and perilous journey, without having seen the transit of Venus; the idea of the disappointment to his king, to his country, to all the philosophers in Europe; threw him into a state of agitation, "which must have been felt to be conceived." At length the black cloud vanished; his hopes affected him almost as much as his fears had done; he fixed his telescope, saw the planet; his eye wandered over the immense space a thousand times in a minute; his secretary stood on one side with his pen in his hand; his assistant, with his eye fixed upon the watch, was stationed on the other side. The moment of the total immersion arrived; the agitated philosopher was seized with an universal shivering, and could scarcely command his thoughts sufficiently to secure the observation.

The uncertainty of reward, and the consequent agitations of hope and fear, operate as unfavourably upon the moral as upon the intellectual character. The favour of princes is an uncertain reward. Courtiers are usually despicable and wretched beings; they live upon hope; but their hope is not connected with exertion. Those who court popularity, are not less despicable or less wretched; their reward is uncertain: what is more uncertain than the affection of the multitude? The Proteus character of Wharton, so admirably drawn by Pope, is a striking picture of a man who has laboured through life with the vague *hope* of obtaining universal applause.

Let us suppose a child to be educated by a variety of persons, all differing in their tastes and tempers, and in their notions of right and wrong; all having the power to reward and punish their common pupil. What must this pupil become? A mixture of incongruous characters; superstitious, enthusiastic, indolent, and perhaps profligate: superstitious, because his own contradictory experience would expose him to fear without reason; enthusiastic, because he would, from the same cause, form absurd expectations; indolent, because the *will* of others has been the measure of his happiness, and his own exertions have never procured him any certain reward; profligate, because, probably from the confused variety of his moral lessons, he has at last concluded that right and wrong are but unmeaning words. Let us change the destiny of this child, by changing his education. Place him under the sole care of a person of an enlarged capacity, and a steady mind; who has formed just notions of right and wrong; and who, in the distribution of reward and punishment, of praise and blame, will be prompt, exact, invariable. His pupil will neither be credulous, rash, nor profligate; and he certainly will not be indolent; his habitual and his rational belief will, in all circumstances, agree with each other; his hope will be the prelude to exertion, and his fear will restrain him only in situations where action is dangerous.

Even amongst children, we must frequently have observed a prodigious difference in the quantity of hope and fear which is felt by those who have been well or ill educated. An ill educated child, is in daily, hourly, alternate agonies of hope and fear; the present never occupies or interests him, but his soul is intent upon some future gratification, which never pays him by its full possession. As soon as he awakens in the morning, he recollects some promised blessing, and, till the happy moment arrives, he is wretched in impatience: at breakfast he is to be blessed with some toy, that he is to have the moment breakfast is finished; and when he finds the toy does not delight him, he is *to be blessed* with a sweet pudding at dinner, or with sitting up half an hour later at night than his usual bed-time. Endeavour to find some occupation that shall amuse him, you will not easily succeed, for he will still anticipate what you are going to say or to do. "What will come next?" "What shall we do after this?" are, as Mr. Williams, in his able lectures upon education, observes, the questions incessantly asked by spoiled children. This species of idle, restless curiosity, does not lead to the acquisition of knowledge, it prevents the possibility of instruction; it is not the animation of a healthy mind, it is the debility of an over-stimulated temper. There is a very sensible letter in Mrs. Macaulay's book upon education, on the impropriety of filling the imagination of young people with prospects of future enjoyment: the foolish system of promising great rewards, and fine presents, she clearly shows creates habitual disorders in the minds of children.

The happiness of life depends more upon a succession of small enjoyments, than upon great pleasures; and those who become incapable of tasting the moderately agreeable sensations, cannot fill up the intervals of their existence between their great delights. The happiness of childhood peculiarly depends upon their enjoyment of *little* pleasures: of these they have a continual variety; they have perpetual occupation for their senses, in observing all the objects around them, and all their faculties may be exercised upon suitable subjects. The pleasure of this exercise is in itself sufficient: we need not say to a child, "Look at the wings of this beautiful butterfly, and I will give you a piece of plum-cake; observe how the butterfly curls his proboscis, how he dives into the honeyed flowers, and I will take you in a coach to pay a visit with me, my dear. Remember the pretty story you read this morning, and you shall have a new coat." Without the new coat, or the visit, or the plum-cake, the child would have had sufficient amusement in the story and the sight of the butterfly's proboscis: the rewards, besides, have no natural connection with the things themselves; and they create, where they are most liked, a taste for factitious pleasures. Would you encourage benevolence, generosity, or prudence, let each have its appropriate reward of affection, esteem, and confidence; [76] but do not by ill-judged bounties attempt to force these virtues into premature display. The rewards which are given to benevolence and generosity in children, frequently encourage selfishness, and sometimes teach them cunning. Lord Kames tells us a story, which is precisely a case in point. Two boys, the sons of the earl of Elgin, were permitted by their father to associate with the poor boys in the neighbourhood of their father's house. One day, the earl's sons being called to dinner, a lad who was playing with them, said that he would wait until they returned—"There is no dinner for me at home," said the poor boy. "Come with us, then," said the earl's sons. The boy refused, and when they asked him if he had any money to buy a dinner, he answered, "No." "Papa," said the eldest of the young gentlemen when he got home, "what was the price of the silver buckles you gave me?" "Five shillings." "Let me have the money, and I'll give you the buckles." It was done accordingly, says Lord Kames. The earl, inquiring privately, found that the money was given to the lad *who had no dinner*. The buckles were returned, and the boy was highly commended for being kind to his companion. The commendations were just, but the buckles should not have been returned: the boy should have been suffered steadily to abide by his own bargain; he should have been let to feel the pleasure, and pay the exact price of his own generosity.

If we attempt to teach children that they can be generous, without giving up some of their own pleasures for the sake of other people, we attempt to teach them what is false. If we once make them amends for any sacrifice they have made, we lead them to expect the same remuneration upon a future occasion; and then, in fact, they act with a direct view to their own interest, and govern themselves by the calculations of prudence, instead of following the dictates of benevolence. It is true, that if we speak with accuracy, we must admit, that the most benevolent and generous persons act from the hope of receiving pleasure, and their enjoyment is more exquisite than that of the most refined selfishness; in the language of M. de Rochefoucault, we should therefore be forced to acknowledge, that the most benevolent is always the most selfish person. This seeming paradox is answered, by observing, that the epithet *selfish* is given to those who prefer pleasures in which other people have no share; we change the meaning of words when we talk of its being selfish to like the pleasures of sympathy or benevolence, because these pleasures cannot be confined solely to the idea of self. When we say that a person pursues his own interest more by being generous than by being covetous, we take into the account the general sum of his agreeable feelings; we do not balance prudentially his loss or gain upon particular occasions. The generous man may himself be convinced, that the sum of his happiness is more increased by the feelings of benevolence, than it could be by the gratification of avarice; but, though his understanding may perceive the demonstration of this moral theorem, though it is the remote principle of his whole conduct, it does not occur to his memory in the form of a prudential aphorism, whenever he is going to do a generous action. It is essential to our ideas of generosity, that no such reasoning should, at that moment, pass in his mind; we know that the feelings of generosity are associated with a number of enthusiastic ideas; we can sympathize with the virtuous insanity of the man who forgets himself whilst he thinks of others; we do not so readily sympathize with the cold strength of mind of the person, who, deliberately preferring *the greatest possible share of happiness*, is benevolent by rule and measure.

Whether we are just or not, in refusing our sympathy to the man of reason, and in giving our spontaneous approbation to the man of enthusiasm, we shall not here examine. But the reasonable man, who has been convinced of this propensity in human nature, will take it into his calculations; he will perceive, that he loses, in losing the pleasure of sympathy, part of the sum total of his possible happiness; he will consequently wish, that he could add this item of pleasure to the credit side of his account. This, however, he cannot accomplish, because, though he can by reason correct his calculations, it is not in the power, even of the most potent reason, suddenly to break habitual associations; much less is it in the power of cool reason to conjure up warm enthusiasm. Yet in this case, enthusiasm *is the thing required*.

What the man of reason cannot do for himself after his associations are strongly formed, might have been easily accomplished in his early education. He might have been taught the same general principles, but with different habits. By early associating the pleasures of sympathy, and praise, and affection with all generous and benevolent actions, his parents might have joined these ideas so forcibly in his mind, that the one set of ideas should never recur without the other. Whenever the words benevolence or generosity were pronounced, the feelings of habitual pleasure would recur; and he would, independently of reason, desire from association to be generous. When enthusiasm is fairly justified by reason, we have nothing to fear from her vehemence.

In rewarding children for the prudential virtues, such as order, cleanliness, economy, temperance, &c. we should endeavour to make the rewards the immediate consequence of the virtues themselves; and at the same time, approbation should be shown in speaking of these useful qualities. A gradation must, however, always be observed in our praises of different virtues; those that are the most useful to society, as truth, justice and humanity, must stand the highest in the scale; those that are most agreeable, claim the next place. Those good qualities, which must wait a considerable time for their reward, such as perseverance, prudence, &c. we must not expect early from young people. Till they have had experience, how can they form any idea about the future? Till they have been punctually rewarded for their industry, or for their prudence, they do not feel the value of prudence and perseverance. Time is necessary to all these lessons, and those who leave time out in their calculations, will always be disappointed in whatever plan of education they may pursue.

Many, to whom the subject is familiar, will be fatigued, probably, by the detailed manner in which it has been thought necessary to explain the principles by which we should guide ourselves in the distribution of rewards and punishments to children. Those who quickly seize, and apply, general ideas, cannot endure, with patience, the tedious minuteness of didactic illustration. Those who are actually engaged in *practical education*, will not, on the contrary, be satisfied with general precepts; and, however plausible any theory may appear, they are well aware that its utility must depend upon a variety of small circumstances, to which writers of theories often neglect to advert. At the hazard of being thought tedious, those must be minute in explanation who desire to be generally useful. An old French writer, [77] more remarkable for originality of thought, than for the graces of style, was once reproached *by a friend* with the frequent repetitions which were to be found in his works. "Name them to me," said the author. The critic, with obliging precision, mentioned all the ideas which had most frequently recurred in the book. "I am satisfied," replied the honest author; "you remember my ideas; I repeated them so often to prevent you from forgetting them. Without my repetitions, we should never have succeeded."

[61] V. The Inquirer, p. 101.

[62] Beccaria, Voltaire, Blackstone, &c.

[63] See Cox's Travels, vol. ii. 189.

[64] See Beccaria, Blackstone, Colquhoun.

[65] Mezentius. *Virgil.*

[66] V. An Enquiry into the Principles of Taxation, p. 37, published in 1790.

[67] Colquhoun. On the Police of the Metropolis.

[68] V. The grand instructions to the commissioners appointed to frame a new code of laws for the Russian empire, p. 183, said to be drawn up by the late Lord Mansfield.

[69] V. Dr. Priestley's Miscellaneous Observations relating to Education, sect. vii. of correction, p. 67.

[70] V. Code of Russian Laws

[71] Colquhoun.

[72] See the judicious Locke's observations upon the subject of *manners*, section 67 of his valuable Treatise on Education.

[73] See vol. ii. of Zoonomia.

[74] We believe this is Williams's idea.

[75] Hume's Dissertation on the Passions.

[76] See Locke, and an excellent little essay of Madame de Lambert's.

[77] The Abbe St. Pierre. See his Eloge by D'Alembert.

CHAPTER X
ON SYMPATHY AND SENSIBILITY

The artless expressions of sympathy and sensibility in children, are peculiarly pleasing; people who, in their commerce with the world, have been disgusted and deceived by falsehood and affectation, listen with delight to the genuine language of nature. Those who have any interest in the education of children, have yet a higher sense of pleasure in observing symptoms of their sensibility; they anticipate the future virtues which early sensibility seems certainly to promise; the future happiness which these virtues will diffuse. Nor are they unsupported by philosophy in these sanguine hopes. No theory was ever developed with more ingenious elegance, than that which deduces all our moral sentiments from sympathy. The direct influence of sympathy upon all social beings, is sufficiently obvious, and we immediately perceive its necessary connection with compassion, friendship, and benevolence; but the subject becomes more intricate when we are to analyse our sense of propriety and justice; of merit and demerit; of gratitude and resentment; self-complacency or remorse; ambition and shame. [78]

We allow, without hesitation, that a being destitute of sympathy, could never have any of these feelings, and must, consequently, be incapable of all intercourse with society; yet we must at the same time perceive, that a being endowed with the most exquisite sympathy, must, without the assistance and education of reason, be, if not equally incapable of social intercourse, far more dangerous to the happiness of society. A person governed by sympathy alone, must be influenced by the bad as well as by the good passions of others; he must feel resentment with the angry man; hatred with the malevolent; jealousy with the jealous; and avarice with the miser: the more lively his sympathy with these painful feelings, the greater must be his misery; the more forcibly he is impelled to action by this sympathetic influence, the greater, probably, must be his imprudence and his guilt. Let us even suppose a being capable of sympathy only with the best feelings of his fellow-creatures, still, without the direction of reason, he would be a nuisance in the world; his pity would stop the hand, and overturn the balance of justice; his love would be as dangerous as his pity; his gratitude would exalt his benefactor at the expense of the whole human race; his sympathy with the rich, the prosperous, the great, and the fortunate, would be so sudden, and so violent, as to leave him no time for reflection upon the consequences of tyranny, or the miseries occasioned by monopoly. No time for reflection, did we say? We forgot that we were speaking of a being destitute of the reasoning faculty! Such a being, no matter what his virtuous sympathies might be, must act either like a madman or a fool. On sympathy we cannot depend, either for the correctness of a man's moral sentiments, or for the steadiness of his moral conduct. It is very common to talk of the excellence of a person's heart, of the natural goodness of his disposition; when these expressions distinctly mean any thing, they must refer to natural sympathy, or a superior degree of sensibility. Experience, however, does not teach us, that sensibility and virtue have any certain connection with each other. No one can read the works of Sterne, or of Rousseau, without believing these men to have been endowed with extraordinary sensibility; yet, who would propose their conduct in life as a model for imitation? That quickness of sympathy with present objects of distress, which constitutes compassion, is usually thought a virtue, but it is a virtue frequently found in persons of an abandoned character. Mandeville, in his essay upon Charity Schools, puts this in a strong light.

"Should any one of us," says he, "be locked up in a ground room, where, in a yard joining to it, there was a thriving good humoured child at play, of two or three years old, so near us, that through the grates of the window we could almost touch it with our hands; and if, whilst we took delight in the harmless diversion, and imperfect prattle, of the innocent babe, a nasty overgrown sow should come in upon the child, set it a screaming, and frighten it out of its wits; it is natural to think that this would make us uneasy, and that with crying out, and making all the menacing noise we could, we should endeavour to drive the sow away—But if this should happen to be an half-starved creature, that, mad with hunger, went roaming about in quest of food, and we should behold the ravenous brute, in spite of our cries, and all the threatening gestures we could think of, actually lay hold of the helpless infant, destroy, and devour it;—to see her widely open her destructive jaws, and the poor lamb beat down with greedy haste; to look on the defenceless posture of tender limbs first trampled upon, then torn asunder; to see the filthy snout digging in the yet living entrails, suck up the smoking blood, and now and then to hear the crackling of the bones, and the cruel animal grunt with savage pleasure over the horrid banquet; to hear and see all this, what torture would it give the soul beyond expression!****** Not only a man of humanity, of good morals, and commiseration, but likewise an highwayman, an house-breaker, or a murderer, could feel anxieties on such an occasion."

Amongst those monsters, who are pointed out by the historian to the just detestation of all mankind, we meet with instances of casual sympathy and sensibility; even their vices frequently prove to us, that they never became utterly indifferent to the opinion and feelings of their fellow-creatures. The dissimulation, jealousy, suspicion, and cruelty of Tiberius, originated, perhaps, more in his anxiety about the opinions which were formed of his character, than in his fears of any conspiracies against his life. The *"judge within," the habit of viewing his own conduct in the light in which it was beheld by the impartial spectator*, prompted him to new crimes; and thus his unextinguished sympathy, and his exasperated sensibility, drove him to excesses, from which a more torpid temperament might have preserved him. [79] When, upon his presenting the sons of Germanicus to the senate, Tiberius beheld the tenderness with which these young men were received, he was moved to such an agony of jealousy, as instantly to beseech the senate that he might resign the empire. We cannot attribute either to policy or fear, this strong emotion, because we know that the senate was at this time absolutely at the disposal of Tiberius, and the lives of the sons of Germanicus depended upon his pleasure.

The desire to excel, according to "Smith's Theory of Moral Sentiments," is to be resolved principally into our love of the sympathy of our fellow-creatures. We wish for their sympathy, either in our success, or in the pleasure we feel in superiority. The desire for this refined modification of sympathy, may be the motive of good and great actions; but it cannot be trusted as a moral principle. Nero's love of sympathy, made him anxious to be applauded on the stage as a fiddler and a buffoon. Tiberius banished one of his philosophic courtiers, and persecuted him till the unfortunate man laid violent hands upon himself, merely because he had discovered that the emperour read books in the morning to prepare himself with questions for his literary society at night. Dionysius, the tyrant of Syracuse, sued in the most abject manner for an Olympic crown, and sent a critic to the galleys for finding fault with his verses. Had not these men a sufficient degree of sensibility to praise, and more than a sufficient desire for the sympathy of their fellow-creatures?

It is not from any perverse love of sophistry, that the word sensibility has been used in these instances instead of *irritability*, which seems better to characterize the temper of a Dionysius, or a Tiberius; but, in fact, irritability, in common language, merely denotes an excessive or ill governed degree of sensibility. The point of excess must be marked: sympathy must be regulated by education, and consequently the methods of directing sensibility to useful and amiable purposes, must be anxiously studied by all who wish either for the happiness or virtue of their pupils.

Long before children can understand reasoning, they can feel sympathy; during this early period of their education, example and habit, slight external circumstances, and the propensity to imitation, govern their thoughts and actions. Imitation is the involuntary effect of sympathy in children; hence those who have the most sympathy, are most liable to be improved or injured by early examples. Examples of the malevolent passions, should therefore be most carefully excluded from the sight of those who have yet no choice in their sympathy; expressions of kindness and affection in the countenance, the voice, the actions, of all who approach, and of all who have the care of infants, are not only immediately and evidently agreeable to the children, but ought also to be used as the best possible means of exciting benevolent sympathies in their mind. Children, who habitually meet with kindness, habitually feel complacency; that species of instinctive, or rather of associated affection, which always rises in the mind from the recollection of past pleasures, is immediately excited in such children by the sight of their parents. By an easy transition of ideas, they expect the same benevolence, even from strangers, which they have experienced from their friends, and their sympathy naturally prepares them to wish for society; this wish is often improperly indulged.

At the age when children begin to unfold their ideas, and to express their thoughts in words, they are such interesting and entertaining companions, that they attract a large portion of our daily attention: we listen eagerly to their simple observations; we enter into their young astonishment at every new object; we are delighted to watch all their emotions; we help them with words to express their ideas; we anxiously endeavour to understand their imperfect reasonings, and are pleased to find, or put them in the right. This season of universal smiles and courtesy, is delightful to children whilst it lasts, but it soon passes away; they soon speak without exciting any astonishment, and instead of meeting with admiration for every attempt to express an idea, they are soon repulsed for troublesome volubility; even when they talk sense, they are suffered to talk unheard, or else they are checked for unbecoming presumption. Children feel this change in public opinion and manners most severely; they are not sensible of any change in themselves, except, perhaps, they are conscious of having improved both in sense and language. This unmerited loss of their late gratuitous allowance of sympathy, usually operates unfavourably upon the temper of the sufferers; they become shy and silent, and reserved, if not sullen; they withdraw from our capricious society, and they endeavour to console themselves with other pleasures. It is difficult to them to feel contented with their own little occupations and amusements, for want of the spectators and the audience which used to be at their command. Children of a timid temper, or of an indolent disposition, are quite dispirited and bereft of all energy in these circumstances; others, with greater vivacity, and more voluntary exertion, endeavour to supply the loss of universal sympathy, by the invention of independent occupations; but they feel anger and indignation, when they are not rewarded with any smiles or any praise for their "virtuous toil." They naturally seek for new companions, either amongst children of their own age, or amongst complaisant servants. Immediately all the business of education is at a stand; for neither these servants, nor these playfellows, are capable of becoming their instructers; nor can tutors hope to succeed, who have transferred their power over the pleasures, and consequently over the affections of their pupils. Sympathy now becomes the declared enemy of all the constituted authorities. What chance is there of obedience or of happiness, under such a government?

Would it not be more prudent to prevent, than to complain of these evils? Sympathy is our first, best friend, in education, and by judicious management, might long continue our faithful ally.

Instead of lavishing our smiles and our attention upon young children for a short period, just at that age when they are amusing playthings, should we not do more wisely if we reserved some portion of our kindness a few years longer? By a proper *economy*, our sympathy may last for many years, and may continually contribute to the most useful purposes. Instead of accustoming our pupils early to such a degree of our attention as cannot be supported long on our parts, we should rather suffer them to feel a little ennui, at that age when they can have but few independent or useful occupations. We should employ ourselves in our usual manner, and converse, without allowing children to interrupt us with frivolous prattle; but whenever they ask sensible questions, make just observations, or show a disposition to acquire knowledge, we should assist and encourage them with praise and affection; gradually as they become capable of taking any part in conversation, they should be admitted into society, and they will learn of themselves, or we may teach them, that useful and agreeable qualities are those by which they must secure the pleasures of sympathy. Esteem, being associated with sympathy, will increase its value, and this connection should be made as soon, and kept as sacred, in the mind as possible.

With respect to the sympathy which children feel for each other, it must be carefully managed, or it will counteract, instead of assisting us, in education. It is natural, that those who are placed nearly in the same circumstances, should feel alike, and sympathize with one another; but children feel only for the present; they have few ideas of the future; and consequently all that they can desire, either for themselves, or for their companions, is what will *immediately* please. Education looks to the future, and frequently we must ensure future advantage, even at the expense of present pain or restraint. The companion and the tutor then, supposing each to be equally good and equally kind, must command, in a very different degree, the sympathy of the child. It may, notwithstanding, be questioned, whether those who are constant companions in their idle hours, when they are *very* young, are likely to be either as fond of one another when they grow up, or even as happy whilst they are children, as those are who spend less time together. Whenever the humours, interests, and passions of others cross our own, there is an end of sympathy, and this happens almost every hour in the day with children; it is generally supposed, that they learn to live in friendship with each other, and to bear with one another's little faults habitually; that they even reciprocally cure these faults, and learn, by experience, those principles of honour and justice on which society depends. We may be deceived in this reasoning by a false analogy.

We call the society of children, *society in miniature*; the proportions of the miniature are so much altered, that it is by no means an accurate resemblance of that which exists in the *civilized* world. Amongst children of different ages, strength, and talents, there must always be tyranny, injustice, and that worst species of inequality, which arises from superior force on the one side, and abject timidity on the other. Of this, the spectators of juvenile disputes and quarrels are sometimes sensible, and they hastily interfere and endeavour to part the combatants, by pronouncing certain moral sentences, such as, "Good boys never quarrel; brothers must love and help one another." But these sentences seldom operate as a charm upon the angry passions; the parties concerned, hearing it asserted that they must love one another, at the very instant when they happen to feel that they cannot, are still further exasperated, and they stand at bay, sullen in hatred, or approach hypocritical in reconciliation. It is more easy to prevent occasions of dispute, than to remedy the bad consequences which petty altercations produce. Young children should be kept asunder at all times, and in all situations, in which it is necessary, or probable, that their appetites and passions should be in direct competition. Two hungry children, with their eager eyes fixed upon one and the same bason of bread and milk, do not sympathize with each other, though they have the same sensations; each perceives, that if the other eats the bread and milk, he cannot eat it. Hunger is more powerful than sympathy; but satisfy the hunger of one of the parties, and immediately he will begin to feel for his companion, and will wish that *his* hunger should also be satisfied. Even Mr. Barnet, the epicure, who is so well described in Moore's excellent novel, [80] *after* he has crammed himself to the throat, asks his wife to "try to eat a bit." Intelligent preceptors will apply the instance of the bason of bread and milk, in a variety of apparently dissimilar circumstances.

We may observe, that the more quickly children reason, the sooner they discover how far their interests are any ways incompatible with the interests of their companions. The more readily a boy calculates, the sooner he will perceive, that if he were to share his bason of bread and milk equally with a dozen of his companions, his own portion must be small. The accuracy of his mental division would prevent him from offering to part with that share which, perhaps, a more ignorant accountant would be ready to surrender at once, without being on that account more generous. Children, who are accurate observers of the countenance, and who have a superior degree of penetration, discover very early the symptoms of displeasure, or of affection, in their friends; they also perceive quickly the dangers of rivalship from their companions. If experience convinces them, that they must lose in proportion as their companions gain, either in fame or in favour, they will necessarily dislike them as rivals; their hatred will be as vehement, as their love of praise and affection is ardent. Thus children, who have the most lively sympathy, are, unless they be judiciously educated, the most in danger of feeling early the malevolent passions of jealousy and envy. It is inhuman, and in every point of view unjustifiable in us, to excite these painful feelings in children, as we too often do, by the careless or partial distribution of affection and applause. Exact justice will best prevent jealousy; each individual submits to justice, because each, in turn, feels the benefit of its protection. Some preceptors, with benevolent intentions, labour to preserve a perfect equality amongst their pupils, and, from the fear of exciting envy in those who are inferior, avoid uttering any encomiums upon superior talents and merit. This management seldom succeeds; the truth cannot be concealed; those who feel their own superiority, make painful reflections upon the injustice done to them by the policy of their tutors; those who are sensible of their own inferiority, are not comforted by the courtesy and humiliating forbearance with which they are treated. It is, therefore, best to speak the plain truth; to give to all their due share of affection and applause: at the same time, we should avoid blaming one child at the moment when we praise another: we should never put our pupils in contrast with one another; nor yet should we deceive them as to their respective excellences and defects. Our comparison should rather be made between what the pupil *has been*, and what he *is*, than between what he *is*, and what any body else *is not*. [81] By this style of praise we may induce children to become emulous of their former selves, instead of being envious of their competitors. Without deceit or affectation, we may also take care to associate general pleasure in a family with particular commendations: thus, if one boy is remarkable for prudence, and another for generosity, we should not praise the generosity of the one at the expense of the prudence of the other, but we should give to each virtue its just measure of applause. If one girl sings, and another draws, remarkably well, we may show that we are pleased with both agreeable accomplishments, without bringing them into comparison. Nor is it necessary that we should be in a desperate hurry to balance the separate degrees of praise which we distribute exactly at the same moment, because if children are sure that the reward of their industry and ingenuity is secured by our justice, they will trust to us, though that reward may be for a few hours delayed. It is only where workmen have no confidence in the integrity or punctuality of their masters, that they are impatient of any accidental delay in the payment of their wages.

With the precautions which have been mentioned, we may hope to see children grow up in real friendship together. The whole sum of their pleasure is much increased by mutual sympathy. This happy moral truth, upon which so many of our virtues depend, should be impressed upon the mind; it should be clearly demonstrated to the reason; it should not be repeated as an a priori, sentimental assertion.

Those who have observed the sudden, violent, and surprising effects of emulation in public schools, will regret the want of this *power* in the intellectual education of their pupils at home. Even the acquisition of talents and knowledge ought, however, to be but a secondary consideration, subordinate to the general happiness of our pupils. If we *could* have superior knowledge, upon condition that we should have a malevolent disposition, and an irritable temper, should we, setting every other moral consideration aside, be willing to make the purchase at such a price? Let any person, desirous to see a striking picture of the effects of scholastic competition upon the moral character, look at the life of that wonder of his age, the celebrated Abeillard. As the taste and manners of the present times are so different from those of the age in which he lived, we see, without any species of deception, the real value of the learning in which he excelled, and we can judge both of his acquirements, and of his character, without prejudice. We see him goaded on by rivalship, and literary ambition, to astonishing exertions at one time; at another, torpid in monkish indolence: at one time, we see him intoxicated with adulation; at another, listless, desponding, abject, incapable of maintaining his own self-approbation without the suffrages of those whom he despised. If his biographer [82] does him justice, a more selfish, irritable, contemptible, miserable being, than the learned Abeillard, could scarcely exist.

A philosopher, [83] who, if we might judge of him by the benignity of his writings, was surely of a most amiable and happy temper, has yet left us a melancholy and discouraging history of the unsociable condition of men of superior knowledge and abilities. He supposes that those who have devoted much time to the cultivation of their understandings, have habitually less sympathy, or less exercise for their sympathy, than those who live less abstracted from the world; that, consequently, "all their social, and all their public affections, lose their natural warmth and vigour," whilst their selfish passions are cherished and strengthened, being kept in constant play by literary rivalship. It is to be hoped, that there are men of the most extensive learning and genius, now living, who could, from their own experience, assure us that those are obsolete observations, no longer applicable to modern human nature. At all events, we, who refer so much to education, are hopefully of opinion, that education can prevent these evils, in common with *almost* all the other evils of life. It would be an errour, fatal to all improvement, to believe that the cultivation of the understanding, impedes the exercise of the social affections. Obviously, a man, who secludes himself from the world, and whose whole life is occupied with abstract studies, cannot enjoy any pleasure from his social affections; his admiration of the dead, is so constant, that he has no time to feel any sympathy with the living. An individual, of this ruminating species, is humorously delineated in Mrs. D'Arblay's Camilla. Men, who are compelled to unrelenting labour, whether by avarice, or by literary ambition, are equally to be pitied. They are not models for imitation; they sacrifice their happiness to some strong passion or interest. Without this ascetic abstinence from the domestic and social pleasures of life, surely persons may cultivate their understandings, and acquire, even by mixing with their fellow-creatures, a variety of useful knowledge.

An ingenious theory [84] supposes the exercise of any of our faculties, is always attended with pleasure, which lasts as long as that exercise can be continued without fatigue. This pleasure, arising from the due exercise of our mental powers, the author of this theory maintains to be the foundation of our most agreeable sentiments. If there be any truth in these ideas, of how many agreeable sentiments must a man of sense be capable! The pleasures of society must to him increase in an almost incalculable proportion; because, in conversation, his faculties can never want subjects on which they may be amply exercised. The dearth of conversation, which every body may have felt in certain company, is always attended with mournful countenances, and every symptom of ennui. Indeed, without the pleasures of conversation, society is reduced to meetings of people, who assemble to eat and drink, to show their fine clothes, to weary and to hate one another. The sympathy of bon vivants is, it must be acknowleged, very lively and sincere towards each other; but this can last only during the hour of dinner, unless they revive, and prolong, by the powers of imagination, the memory of the feast. Some foreign traveller [85] tells us, that "every year, at Naples, an officer of the police goes through the city, attended by a trumpeter, who proclaims in all the squares and cross-ways, how many thousand oxen, calves, lambs, hogs, &c. the Neapolitans have had the honour of eating in the course of the year." The people all listen with extreme attention to this proclamation, and are immoderately delighted at the huge amount.

A degree, and scarcely one degree, above the brute sympathy of good eaters, is that gregarious propensity which is sometimes honoured with the name of sociability. The current sympathy, or appearance of sympathy, which is to be found amongst the idle and frivolous in fashionable life, is wholly unconnected with even the idea of esteem. It is therefore pernicious to all who partake of it; it excites to no great exertions; it rewards neither useful nor amiable qualities: on the contrary, it is to be obtained by vice, rather than by virtue; by folly much more readily than by wisdom. It is the mere follower of fashion, and of dissipation, and it keeps those in humour and countenance, who ought to hear the voice of public reproach, and who might be roused by the fear of disgrace, or the feelings of shame, to exertions which should justly entitle them to the approbation and affection of honourable friends.

Young people, who are early in life content with this *convivial* sympathy, may, in the common phrase, become *very good, pleasant companions*; but there is little chance that they should ever become any thing more, and there is great danger that they may be led into any degree of folly, extravagance, or vice, to which fashion and the voice of numbers invite. It sometimes happens, that men of superior abilities, have such an indiscriminate love of applause and sympathy, that they reduce themselves to the standard of all their casual companions, and vary their objects of ambition with the opinion of the silly people with whom they chance to associate. In public life, party spirit becomes the ruling principle of men of this character; in private life, they are addicted to clubs, and associations of all sorts, in which the contagion of sympathy has a power which the sober influence of reason seldom ventures to correct. The waste of talents, and the total loss of principle, to which this indiscriminate love of sympathy leads, should warn us to guard against its influence by early education. The gregarious propensity in childhood, should not be indulged without precautions: unless their companions are well educated, we can never be reasonably secure of the conduct or happiness of our pupils: from sympathy, they catch all the wishes, tastes, and ideas of those with whom they associate; and what is still worse, they acquire the dangerous habits of resting upon the support, and of wanting the stimulus of numbers. It is, surely, far more prudent to let children feel a little ennui, from the want of occupation and of company, than to purchase for them the juvenile pleasures of society at the expense of their future happiness. Childhood, as a part of our existence, ought to have as great a share of happiness as it can enjoy compatibly with the advantage of the other seasons of life. By this principle, we should be guided in all which we allow, and in all which we refuse, to children; by this rule, we may avoid unnecessary severity, and pernicious indulgence.

As young people gradually acquire knowledge, they will learn to *converse*, and when they have the habits of conversing rationally, they will not desire companions who can only chatter. They will prefer the company of friends, who can sympathize in their occupations, to the presence of ignorant idlers, who can fill up the void of ideas with nonsense and noise. Some people have a notion that the understanding and the *heart* are not to be educated at the same time; but the very reverse of this is, perhaps, true; neither can be brought to any perfection, unless both are cultivated together.

We should not, therefore, expect premature virtues. During childhood, there occur but few opportunities of exerting the virtues which are recommended in books, such as humanity and generosity.

The *humanity* of children cannot, perhaps, properly be said to be exercised upon animals; they are frequently extremely fond of animals, but they are not always equable in their fondness; they sometimes treat their favourites with that caprice which favourites are doomed to experience; this caprice degenerates into cruelty, if it is resented by the sufferer. We must not depend merely upon the natural feelings of compassion, as preservatives against cruelty; the *instinctive* feelings of compassion, are strong amongst uneducated people; yet these do not restrain them from acts of cruelty. They take delight, it has been often observed, in all tragical, sanguinary spectacles, because these excite emotion, and relieve them from the listless state in which their days usually pass. It is the same with all persons, in all ranks of life, whose minds are uncultivated. [86] Until young people have fixed *habits* of benevolence, and a taste for occupation, perhaps it is not prudent to trust them with the care or protection of animals. Even when they are enthusiastically fond of them, they cannot, by their utmost ingenuity, make the animal so happy in a state of captivity, as they would be in a state of liberty. They are apt to insist upon doing animals good against their will, and they are often unjust in the defence of their favourites. A boy of seven years old, once knocked down his sister, to prevent her crushing his caterpillar. [87]

Children should not be taught to confine their benevolence to those animals which are thought beautiful; the fear and disgust which we express at the sight of certain unfortunate animals, whom we are pleased to call ugly and shocking, are observed by children, and these associations lead to cruelty. If we do not prejudice our pupils by foolish exclamations; if they do not, from sympathy, catch our absurd antipathies, their benevolence towards the animal world, will not be illiberally confined to favourite lap-dogs and singing-birds. From association, most people think that frogs are ugly animals. L——, a boy between five and six years old, once begged his mother to come out to look at a *beautiful* animal which he had just found; she was rather surprised to find that this beautiful creature was a frog.

If children never see others torment animals, they will not think that cruelty can be an amusement; but they may be provoked to revenge the pain which is inflicted upon them; and therefore we should take care not to put children in situations where they are liable to be hurt or terrified by animals. Could we possibly expect, that Gulliver should love the Brobdignagian wasp that buzzed round his cake, and prevented him from eating his breakfast? Could we expect that Gulliver should be ever reconciled to the rat against whom he was obliged to draw his sword? Many animals are, to children, what the wasp and the rat were to Gulliver. Put bodily fear out of the case, it required all uncle Toby's benevolence to bear the buzzing of a gnat while he was eating his dinner. Children, even when they have no cause to be afraid of animals, are sometimes in situations to be provoked by them; and the nice casuist will find it difficult to do strict justice upon the offended and the offenders.

October 2, 1796. S——, nine years old, took care of his brother H—— 's hot-bed for some time, when H—— was absent from home. He was extremely anxious about his charge; he took one of his sisters to look at the hot-bed, showed her a hole where the mice came in, and expressed great hatred against the whole race. He the same day asked his mother for a bait for the mouse-trap; his mother refused to give him one, telling him that she did not wish he should learn to kill animals. How good nature sometimes leads to the opposite feeling! S——'s love for his brother's cucumbers made him *imagine* and compass the death of the mice. Children should be protected against animals, which we do not wish that they should hate; if cats scratch them, and dogs bite them, and mice devour the fruits of their industry, children must consider these animals as enemies; they cannot love them, and they may learn the habit of revenge, from being exposed to their insults and depredations. Pythagoras himself would have insisted upon his exclusive right to the vegetables on which he was to subsist, especially if he had raised them by his own care and industry. Buffon, [88] notwithstanding all his benevolent philosophy, can scarcely speak with patience of his enemies the field mice; who, when he was trying experiments upon the culture of forest trees, tormented him perpetually by their insatiable love of acorns. *"I was terrified,"* says he, "at the discovery of half a bushel, and often a whole bushel, of acorns in each of the holes inhabited by these little animals; they had collected these acorns for their winter provision." The philosopher gave orders immediately for the erection of a great number of traps, and snares baited with broiled nuts; in less than three weeks nearly three hundred field mice were killed *or taken prisoners.* Mankind are obliged to carry on a defensive war with the animal world. "Eat or be eaten," says Dr. Darwin, is the great law of nature. It is fortunate for us that there are butchers by profession in the world, and rat-catchers, and cats, otherwise our habits of benevolence and sympathy would be utterly destroyed. Children, though they must perceive the necessity for destroying certain animals need not be themselves executioners; they should not conquer the natural repugnance to the sight of the struggles of pain, and the convulsions of death; their aversion of being the cause of pain should be preserved, both by principle and habit. Those who have not been habituated to the bloody form of cruelty, can never fix their eye upon her without shuddering; even those to whom she may have, in some instances, been early familiarized, recoil from her appearance in any shape to which they have not been accustomed. At one of the magnificent shows with which Pompey [89] entertained the Roman people for five days successively, the populace enjoyed the death of wild beasts; five hundred lions were killed; but, on the last day, when twenty elephants were put to death, the people, unused to the sight, and moved by the lamentable howlings of these animals, were seized with sudden compassion; they execrated Pompey himself for being the author of so much cruelty.

Charity for the poor, is often inculcated in books for children; but how is this virtue to be actually brought into practice in childhood? Without proper objects of charity are selected by the parents, children have no opportunities of discovering them; they have not sufficient knowledge of the world to distinguish truth from falsehood in the complaints of the distressed: nor have they sufficiently enlarged views to discern the best means of doing good to their fellow-creatures. They may give away money to the poor, but they do not always feel the value of what they give: they give counters: supplied with all the necessaries and luxuries of life, they have no use for money; they feel no privation; they make no sacrifice in giving money away, or at least, none worthy to be extolled as heroic. When children grow up, they learn the value of money; their generosity will then cost them rather more effort, and yet can be rewarded only with the same expressions of gratitude, with the same blessings from the beggar, or the same applause from the spectator.

Let us put charity out of the question, and suppose that the generosity of children is displayed in making presents to their companions, still there are difficulties. These presents are usually baubles, which at the best can encourage only a frivolous taste. But we must further consider, that even generous children are apt to expect generosity equal to their own from their companions; then come tacit or explicit comparisons of the value or elegance of their respective gifts; the difficult rules of exchange and barter are to be learned; and nice calculations of *Tare and Tret* are entered into by the repentant borrowers and lenders. A sentimental, two often ends in a commercial intercourse; and those who begin with the most munificent dispositions, sometimes end with selfish discontent, low cunning, or disgusting ostentation. Whoever has carefully attended to young makers of presents, and makers of bargains, will not think this account of them much exaggerated.

"Then what is to be done? How are the social affections to be developed? How is the sensibility of children to be tried? How is the young heart to display its most amiable feelings?" a sentimental preceptress will impatiently inquire.

The amiable feelings of the heart need not be displayed; they may be sufficiently exercised without the stimulus either of our eloquence or our applause. In madame de Silleri's account of the education of the children of the duke of Orleans, there appears rather too much sentimental artifice and management. When the Duchess of Orleans was ill, the children were instructed to write "charming notes" from day to day, and from hour to hour, to inquire how she did. Once when a servant was going from Saint Leu to Paris, madame de Silleri asked her pupils if they had any commissions; the little duke de Chartres says yes, and gave a message about a bird-cage, but he did not recollect to write to his mother, till somebody whispered to him that he had forgotten it. Madame de Silleri calls this childish forgetfulness a "heinous offence;" but was not it very natural, that the boy should think of his bird cage? and what mother would wish that her children should have it put into their head, to inquire after her health in the complimentary style? Another time, madame de Silleri is displeased with her pupils, because they did not show sufficient sympathy and concern for her when she had a headache or sore throat. The exact number of messages which, consistently with the strict duties of friendship, they ought to have sent, are upon another occasion prescribed.

"I had yesterday afternoon a violent attack of the colic, and you discovered the greatest sensibility. By the journal of M. le Brun, I find it was the duke de Montpensier who thought this morning of writing to inquire how I did. You left me yesterday in a very calm state, and there was no reason for anxiety; but, consistently with the strict duties of friendship, you ought to have given orders before you went to bed, for inquiries to be made at eight o'clock in the morning, to know whether I had had any return of my complaint during the night; and you should again have sent at ten, to learn from myself, the instant I awoke, the exact state of my health. Such are the benevolent and tender cares which a lively and sincere friendship dictates. You must accustom yourselves to the observance of them, if you wish to be beloved."

Another day madame de Silleri told the duke de Chartres, that he had a very idiotic appearance, because, when he went to see his mother, his attention was taken up by two paroquets which happened to be in the room. All these reproaches and documents could not, we should apprehend, tend to increase the real sensibility and affection of children. Gratitude is one of the most certain, but one of the latest, rewards, which preceptors and parents should expect from their pupils. Those who are too impatient to wait for the gradual development of the affections, will obtain from their children, instead of warm, genuine, enlightened gratitude, nothing but the expression of cold, constrained, stupid hypocrisy. During the process of education, a child cannot perceive its ultimate end; how can he judge whether the means employed by his parents, are well adapted to effect their purposes? Moments of restraint and of privation, or, perhaps, of positive pain, must be endured by children under the mildest system of education: they must, therefore, perceive, that their parents are the immediate cause of some evils to them; the remote good is beyond their view. And can we expect from an infant the systematic resignation of an optimist? Belief upon trust, is very different from that which arises from experience; and no one, who understands the human heart, will expect incompatible feelings: in the mind of a child, the feeling of present pain is incompatible with gratitude. Mrs. Macaulay mentions a striking instance of extorted gratitude. A poor child, who had been taught to return thanks for every thing, had a bitter medicine given to her; when she had drank it, she curtesied, and said, "Thank you for my good stuff." There was a mistake in the medicine, and the child died the next morning.

Children who are not sentimentally educated, often offend by their simplicity, and frequently disgust people of impatient feelings, by their apparent indifference to things which are expected to touch their sensibility. Let us be content with nature, or rather let us never exchange simplicity for affection. Nothing hurts young people more than to be watched continually about their feelings, to have their countenances scrutinized, and the degrees of their sensibility measured by the surveying eye of the unmerciful spectator. Under the constraint of such examinations, they can think of nothing, but that they are looked at, and feel nothing but shame or apprehension: they are afraid to lay their minds open, lest they should be convicted of some deficiency of feeling. On the contrary, children who are not in dread of this sentimental inquisition, speak their minds, the truth, and the whole truth, without effort or disguise: they lay open their hearts, and tell their thoughts as they arise, with simplicity that would not fear to enter even "The palace of Truth." [90]

A little girl, Ho— —, who was not quite four years old, asked her mother to give her a plaything: one of her sisters had just before asked for the same thing. "I cannot give it to you both," said the mother.

Ho— —. No, but I wish you to give it to me, and not to E— —.

Mother. Don't you wish your sister to have what she wants?

Ho— —. Mother, if I say that I *don't* wish so, will you give it to me?

Perhaps this *naivete* might have displeased some scrupulous admirers of politeness, who could not discover in it symptoms of that independent simplicity of character, for which the child who made this speech was distinguished.

"Do you *always* love me?" said a mother to her son, who was about four years old.

"Always," said the child, "except when I am asleep."

Mother. "And why do you not love me when you are asleep?"

Son. "Because I do not think of you then."

This sensible answer showed, that the boy reflected accurately upon his own feelings, and a judicious parent must consequently have a sober certainty of his affection. The thoughtless caresses of children who are never accustomed to reason, are lavished alike upon strangers and friends, and their fondness of to-day may, without any reasonable cause, become aversion by to-morrow.

Children are often asked to tell which of their friends they love the best, but they are seldom required to assign any reason for their choice. It is not prudent to question them frequently about their own feelings; but whenever they express any decided preference, we should endeavour to *lead*, not to *drive* them to reflect upon the reasons for their affection. They will probably at first mention some particular instance of kindness, which they have lately received from the person whom they prefer. "I like such a person because he mended my top." "I like such another because he took me out to walk with him and let me gather flowers." By degrees we may teach children to generalize their ideas, and to perceive that they like people for being either useful or agreeable.

The desire to return kindness by kindness, arises very early in the mind; and the hope of conciliating the good will of the powerful beings by whom they are surrounded, is one of the first wishes that appears in the minds of intelligent and affectionate children. From this sense of mutual dependence, the first principles of social intercourse are deduced, and we may render our pupils either mean sycophants, or useful and honourable members of society, by the methods which we use to direct their first efforts to please. It should be our object to convince them, that the exchange of mutual good offices contributes to happiness; and whilst we connect the desire to assist others with the perception of the beneficial consequences that eventually arise to themselves, we may be certain that children will never become blindly selfish, or idly sentimental. We cannot help admiring the simplicity, strength of mind, and good sense, of a little girl of four years old, who, when she was put into a stage coach with a number of strangers, looked round upon them all, and, after a few minutes silence, addressed them, with the imperfect articulation of infancy, in the following words:

"If you'll be good to me, I'll be good to you."

Whilst we were writing upon sympathy and sensibility, we met with the following apposite passage:

"In 1765, I was," says M. de St. Pierre, "at Dresden, at a play acted at court; it was the Pere de Famille. The electoress came in with one of her daughters, who might be about five or six years old. An officer of the Saxon guards, who came with me to the play, whispered, 'That child will interest you as much as the play.' As soon as she was seated, she placed both her hands on the front of the box, fixed her eyes upon the stage, and continued with her mouth open, all attention to the motions of the actors. It was truly touching to see their different passions painted on her face as in a glass. There appeared in her countenance successively, anxiety, surprise, melancholy, and grief; at length the interest increasing in every scene, tears began to flow, which soon ran in abundance down her little cheeks; then came agitation, sighs, and loud sobs; at last they were obliged to carry her out of the box, lest she should choke herself with crying. My next neighbour told me, that every time that this young princess came to a pathetic play, she was obliged to leave the house before the catastrophe."

"I have seen," continues M. de St. Pierre, "instances of sensibility still more touching amongst the children of the common people, because the emotion was not here produced by any theatrical effect. As I was walking some years ago in the Pre St. Gervais, at the beginning of winter, I saw a poor woman lying on the ground, busied in weeding a bed of sorrel; near her was a little girl of six years old at the utmost, standing motionless, and all purple with cold. I addressed myself to this woman, who appeared to be ill, and I asked her what was the matter with her. Sir, said she, for these three months I have suffered terribly from the rheumatism, but my illness troubles me less than this child, she never will leave me; if I say to her, Thou art quite frozen, go and warm thyself in the house, she answers me, Alas! mamma, if I leave you, you'll certainly fall ill again!"

"Another time, being at Marly, I went to see, in the groves of that magnificent park, that charming group of children who are feeding with vine leaves and grapes a goat who seems to be playing with them. Near this spot is an open summer house, where Louis XV. on fine days, used sometimes to take refreshment. As it was showery weather, I went to take shelter for a few minutes. I found there three children, who were much more interesting than children of marble. They were two little girls, very pretty, and very busily employed in picking up all round the summer house dry sticks, which they put into a sort of wallet which was lying upon the king's table, whilst a little ill clothed thin boy was devouring a bit of bread in one corner of the room. I asked the tallest of the children, who appeared to be between eight and nine years old, what she meant to do with the wood which she was gathering together with so much eagerness. She answered, 'Sir, you see that little boy, he is very unhappy. He has a mother-in-law' (Why always *a mother-in-law*?) 'He has a mother-in-law, who sends him all day long to look for wood; when he does not bring any home, he is beaten; when he has got any, the Swiss who stands at the entrance of the park takes it all away from him, and keeps it for himself. The boy is almost starved with hunger, and we have given him our breakfast.' After having said these words, she and her companion finished filling the little wallet, they packed it upon the boy's shoulders, and they ran before their unfortunate friend to see that he might pass in safety."

We have read these three anecdotes to several children, and have found that the *active* friends of the little wood-cutter were the most admired. It is probable, that amongst children who have been much praised for expressions of sensibility, the young lady who wept so bitterly at the play-house, would be preferred; affectionate children will like the little girl who stood purple with cold beside her sick mother; but if they have been well educated, they will probably express some surprise at her motionless attitude; they will ask why she did not try to help her mother to weed the bed of sorrel.

It requires much skill and delicacy in our conduct towards children, to preserve a proper medium between the indulging and the repressing of their sensibility. We are cruel towards them when we suspect their genuine expressions of affection; nothing hurts the temper of a generous child more than this species of injustice. Receive his expressions of kindness and gratitude with cold reserve, or a look that implies a doubt of his truth, and you give him so much pain, that you not only repress, but destroy his affectionate feelings. On the contrary, if you appear touched and delighted by his caresses, from the hope of pleasing, he will be naturally inclined to repeat such demonstrations of sensibility: this repetition should be gently discouraged, lest it should lead to affectation. At the same time, though we take this precaution, we should consider, that children are not early sensible that affectation is either ridiculous or disgusting; they are not conscious of doing any thing wrong by repeating what they have once perceived to be agreeable in their own, or in the manners of others. They frequently imitate, without any idea that imitation is displeasing; their object, as Locke observes, is to please by affectation; they only mistake the means: we should rectify this mistake without treating it as a crime.

A little girl of five years old stood beside her mother, observing the distribution of a dish of strawberries, the first strawberries of the year; and seeing a number of people busily helping, and being helped to cream and sugar, said in a low voice, not meant to attract attention, "I like to see people helping one another." Had the child, at this instant, been praised for this natural expression of sympathy, the pleasure of praise would have been immediately substituted in her mind, instead of the feeling of benevolence, which was in itself sufficiently agreeable; and, perhaps, from a desire to please, she would, upon the next favourable occasion, have repeated the same sentiment; this we should immediately call affectation; but how could the child foresee, that the repetition of what we formerly liked, would be offensive? We should not first extol sympathy, and then disdain affectation; our encomiums frequently produce the faults by which we are disgusted. Sensibility and sympathy, when they have proper objects, and full employment, do not look for applause; they are sufficiently happy in their own enjoyments. Those who have attempted to teach children, must have observed, that sympathy is immediately connected with all the imitative arts; the nature of this connection, more especially in poetry and painting, has been pointed out with ingenuity and eloquence by those [91] whose excellence in these arts entitle their theories to our prudent attention. We shall not attempt to repeat; we refer to their observations. Sufficient occupation for sympathy, may be found by cultivating the talents of young people.

Without repeating here what has been said in many other places, it may be necessary to remind all who are concerned in *female* education, that peculiar caution is necessary to manage female sensibility: to make, what is called the heart, a source of permanent pleasure, we must cultivate the reasoning powers at the same time that we repress the enthusiasm of *fine feeling*. Women, from their situation and duties in society, are called upon rather for the daily exercise of quiet domestic virtues, than for those splendid acts of generosity, or those exaggerated expressions of tenderness, which are the characteristics of heroines in romance. Sentimental authors, who paint with enchanting colours all the graces and all the virtues in happy union, teach us to expect that this union should be indissoluble. Afterwards, from the natural influence of association, we expect in real life to meet with virtue when we see grace, and we are disappointed, almost disgusted, when we find virtue unadorned. This false association has a double effect upon the conduct of women; it prepares them to be pleased, and it excites them to endeavour to please by adventitious charms, rather than by those qualities which merit esteem. Women, who have been much addicted to common novel-reading, are always acting in imitation of some Jemima, or Almeria, who never existed, and they perpetually mistake plain William and Thomas for "*My Beverly!*" They have another peculiar misfortune; they require continual great emotions to keep them in tolerable humour with themselves; they must have tears in their eyes, or they are apprehensive that their hearts are growing hard. They have accustomed themselves to such violent stimulus, that they cannot endure the languor to which they are subject in the intervals of delirium. Pink appears pale to the eye that is used to scarlet; and common food is insipid to the taste which has been vitiated by the high seasonings of art.

A celebrated French actress, in the wane of her charms, and who, for that reason, began to feel weary of the world, exclaimed, whilst she was recounting what she had suffered from a faithless lover, "Ah! c'étoit le bon temps, j'étois bien malheureuse!" [92]

The happy age in which women can, with any grace or effect, be romantically wretched, is, even with the beautiful, but a short season of felicity. The sentimental sorrows of any female mourner, of more than thirty years standing, command but little sympathy, and less admiration; and what other consolations are suited to sentimental sorrows?

Women, who cultivate their reasoning powers, and who acquire tastes for science and literature, find sufficient variety in life, and do not require the *stimulus* of dissipation, or of romance. Their sympathy and sensibility are engrossed by proper objects, and connected with habits of useful exertion: they usually feel the affection which others profess, and actually enjoy the happiness which others describe.

[78] Adam Smith.

[79] See Smith.

[80] Edward.

[81] V. Rousseau and Williams.

[82] Berington. See his Life of Abeillard.

[83] Dr. John Gregory. Comparative View of the State and Faculties of Man with those of the Animal World. See vol. ii. of Works, from page 100 to 114.

[84] Vernet's Théorie des Sentiments Agréables.

[85] V. Varieties of Literature, vol. i.

[86] Can it be true, that an English nobleman, in the 18th century, won a bet by procuring a man to eat a cat alive?

[87] See Moore's Edward for the boy and larks, an excellent story for children.

[88] Mem. de l'Acad. R. for the year 1742, p. 332.

[89] V. Middleton's Life of Cicero, vol. i. page 474.

[90] V. Le Palais de la Verite.—Madame de Genlis Veillées du Château.

[91] Sir Joshua Reynolds's Discourses. Dr. Darwin's Critical Interludes in the Botanic Garden, and his chapter on Sympathy and Imitation in Zoonomia.

[92] D'Alembert.

CHAPTER XI
ON VANITY, PRIDE, AND AMBITION

We shall not weary the reader by any common-place declamations upon these moral topics. No great subtilty of distinction is requisite to mark the differences between Vanity and Pride, since those differences have been pointed out by every moralist, who has hoped to please mankind by an accurate delineation of the failings of human nature. Whatever distinctions exist, or may be supposed to exist, between the characters in which pride or vanity predominates, it will readily be allowed, that there is one thing in which they both agree—they both receive pleasure from the approbation of others, and from their own. We are disgusted with the vain man, when he intemperately indulges in praise of himself, however justly he may be entitled to that praise, because he offends against those manners which we have been accustomed to think polite, and he claims from us a greater portion of sympathy than we can possibly afford to give him. We are not, however, pleased by the negligence with which the proud man treats us; we do not like to see that he can exist in independent happiness, satisfied with a cool internal sense of his own merits; he loses our sympathy, because he does not appear to value it.

If we could give our pupils exactly the character we wish, what degrees of vanity and pride should we desire them to have, and how should we regulate these passions? Should we not desire, that their ambition to excel might be sufficient to produce the greatest possible exertions, directed to the best possible objects; that their opinion of themselves should be strictly just, and should never be expressed in such a manner as to offend against propriety, or so as to forfeit the sympathy of mankind? As to the degree of pleasure which they should feel from their secret reflections upon their own meritorious conduct, we should certainly desire this to be as lasting, and as exquisite, as possible. A considerable portion of the happiness of life arises from the sense of self-approbation; we should, therefore, secure this gratification in its utmost perfection. We must observe, that, however independent the proud man imagines himself to be of the opinions of all around him, he must form his judgment of his own merits from some standard of comparison, by some laws drawn from observation of what mankind in general, or those whom he particularly esteems, think wise or amiable. He must begin then in the same manner with the vain man, whom he despises, by collecting the suffrages of others; if he selects, with perfect wisdom, the opinions which are most just, he forms his character upon excellent principles; and the more steadily he abides by his first views, the more he commands and obtains respect. But if, unfortunately, he makes a mistake at first, his obstinacy in errour is not to be easily corrected, for he is not affected by the general voice of disapprobation, nor by the partial loss of the common pleasures of sympathy. The vain man, on the contrary, is in danger, let him form his first notions of right and wrong ever so justly, of changing them when he happens to be in society with any persons who do not agree with him in their moral opinions, or who refuse him that applause which supports his own feeble self-approbation. We must, in education, endeavour to guard against these opposite dangers; we must enlighten the understanding, to give our pupils the power of forming their rules of conduct rightly, and we must give them sufficient strength of mind to abide by the principles which they have formed. When we first praise children, we must be careful to associate pleasure with those things which are really deserving of approbation. If we praise them for beauty, or for any happy expressions which entertain us, but which entertain us merely as the sprightly nonsense of childhood, we create vanity in the minds of our pupils; we give them false ideas of merit, and, if we excite them to exertions, they are not exertions directed to any valuable objects. Praise is a strong stimulus to industry, if it be properly managed; but if we give it in too large and lavish quantities early in life, we shall soon find that it loses its effect, and yet that the *patient* languishes for want of the excitation which custom has rendered almost essential to his existence. We say the *patient*, for this mental languor may be considered entirely as a disease. For its cure, see the second volume of Zoonomia, under the article Vanity.

Children, who are habituated to the daily and hourly food of praise, continually require this sustenance unless they are attended to; but we may gradually break bad habits. It is said, that some animals can supply themselves at a single draught with what will quench their thirst for many days. The human animal may, perhaps, by education, be taught similar foresight and abstinence in the management of his thirst for flattery. Young people, who live with persons that seldom bestow praise, do not expect that stimulus, and they are content if they discover by certain signs, either in the countenance, manner, or tone of voice, of those whom they wish to please, that they are tolerably well satisfied. It is of little consequence by what language approbation is conveyed, whether by words, or looks, or by that silence which speaks with so much eloquence; but it is of great importance that our pupils should set a high value upon the expressions of our approbation. They will value it in proportion to their esteem and their affection for us; we include in the word *esteem*, a belief in our justice, and in our discernment. Expressions of affection, associated with praise, not only increase the pleasure, but they alter the nature the of that pleasure; and if they gratify vanity, they at the same time excite some of the best feelings of the heart. The selfishness of vanity is corrected by this association; and the two pleasures of sympathy and self-complacency should never, when we can avoid it, be separated.

Children, who are well educated, and who have acquired an habitual desire for the approbation of their friends, may continue absolutely indifferent to the praise of strangers, or of *common* acquaintance; nor is it probable that this indifference should suddenly be conquered, because the greatest part of the pleasure of praise in their mind, depends upon the esteem and affection which they feel for the persons by whom it is bestowed. Instead of desiring that our pupils should entirely repress, in the company of their own family, the pleasure which they feel from the praise that is given to them by their friends, we should rather indulge them in this natural expansion of mind; we should rather permit their youthful vanity to display itself openly to those whom they most love and esteem, than drive them, by unreasonable severity, and a cold refusal of sympathy, into the society of less rigid observers. Those who have an aversion to vanity, will not easily bear with its uncultivated intemperance of tongue; but they should consider, that much of what disgusts them, is owing to the simplicity of childhood, which must be allowed time to learn that respect for the feelings of others, which teaches us to restrain our own: but we must not be in haste to restrain, lest we teach hypocrisy, instead of strength of mind, or real humility. If we expect that children should excel, and should not know that they excel, we expect impossibilities; we expect at the same time, intelligence and stupidity. If we desire that they should be excited by praise, and that, at the same time, they should feel no pleasure in the applause which they have earned, we desire things that are incompatible. If we encourage children to be frank and sincere, and yet, at the same time, reprove them whenever they naturally express their opinions of themselves, or the pleasurable feelings of self-approbation, we shall counteract our own wishes. Instead of hastily blaming children for the sincere and simple expression of their self-complacency, or of their desire for the approbation of others, we should gradually point out to them the truth—that those who refrain from that display of their own perfections which we call vanity, in fact are well repaid for the constraint which they put upon themselves, by the superior degree of respect and sympathy which they obtain; that vain people effectually counteract their own wishes, and meet with contempt, instead of admiration. By appealing constantly, when we praise, to the judgment of the pupils themselves, we shall at once teach them the habit of re-judging flattery, and substitute, by insensible degrees, patient, steady confidence in themselves, for the wavering, weak, impatience of vanity. In proportion as any one's confidence in himself increases, his anxiety for the applause of others diminishes: people are very seldom vain of any accomplishments in which they obviously excel, but they frequently continue to be vain of those which are doubtful. Where mankind have not confirmed their own judgment, they are restless, and continually aim either at convincing others, or themselves, that they are in the right. Hogarth, who invented a new and original manner of satirizing the follies of mankind, was not vain of this talent, but was extremely vain of his historical paintings, which were indifferent performances. Men of acknowledged literary talents, are seldom fond of amateurs; but, if they are but half satisfied of their own superiority, they collect the tribute of applause with avidity, and without discrimination or delicacy. Voltaire has been reproached with treating strangers rudely who went to Ferney, to see and admire a philosopher as a prodigy. Voltaire valued his time more than he did this vulgar admiration; his visiters, whose understanding had not gone through exactly the same process, who had not, probably, been satisfied with public applause, and who set, perhaps, a considerable value upon their own praise, could not comprehend this appearance of indifference to admiration in Voltaire, especially when it was well known that he was not insensible of fame. He was, at an advanced age, exquisitely anxious about the fate of one of his tragedies; and a public coronation at the theatre at Paris, had power to inebriate him at eighty-four. Those who have exhausted the stimulus of wine, may yet be intoxicated by opium. The voice of numbers appears to be sometimes necessary to give delight to those who have been fatigued with the praise of individuals; but this taste for *acclamation* is extremely dangerous. A multitude of good judges seldom meet together.

By a slight difference in their manner of reasoning, two men of abilities, who set out with the same desire for fame, may acquire different habits of pride, or of vanity; the one may value the number, the other may appreciate the judgment of his admirers. There is something not only more wise, but more elevated, in this latter species of select triumph; the noise is not so great; the music is better. "If I listened to the music of praise," says an historian, who obviously was not insensible to its charms, "I was more seriously satisfied with the approbation of my *judges*. The candour of Dr. Robertson embraced his disciple. A letter from Mr. Hume overpaid the labour of ten years." [93] Surely no one can be displeased with this last generous expression of enthusiasm; we are not so well satisfied with Buffon, when he ostentatiously displays the epistles of a prince and an empress. [94]

Perhaps, by pointing out at proper opportunities the difference in our feelings with respect to vulgar and refined vanity, we might make a useful impression upon those who have yet their habits to form. The conversion of vanity into pride, is not so difficult a process as those, who have not analyzed both, might, from the striking difference of their appearance, imagine. By the opposite tendencies of education, opposite characters from the same original dispositions are produced. Cicero, had he been early taught to despise the applause of the multitude, would have turned away like the proud philosopher, who asked his friends what absurdity he had uttered, when he heard the populace loud in acclamations of his speech; and the cynic, whose vanity was seen through the holes in his cloak, might, perhaps, by a slight difference in his education, have been rendered ambitious of the Macedonian purple.

In attempting to convert vanity into pride, we must begin by exercising the vain patient in forbearance of present pleasure; it is not enough to convince his understanding, that the advantages of proud humility are great; he may be perfectly sensible of this, and may yet have so little command over himself, that his loquacious vanity may get the better, from hour to hour, of his better judgment. Habits are not to be instantaneously conquered by reason; if we do not keep this fact in our remembrance, we shall be frequently disappointed in education; and we shall, perhaps, end by thinking that reason can do nothing, if we begin by thinking that she can do every thing. We must not expect that a vain child should suddenly break and forget all his past associations; but we may, by a little early attention, prevent much of the trouble of curing, or converting, the disease of vanity.

When children first begin to learn accomplishments, or to apply themselves to literature, those who instruct, are apt to encourage them with too large a portion of praise; *the smallest quantity of stimulus that can produce the exertion we desire, should be used*; if we use more, we waste our power, and injure our pupil. As soon as habit has made any exertion familiar, and consequently easy, we may withdraw the original excitation, and the exertion will still continue. In learning, for instance, a new language, at first, whilst the pupil is in the midst of the difficulties of regular and irregular verbs, and when, in translation, a dictionary is wanted at every moment, the occupation itself cannot be very agreeable; but we are excited by the hope that our labour will every day diminish, and that we shall at last enjoy the entertainment of reading useful and agreeable books. Children, who have not learnt by experience the pleasures of literature, cannot feel this hope as strongly as we do, we, therefore, excite them by praise; but by degrees they begin to feel the pleasure of success and occupation; when these are felt, we may and ought to withdraw the unnecessary excitements of praise. If we continue, we mislead the child's mind, and, whilst we deprive him of his natural reward, we give him a factitious taste. When any moral habit is to be acquired, or when we wish that our pupil should cure himself of any fault, we must employ at first strong excitement, and reward with warmth and eloquence of approbation; when the fault is conquered, when the virtue is acquired, the extraordinary excitement should be withdrawn, and all this should not be done with an air of mystery and artifice; the child should know all that we do, and why we do it; the sooner he learns how his own mind is managed, the better—the sooner he will assist in his own education.

Every body must have observed, that languor of mind succeeds to the intoxication of vanity; if we can avoid the intoxication, we shall avoid the languor. Common sayings often imply those sensible observations which philosophers, when they theorize only, express in other words. We frequently hear it said to a child, "Praise spoils you; my praise did you harm; you can't bear praise well; you grow conceited; you become idle; you are good for nothing, because you have been too much flattered." All these expressions show, that the consequences of over-stimulating the mind by praise, have been vaguely taken notice of in education; but no general rules have been deduced from these observations. With children of different habits and temperaments, the same degree of excitement acts differently, so that it is scarcely possible to fix upon any positive quantity fit for all dispositions—the quantity must be relative; but we may, perhaps, fix upon a criterion by which, in most cases, the proportion may be ascertained. The golden rule, [95] which an eminent physician has given to the medical world for ascertaining the necessary and useful quantity of stimulus for weak and feverish patients, may, with advantage, be applied in education. Whenever praise produces the intoxication of vanity, it is hurtful; whenever the appearances of vanity diminish in consequence of praise, we may be satisfied that it does good, that it increases the pupil's confidence in himself, and his strength of mind. We repeat, that persons who have confidence in themselves, may be proud, but are never vain; that vanity cannot support herself without the concurring flattery of others; pride is satisfied with his own approbation. In the education of children who are more inclined to pride than to vanity, we must present large objects to the understanding, and large motives must be used to excite voluntary exertion. If the understanding of proud people be not early cultivated, they frequently fix upon some false ideas of honour or dignity, to which they are resolute martyrs through life. Thus the high-born Spaniards, if we may be allowed to reason from the imperfect history of national character. The Spaniards, who associate the ideas of dignity and indolence, would rather submit to the evils of poverty, than to the imaginary disgrace of working for their bread. Volney, and the baron de Tott, give us some curious instances of the pride of the Turks, which prevents them from being taught any useful arts by foreigners. To show how early false associations are formed and supported by pride, we need but recollect the anecdote of the child mentioned by de Tott. [96] The baron de Tott bought a pretty toy for a present for a little Turkish friend, but the child was too proud to seem pleased with the toy; the child's grandfather came into the room, saw, and was delighted with the toy, sat down on the carpet, and played with it until he broke it. We like the second childhood of the grandfather better than the premature old age of the grandson.

The self-command which the fear of disgrace insures, can produce either great virtues, or great vices. Revenge and generosity are, it is said, to be found in their highest state amongst nations and individuals characterized by pride. The early objects which are associated with the idea of honour in the mind, are of great consequence; but it is of yet more consequence to teach proud minds early to bend to the power of reason, or rather to glory in being governed by reason. They should be instructed, that the only possible means of maintaining their opinions amongst persons of sense, is to support them by unanswerable arguments. They should be taught, that, to secure respect, they must deserve it; and their self-denial, or self-command, should never obtain that tacit admiration which they most value, except where it is exerted for useful and rational purposes. The constant custom of appealing, in the last resort, to their own judgment, which distinguishes the proud from the vain, makes it peculiarly necessary that the judgment, to which so much is trusted, should be highly cultivated. A vain man may be tolerably well conducted in life by a sensible friend; a proud man ought to be able to conduct himself perfectly well, because he will not accept of any assistance. It seems that some proud people confine their benevolent virtues within a smaller sphere than others; they value only their own relations, their friends, their country, or whatever is connected with themselves. This species of pride may be corrected by the same means which are used to increase sympathy. [97] Those who, either from temperament, example, or accidental circumstances, have acquired the habit of repressing and commanding their emotions, must be carefully distinguished from the selfish and insensible. In the present times, when the affectation of sensibility is to be dreaded, we should rather encourage that species of pride which disdains to display the affections of the heart. "You Romans triumph over your tears, and call it virtue! I triumph in my tears," says Caractacus; his tears were respectable, but in general the Roman triumph would command the most sympathy.

Some people attribute to pride all expressions of confidence in one's self: these may be offensive to common society, but they are sometimes powerful over the human mind, and where they are genuine, mark somewhat superior in character. Much of the effect of lord Chatham's eloquence, much of his transcendent influence in public, must be attributed to the confidence which he showed in his own superiority. "I trample upon impossibilities!" was an exclamation which no inferiour mind would dare to make. Would the house of commons have permitted any one but lord Chatham to have answered an oration by "Tell me, gentle shepherd, where?" The danger of failing, the hazard that he runs of becoming ridiculous who verges upon the moral sublime, is taken into our account when we judge of the action, and we pay involuntary tribute to courage and success: but how miserable is the fate of the man who mistakes his own powers, and upon trial is unable to support his assumed superiority; mankind revenge themselves without mercy upon his ridiculous pride, eager to teach him the difference between insolence and magnanimity. Young people inclined to over-rate their own talents, or to under-value the abilities of others, should frequently have instances given to them from real life, of the mortifications and disgrace to which imprudent boasters expose themselves. Where they are able to demonstrate their own abilities, they run no risk in speaking with decent confidence; but where their success depends, in any degree, either upon fortune or opinion, they should never run the hazard of presumption. Modesty prepossesses mankind in favour of its possessor, and has the advantage of being both graceful and safe: this was perfectly understood by the crafty Ulysses, who neither raised his eyes, nor stretched his sceptered hand, "when he first rose to speak." We do not, however, recommend this artificial modesty; its trick is soon discovered, and its sameness of dissimulation presently disgusts. Prudence should prevent young people from hazardous boasting; and good nature and good sense, which constitute real politeness, will restrain them from obtruding their merits to the mortification of their companions: but we do not expect from them total ignorance of their own comparative merit. The affectation of humility, when carried to the extreme, to which all affectation is liable to be carried, appears full as ridiculous as troublesome, and offensive as any of the graces of vanity, or the airs of pride. Young people are cured of presumption by mixing with society, but they are not so easily cured of any species of affectation.

In the chapter on female accomplishments, we have endeavoured to point out, that the enlargement of understanding in the fair sex, which must result from their increasing knowledge, will necessarily correct the feminine foibles of vanity and affectation.

Strong, prophetic, eloquent praise, like that which the great lord Chatham bestowed on his son, would rather inspire in a generous soul noble emulation, than paltry vanity. "On this boy," said he, laying his hand upon his son's head, "descends my mantle, with a double portion of my spirit!" Phillip's praise of his son Alexander, when the boy rode the unmanageable horse, [98] is another instance of the kind of praise capable of exciting ambition.

As to ambition, we must decide what species of ambition we mean, before we can determine whether it ought to be encouraged or repressed; whether it should be classed amongst virtues or vices; that is to say, whether it adds to the happiness or the misery of human creatures. "The inordinate desire of fame," which often destroys the lives of millions when it is connected with ideas of military enthusiasm, is justly classed amongst the *"diseases of volition:"* for its description and cure we refer to Zoonomia, vol. ii. Achilles will there appear to his admirers, perhaps, in a new light.

The ambition to rise in the world, usually implies a mean, sordid desire of riches, or what are called honours, to be obtained by the common arts of political intrigue, by cabal to win popular favour, or by address to conciliate the patronage of the great. The experience of those who have been governed during their lives by this passion, if passion it may be called, does not show that it can confer much happiness either in the pursuit or attainment of its objects. See Bubb Doddington's Diary, a most useful book; a journal of the petty anxieties, and constant dependence, to which an ambitious courtier is necessarily subjected. See also Mirabeau's "Secret History of the Court of Berlin," for a picture of a man of great abilities degraded by the same species of low unprincipled competition. We may find in these books, it is to be hoped, examples which will strike young and generous minds, and which may inspire them with contempt for the objects and the means of vulgar ambition. There is a more noble ambition, by which the enthusiastic youth, perfect in the theory of all the virtues, and warm with yet unextinguished benevolence, is apt to be seized; his heart beats with the hope of immortalizing himself by noble actions; he forms extensive plans for the improvement and the happiness of his fellow creatures; he feels the want of power to carry these into effect; power becomes the object of his wishes. In the pursuit, in the attainment of this object, how are his feelings changed! M. Necker, in the preface to his work on French finance, [99] paints, with much eloquence, and with an appearance of perfect truth, the feelings of a man of virtue and genius, before and after the attainment of political power. The moment when a minister takes possession of his place, surrounded by crowds and congratulations, is well described; and the succeeding moment, when clerks with immense portfolios enter, is a striking contrast. Examples from romance can never have such a powerful effect upon the mind, as those which are taken from real life; but in proportion to the just and lively representation of situations, and passions resembling reality, fictions may convey useful moral lessons. In the Cyropædia there is an admirable description of the day spent by the victorious Cyrus, giving audience to the unmanageable multitude, after the taking of Babylon had accomplished the fullness of his ambition. [100]

It has been observed, that these examples of the insufficiency of the objects of ambition to happiness, seldom make any lasting impression upon the minds of the ambitious. This may arise from two causes; from the reasoning faculty's not having been sufficiently cultivated, or from the habits of ambition being formed before proper examples are presented to the judgment for comparison. Some ambitious people, when they reason coolly, acknowledge and feel the folly of their pursuits; but still, from the force of habit, they act immediately in obedience to the motives which they condemn: others, who have never been accustomed to reason firmly, believe themselves to be in the right in the choice of their objects; and they cannot comprehend the arguments which are used by those who have not the same way of thinking as themselves. If we fairly place facts before young people, who have been habituated to reason, and who have not yet been inspired with the passion, or enslaved by the habits of vulgar ambition, it is probable, that they will not be easily effaced from the memory, and that they will influence the conduct through life.

It sometimes happens to men of a sound understanding, and a philosophic turn of mind, that their ambition decreases with their experience. They begin with some ardor, perhaps, an ambitious pursuit; but by degrees they find the pleasure of the occupation sufficient without the fame, which was their original object. This is the same process which we have observed in the minds of children with respect to the pleasures of literature, and the taste for sugar-plums.

Happy the child who can be taught to improve himself without the stimulus of sweetmeats! Happy the man who can preserve activity without the excitements of ambition!

[93] Gibbon. Memoirs of his Life and Writings, page 148.—Perhaps Gibbon had this excellent line of Mrs. Barbauld's in his memory:

"And pay a life of hardships with a line."

[94] See Peltier's state of Paris in the years 1795 and 1796.

[95] See Zoonomia, vol. i. p. 99.

[96] V. De Tott's Memoirs, p. 138, a note.

[97] V. Sympathy.

[98] V. Plutarch.

[99] Necker de l'Administration des Finances de la France, vol. i. p. 98.

[100] Cyropædia, vol. ii. page 303.

CHAPTER XII
BOOKS

The first books which are now usually put into the hands of a child, are Mrs. Barbauld's Lessons; they are by far the best books of the kind that have ever appeared; those only who know the difficulty and the importance of such compositions in education, can sincerely rejoice, that the admirable talents of such a writer have been employed in such a work. We shall not apologize for offering a few remarks on some passages in these little books, because we are convinced that we shall not offend.

Lessons for children from three to four years old, should, we think, have been lessons for children from four to five years old; few read, or ought to read, before that age.

"Charles shall have a pretty new lesson."

In this sentence the words pretty and new are associated; but they represent ideas which ought to be kept separate in the mind of a child. The love of novelty is cherished in the minds of children by the common expressions that we use to engage them to do what we desire. "You shall have a new whip, a new hat," are improper modes of expression to a child. We have seen a boy who had literally twenty new whips in one year, and we were present when his father, to comfort him when he was in pain, went out to buy him a *new* whip, though he had two or three scattered about the room.

The description, in the first part of Mrs. Barbauld's Lessons, of the naughty boy who tormented the robin, and who was afterwards supposed to be eaten by bears, is more objectionable than any in the book: the idea of killing is in itself very complex, and, if explained, serves only to excite terror; and how can a child be made to comprehend why a cat *should* catch mice, and not kill birds? or why should this species of honesty be expected from an animal of prey?

"I want my dinner."

Does Charles take it for granted, that what he eats is his own, and that he *must* have his dinner? These and similar expressions are words of course;

but young children should not be allowed to use them: if they are permitted to assume the tone of command, the feelings of impatience and ill temper quickly follow, and children become the little tyrants of a family. Property is a word of which young people have general ideas, and they may, with very little trouble, be prevented from claiming things to which they have no right. Mrs. Barbauld has judiciously chosen to introduce a little boy's daily history in these books; all children are extremely interested for Charles, and they are very apt to expect that every thing which happens to him, is to happen to them; and they believe, that every thing he does, is right; therefore, his biographer should, in another edition, revise any of his expressions which may mislead the future tribe of his little imitators.

"Maid, come and dress Charles."

After what we have already said with respect to servants, we need only observe, that this sentence for Charles should not be read by a child; and that in which the maid is said to bring home a gun, &c. it is easy to strike a pencil line across it. All the passages which might have been advantageously omitted in these excellent little books, have been carefully obliterated before they were put into the hands of children, by a mother who knew the danger of early false associations.

"Little boys don't eat butter."

"No body wears a hat in the house."

This is a very common method of speaking, but it certainly is not proper towards children. Affirmative sentences should always express real facts. Charles must know that some little boys do eat butter; and that some people wear their hats in their houses. This mode of expression, "No body does that!" "Every body does this!" lays the foundation for prejudice in the mind. This is the language of fashion, which, more than conscience, makes cowards of us all.

"I want some wine."

Would it not be better to tell Charles, in reply to this speech, that wine is not good for him, than to say, "Wine for little boys! I never heard of such a thing!" If Charles were to be ill, and it should be necessary to give him wine; or were he to see another child drink it, he would lose confidence in what was said to him. We should be very careful of our words, if we expect our pupils to have confidence in us; and if they have not, we need not attempt to educate them.

"The moon shines at night, when the sun is gone to bed."

When the sun is out of sight, would be more correct, though not so pleasing, perhaps, to the young reader. It is very proper to teach a child, that when the sun disappears, when the sun is below the horizon, it is the time when most animals go to rest; but we should not do this by giving so false an idea, as that the sun is gone to bed. Every thing relative to the system of the universe, is above the comprehension of a child; we should, therefore, be careful to prevent his forming erroneous opinions. We should wait for a riper period of his understanding, before we attempt positive instruction upon abstract subjects.

The enumeration of the months in the year, the days in the week, of metals, &c. are excellent lessons for a child who is just beginning to learn to read. The classification of animals into quadrupeds, bipeds, &c. is another useful specimen of the manner in which children should be taught to generalize their ideas. The pathetic description of the poor timid hare running from the hunters, will leave an impression upon the young and humane heart, which may, perhaps, save the life of many a hare. The poetic beauty and eloquent simplicity of many of Mrs. Barbauld's Lessons, cultivate the imagination of children, and their taste, in the best possible manner.

The description of the white swan with her long arched neck, "winning her easy way" through the waters, is beautiful; so is that of the nightingale singing upon her lone bush by moon-light. Poetic descriptions of real objects, are well suited to children; apostrophe and personification they understand; but all allegoric poetry is difficult to manage for them, because they mistake the poetic attributes for reality, and they acquire false and confused ideas. With regret children close Mrs. Barbauld's little books, and parents become yet more sensible of their value, when they perceive that none can be found immediately to supply their place, or to continue the course of agreeable ideas which they have raised in the young pupil's imagination.

"Evenings at Home," do not immediately join to Lessons for Children from three to four years old; and we know not where to find any books to fill the interval properly. The popular character of any book is easily learned, and its general merit easily ascertained; this may satisfy careless, indolent tutors, but a more minute investigation is necessary to parents who are anxious for the happiness of their family, or desirous to improve the art of education. Such parents will feel it to be their duty to look over every page of a book before it is trusted to their children; it is an arduous task, but none can be too arduous for the enlightened energy of parental affection. We are acquainted with the mother of a family, who has never trusted any book to her children, without having first examined it herself with the most scrupulous attention; her care has been repaid with that success in education, which such care can alone ensure. We have several books before us marked by her pencil, and volumes which, having undergone some necessary operations by her scissors, would, in their mutilated state, shock the sensibility of a nice librarian. But shall the education of a family be sacrificed to the beauty of a page, or even to the binding of a book? Few books can safely be given to children without the previous use of the pen, the pencil, and the scissors. In the books which we have before us, in their corrected state, we see sometimes a few words blotted out, sometimes half a page, sometimes many pages are cut out. In turning over the leaves of "The Children's Friend," we perceive, that the different ages at which different stories should be read, have been marked; and we were surprised to meet with some stories marked for six years old, and some for sixteen, in the same volume. We see that different stories have been marked with the initials of different names by this cautious mother, who considered the temper and habits of her children, as well as their ages.

As far as these notes refer peculiarly to her own family, they cannot be of use to the public; but the principles which governed a judicious parent in her selection, must be capable of universal application.

It may be laid down as a first principle, that we should preserve children from the knowledge of any vice, or any folly, of which the idea has never yet entered their minds, and which they are not necessarily disposed to learn by early example. Children who have never lived with servants, who have never associated with ill educated companions of their own age, and who, in their own family, have heard nothing but good conversation, and seen none but good examples, will, in their language, their manners, and their whole disposition, be not only free from many of the faults common amongst children, but they will absolutely have no idea that there are such faults. The language of children who have heard no language but what is good, must be correct. On the contrary, children who hear a mixture of low and high vulgarity before their own habits are fixed, must, whenever they speak, continually blunder; they have no rule to guide their judgment in their selection from the variety of dialects which they hear; probably they may often be reproved for their mistakes, but these reproofs will be of no avail, whilst the pupils continue to be puzzled between the example of the nursery and of the drawing-room. It will cost much time and pains to correct these defects, which might have been with little difficulty prevented. It is the same with other bad habits. Falsehood, caprice, dishonesty, obstinacy, revenge, and all the train of vices which are the consequences of mistaken or neglected education, which are learned by bad example, and which are not inspired by nature, need scarcely be known to children whose minds have from their infancy been happily regulated. Such children should sedulously be kept from contagion. No books should be put into the hands of this happy class of children, but such as present the best models of virtue: there is no occasion to shock them with caricatures of vice. Such caricatures they will even understand to be well drawn, because they are unacquainted with any thing like the originals. Examples to deter them from faults to which they have no propensity, must be useless, and may be dangerous. For the same reason that a book written in bad language, should never be put into the hands of a child who speaks correctly, a book exhibiting instances of vice, should never be given to a child who thinks and acts correctly. The love of novelty and of imitation, is so strong in children, that even for the pleasure of imitating characters described in a book, or actions which strike them as singular, they often commit real faults.

To this danger of catching faults by sympathy, children of the greatest simplicity are, perhaps, the most liable, because they least understand the nature and consequences of the actions which they imitate.

During the age of imitation, children should not be exposed to the influence of any bad examples until their habits are formed, and until they have not only the sense to choose, but the fortitude to abide by, their own choice. It may be said, that "children must know that vice exists; that, even amongst their own companions, there are some who have bad dispositions; they cannot mix even in the society of children, without seeing examples which they ought to be prepared to avoid."

These remarks are just with regard to pupils who are intended for a public school, and no great nicety in the selection of their books is necessary; but we are now speaking of children who are to be brought up in a private family. Why should they be prepared to mix in the society of children who have bad habits or bad dispositions? Children should not be educated for the society of children; nor should they live in that society during their education. We must not expect from them premature prudence, and all the social virtues, before we have taken any measures to produce these virtues, or this tardy prudence. In private education, there is little chance that one errour should balance another; the experience of the pupil is much confined; the examples which he sees, are not so numerous and various as to counteract each other. Nothing, therefore, must be expected from the counteracting influence of opposing causes; nothing should be trusted to chance. Experience must preserve one uniform tenour; and examples must be selected with circumspection. The less children associate with companions of their own age, the less they know of the world; the stronger their taste for literature; the more forcible will be the impression that will be made upon them by the pictures of life, and the characters and sentiments which they meet with in books. Books for such children, ought to be *sifted* by an academy [101] of enlightened parents.

Without particular examples, the most obvious truths are not brought home to our business. We shall select a few examples from a work of high and deserved reputation, from a work which we much admire, "Berquin's Children's Friend." We do not mean to criticise this work as a literary production; but simply to point out to parents, that, even in the best books for children, much must still be left to the judgment of the preceptor; much in the choice of stories, and particular passages suited to different pupils.

In "The Children's Friend," there are several stories well adapted to one class of children, but entirely unfit for another. In the story called the Hobgoblin, Antonia, a little girl "who has been told a hundred foolish stories by her maid, particularly one about a black-faced goblin," is represented as making a lamentable outcry at the sight of a chimney-sweeper; first she runs for refuge to the kitchen, the last place to which she should run; then to the pantry; thence she jumps out of the window, "half dead with terror," and, in the elegant language of the translator, *almost splits her throat with crying out Help! Help!* — In a few minutes she discovers her errour, is heartily ashamed, and "ever afterwards Antonia was the first to laugh at silly stories, told by silly people, of hobgoblins and the like, to frighten her."

For children who have had the misfortune to have heard the hundred foolish stories of a foolish maid, this apparition of the chimney-sweeper is well managed; though, perhaps, ridicule might not effect so sudden st cure in all cases as it did in that of Antonia. By children who have not acquired terrors of the black-faced goblin, and who have not the habit of frequenting the kitchen and the pantry, this story should never be read.

"The little miss deceived by her maid," who takes her mamma's keys out of her drawers, and who steals sugar and tea for her maid, that she may have the pleasure of playing with a cousin whom her mother had forbidden her to see, is not an example that need be introduced into any well regulated family. The picture of Amelia's misery, is drawn by the hand of a master. Terror and pity, we are told by the tragic poets, purify the mind; but there are minds that do not require this species of purification. Powerful antidotes are necessary to combat powerful poisons; but where no poison has been imbibed, are not antidotes more dangerous than useful?

The stories called "The Little Gamblers; Blind Man's Buff; and Honesty the best Policy," are stories which may do a great deal of good to bad children, but they should never be given to those of another description. The young gentlemen who cheat at cards, and who pocket silver fish, should have no admittance any where. It is not necessary to put *children* upon their guard against associates whom they are not likely to meet; nor need we introduce The Vulgar and Mischievous School-Boy, to any but school-boys. Martin, who throws squibs at people in the street, who fastens rabbits' tails behind their backs, who fishes for their wigs, who sticks up pins in his friends' chairs, who carries a hideous mask in his pocket to frighten little children, and who is himself frightened into repentance by a spectre with a speaking trumpet, is a very objectionable, though an excellent dramatic character. The part of the spectre is played by the groom; this is ill contrived in a drama for children; grooms should have nothing to do with their entertainments; and Cæsar, who is represented as a pleasing character, should not be supposed to make the postillion a party in his inventions.

"*A good heart compensates for many indiscretions,*" is a dangerous title for a play for young people; because *many* is an indefinite term; and in settling how many, the calculations of parents and children may vary materially. This little play is so charmingly written, the character of the imprudent and generous Frederick is so likely to excite imitation, that we must doubly regret his intimacy with the coachman, his running away from school, and drinking beer at an ale-house in a fair. The coachman is an excellent old man; he is turned away for having let master Frederick mount his box, assume the whip, and overturn a handsome carriage. Frederick, touched with gratitude and compassion, gives the old man all his pocket money, and sells a watch and some books to buy clothes for him. The motives of Frederick's conduct are excellent, and, as they are misrepresented by a treacherous and hypocritical cousin, we sympathize more strongly with the hero of the piece; and all his indiscretions appear, at least, amiable defects. A nice observer [102] of the human heart says, that we are never inclined to to cure ourselves of any defect which makes us agreeable. Frederick's real virtues will not, probably, excite imitation so much as his imaginary excellences. We should take the utmost care not to associate in the mind the ideas of imprudence and of generosity; of hypocrisy and of prudence: on the contrary, it should be shown that prudence is necessary to real benevolence; that no virtue is more useful, and consequently more respectable, than justice. These homely truths will never be attended to as the counter-check moral of an interesting story; stories which require such morals, should, therefore, be avoided.

It is to be hoped, that select parts of The Children's Friend, [103] translated by some able hand, will be published hereafter for the use of private families. Many of the stories, to which we have ventured to object, are by no means unfit for school-boys, to whom the characters which are most exceptionable cannot be new. The vulgarity of language which we have noticed, is not to be attributed to M. Berquin, but to his wretched translator. L'Ami des Enfans, is, in French, remarkably elegantly written. The Little Canary Bird, Little George, The Talkative Little Girl, The Four Seasons, and many others, are excellent both in point of style and dramatic effect; they are exactly suited to the understandings of children; and they interest without any improbable events, or unnatural characters.

In fiction it is difficult to avoid giving children false ideas of virtue, and still more difficult to keep the different virtues in their due proportions. This should be attended to with care in all books for young people; nor should we sacrifice the understanding to the enthusiasm of eloquence, or the affectation of sensibility. Without the habit of reasoning, the best dispositions can give us no solid security for happiness; therefore, we should early cultivate the reasoning faculty, instead of always appealing to the imagination. By sentimental persuasives, a child may be successfully governed for a time, but that time will be of short duration, and no power can continue the delusion long.

In the dialogue upon this maxim, "that a competence is best," the reasoning of the father is not a match for that of the son; by using less eloquence, the father might have made out his case much better. The boy sees that many people are richer than his father, and perceiving that their riches procure a great number of conveniences and comforts for them, he asks why his father, who is as good as these opulent people, should not also be as rich. His father tells him, that he is rich, that he has a large garden, and a fine estate; the boy asks to see it, and his father takes him to the top of a high hill, and, showing him an extensive prospect, says to him, "All this is my estate." The boy cross questions his father, and finds out that it is not his estate, but that he may enjoy the pleasure of looking at it; that he can buy wood when he wants it for firing; venison, without hunting the deer himself; fish, without fishing; and butter, without possessing all the cows that graze in the valley; therefore he calls himself master of the woods, the deer, the herds, the huntsmen, and the labourers that he beholds. This is [104] poetic philosophy, but it is not sufficiently accurate for a child; it would confound his ideas of property, and it would be immediately contradicted by his experience. The father's reasoning is perfectly good, and well adapted to his pupil's capacity, when he asks, "whether he should not require a superfluous appetite to enjoy superfluous dishes at his meals." In returning from his walk, the boy sees a mill that is out of repair, a meadow that is flooded, and a quantity of hay spoiled; he observes, that the owners of these things must be sadly vexed by such accidents, and his father congratulates himself upon their not being his property. Here is a direct contradiction; for a few minutes before he had asserted that they belonged to him. Property is often the cause of much anxiety to its possessor; but the question is, whether the pains, or the pleasures of possessing it, predominate; if this question could not be fully discussed, it should not be partially stated. To silence a child in argument is easy, to convince him is difficult; sophistry or wit should never be used to confound the understanding. Reason has equal force from the lips of the giant and of the dwarf.

These minute criticisms may appear invidious; but it is hoped that they will be considered only as illustrations of general principles; illustrations necessary to our subject. We have chosen M. Berquin's work because of its universal popularity; probably all the examples which have been selected, are in the recollection of most readers, or at least it is easy to refer to them, because "The Children's Friend" is to be found in every house where there are any children. The principles by which we have examined Berquin, may be applied to all books of the same class. Sandford and Merton, Madame de Silleri's Theatre of Education, and her Tales of the Castle, Madame de la Fite's Tales and Conversations, Mrs. Smith's Rural Walks, with a long list of other books for children, which have considerable merit, would deserve a separate analysis, if literary criticism were our object. A critic once, with indefatigable ill-nature, picked out all the faults of a beautiful poem, and presented them to Apollo. The god ordered a bushel of his best Parnassian wheat to be carefully winnowed, and he presented the critic with the chaff. Our wish is to separate the small portion of what is useless, from the excellent nutriment contained in the books we have mentioned.

With respect to sentimental stories, [105] and books of mere entertainment, we must remark, that they should be sparingly used, especially in the education of girls. This species of reading, cultivates what is called the heart prematurely; lowers the tone of the mind, and induces indifference for those common pleasures and occupations which, however trivial in themselves, constitute by far the greatest portion of our daily happiness. Stories are the novels of childhood. We know, from common experience, the effects which are produced upon the female mind by immoderate novel reading. To those who acquire this taste, every object becomes disgusting which is not in an attitude for poetic painting; a species of moral picturesque is sought for in every scene of life, and this is not always compatible with sound sense, or with simple reality. Gainsborough's Country Girl, as it has been humorously [106] remarked, "is a much more picturesque object, than a girl neatly dressed in a clean white frock; but for this reason, are all children to go in rags?" A tragedy heroine, weeping, swooning, dying, is a moral picturesque object; but the frantic passions, which have the best effect upon the stage, might, when exhibited in domestic life, appear to be drawn upon too large a scale to please. The difference between reality and fiction, is so great, that those who copy from any thing but nature, are continually disposed to make mistakes in their conduct, which appear ludicrous to the impartial spectator. Pathos depends on such nice circumstances, that domestic, sentimental distresses, are in a perilous situation; the sympathy of their audience, is not always in the power of the fair performers. Frenzy itself may be turned to farce. [107] "Enter the princess mad in white satin, and her attendant mad in white linen."

Besides the danger of creating a romantic taste, there is reason to believe, that the species of reading to which we object, has an effect directly opposite to what it is intended to produce. It diminishes, instead of increasing, the sensibility of the heart; a combination of romantic imagery, is requisite to act upon the associations of sentimental people, and they are virtuous only when virtue is in perfectly good taste. An eloquent philosopher [108] observes, that in the description of scenes of distress in romance and poetry, the distress is always made *elegant*; the imagination, which has been accustomed to this delicacy in fictitious narrations, revolts from the disgusting circumstances which attend real poverty, disease and misery; the emotions of pity, and the exertions of benevolence, are consequently repressed precisely at the time when they are necessary to humanity.

With respect to pity, it is a spontaneous, natural emotion, which is strongly felt by children, but they cannot properly be said to feel benevolence till they are capable of reasoning. Charity must, in them, be a very doubtful virtue; they cannot be competent judges as to the general utility of what they give. Persons of the most enlarged understanding, find it necessary to be extremely cautious in charitable donations, lest they should do more harm than good. Children cannot see beyond the first link in the chain which holds society together; at the best, then, their charity can be but a partial virtue. But in fact, children have nothing to give; they think that they give, when they dispose of property of their parents; they suffer no privation from this sort of generosity, and they learn ostentation, instead of practising self-denial. Berquin, in his excellent story of "The Little Needle Woman," has made the children give their own work; here the pleasure of employment is immediately connected with the gratification of benevolent feelings; their pity is not merely passive, it is active and useful.

In fictitious narratives, affection for parents, and for brothers and sisters, is often painted in agreeable colours, to excite the admiration and sympathy of children. Caroline, the charming little girl, who gets upon a chair to wipe away the tears that trickle down her eldest sister's cheek when her mother is displeased with her, [109] forms a natural and beautiful picture; but the desire to imitate Caroline must produce affectation. All the simplicity of youth, is gone the moment children perceive that they are extolled for the expression of fine feelings, and fine sentiments. Gratitude, esteem and affection, do not depend upon the table of consanguinity; they are involuntary feelings, which cannot be raised at pleasure by the voice of authority; they will not obey the dictates of interest; they secretly despise the anathemas of sentiment. Esteem and affection, are the necessary consequences of a certain course of conduct, combined with certain external circumstances, which are, more or less, in the power of every individual. To arrange these circumstances prudently, and to pursue a proper course of conduct steadily, something more is necessary than the transitory impulse of sensibility, or of enthusiasm.

There is a class of books which amuse the imagination of children, without acting upon their feelings. We do not allude to fairy tales, for we apprehend that these are not now much read; but we mean voyages and travels; these interest young people universally. Robinson Crusoe, Gulliver, and the Three Russian Sailors, who were cast away upon the coast of Norway, are general favourites. No child ever read an account of a shipwreck, or even a storm, without pleasure. A desert island is a delightful place, to be equalled only by the skating land of the rein-deer, or by the valley of diamonds in the Arabian Tales. Savages, especially if they be cannibals, are sure to be admired, and the more hair-breadth escapes the hero of the tale has survived, and the more marvellous his adventures, the more sympathy he excites. [110]

Will it be thought to proceed from a spirit of contradiction, if we remark, that this species of reading should not early be chosen for boys of an enterprising temper, unless they are intended for a sea-faring life, or for the army? The taste for adventure, is absolutely incompatible with the sober perseverance necessary to success in any other liberal professions. To girls, this species of reading cannot be as dangerous as it is to boys; girls must very soon perceive the impossibility of their rambling about the world in quest of adventures; and where there appears an obvious impossibility in gratifying any wish, it is not likely to become, or at least to continue, a torment to the imagination. Boys, on the contrary, from the habits of their education, are prone to admire, and to imitate, every thing like enterprise and heroism. Courage and fortitude, are the virtues of men, and it is natural that boys should desire, if they believe that they possess these virtues, to be placed in those great and extraordinary situations which can display them to advantage. The taste for adventure, is not repressed in boys by the impossibility of its indulgence; the world is before them, and they think that fame promises the highest prize to those who will most boldly venture in the lottery of fortune. The rational probability of success, few young people are able, fewer still are willing, to calculate; and the calculations of prudent friends, have little power over their understandings, or at least, over their imagination, the part of the understanding which is most likely to decide their conduct.—From general maxims, we cannot expect that young people should learn much prudence; each individual admits the propriety of the rule, yet believes himself to be a privileged exception. Where any prize is supposed to be in the gift of fortune, every man, or every young man, takes it for granted that he is a favourite, and that it will be bestowed upon him. The profits of commerce and of agriculture, the profits of every art and profession, can be estimated with tolerable accuracy; the value of activity, application and abilities, can be respectively measured by some certain standard. Modest, or even prudent people, will scruple to rate themselves in all of these qualifications superior to their neighbours; but every man will allow that, in point of good fortune, at any game of chance, he thinks himself upon a fair level with every other competitor.

When a young man deliberates upon what course of life he shall follow, the patient drudgery of a trade, the laborious mental exertions requisite to prepare him for a profession, must appear to him in a formidable light, compared with the alluring prospects presented by an adventuring imagination. At this time of life, it will be too late suddenly to change the taste; it will be inconvenient, if not injurious, to restrain a young man's inclinations by force or authority; it will be imprudent, perhaps fatally imprudent, to leave them uncontroled. Precautions should therefore be taken long before this period, and the earlier they are taken, the better. It is not idle refinement to assert, that the first impressions which are made upon the imagination, though they may be changed by subsequent circumstances, yet are discernible in every change, and are seldom entirely effaced from the mind, though it may be difficult to trace them through all their various appearances. A boy, who at seven years old, longs to be Robinson Crusoe, or Sinbad the sailor, may at seventeen, retain the same taste for adventure and enterprise, though mixed so as to be less discernible, with the incipient passions of avarice and ambition; he has the same dispositions modified by a slight knowledge of real life, and guided by the manners and conversation of his friends and acquaintance. Robinson Crusoe and Sinbad, will no longer be his favourite heroes; but he will now admire the soldier of fortune, the commercial adventurer, or the nabob, who has discovered in the east the secret of Aladdin's wonderful lamp; and who has realized the treasures of Aboulcasem.

The history of realities, written in an entertaining manner, appears not only better suited to the purposes of education, but also more agreeable to young people than improbable fictions. We have seen the reasons why it is dangerous to pamper the taste early with mere books of entertainment; to voyages and travels, we have made some objections. Natural history, is a study particularly suited to children: it cultivates their talents for observation, applies to objects within their reach, and to objects which are every day interesting to them. The histories of the bee, the ant, the caterpillar, the butterfly, the silk-worm, are the first things that please the taste of children, and these are the histories of realities.

Amongst books of mere entertainment, no one can be so injudicious, or so unjust, as to class the excellent "Evenings at Home." Upon a close examination, it appears to be one of the best books for young people from seven to ten years old, that has yet appeared. We shall not pretend to enter into a minute examination of it; because, from what we have already said, parents can infer our sentiments, and we wish to avoid tedious, unnecessary detail. We shall, however, just observe, that the lessons on natural history, on metals, and on chemistry, are particularly useful, not so much from the quantity of knowledge which, they contain, as by the agreeable manner in which it is communicated: the mind is opened to extensive views, at the same time that nothing above the comprehension of children is introduced. The mixture of moral and, scientific lessons, is happily managed so as to relieve the attention; some of the moral lessons, contain sound argument, and some display just views of life. "Perseverance against Fortune;" "The Price of Victory;" "Eyes and no Eyes," have been generally admired as much by parents as by children.

There is a little book called "Leisure Hours," which contains a great deal of knowledge suited to young people; but they must observe, that the style is not elegant; perhaps, in a future edition, the style may be revised. The "Conversations d'Emile," are elegantly written, and the character of the mother and child admirably well preserved. White of Selborne's Naturalist's Calendar, we can recommend with entire approbation: it is written in a familiar, yet elegant style; and the journal form, gives it that air of reality which is so agreeable and interesting to the mind. Mr. White will make those who have observed, observe the more, and will excite the spirit of observation in those who never before observed.

Smellie's Natural History, is a useful, entertaining book; but it *must* be carefully looked over, and many pages and half pages must be entirely sacrificed. And here one general caution may be necessary. It is hazarding too much, to make children promise not to read parts of any book which is put into their hands; when the book is too valuable, in the parent's estimation, to be cut or blotted, let it not be given to children when they are alone; in a parent's presence, there is no danger, and the children will acquire the habit of reading the passages that are selected without feeling curiosity about the rest. As young people grow up, they will judge of the selections that have been made for them; they will perceive why such a passage was fit for their understanding at one period, which they could not have understood at another. If they are never forced to read what is tiresome, they will anxiously desire to have passages selected for them; and they will not imagine that their parents are capricious in these selections; but they will, we speak from experience, be sincerely grateful to them for the time and trouble bestowed in procuring their literary amusements.

When young people have established their character for truth and exact integrity, they should be entirely trusted with books as with every thing else. A slight pencil line at the side of a page, will then be all that is necessary to guide them to the best parts of any book. Suspicion would be as injurious, as too easy a faith is imprudent: confidence confirms integrity; but the habits of truth must be formed before dangerous temptations are presented. We intended to have given a list of books, and to have named the pages in several authors, which have been found interesting to children from seven to nine or ten years old. The Reviews; The Annual Registers; Enfield's Speaker; *Elegant Extracts*; The Papers of the Manchester Society; The French Academy of Sciences; Priestley's History of Vision; and parts of the Works of Franklin, of Chaptal, Lavoisier and Darwin, have supplied us with our best materials. Some periodical papers from the World, Rambler, Guardian, and Adventurer, have been chosen: these are books with which all libraries are furnished. But we forbear to offer any list; the passages we should have mentioned, have been found to please in one family; but we are sensible, that as circumstances vary, the choice of books for different families, ought to be different. Every parent must be capable of selecting those passages in books which are most suited to the age, temper, and taste of their children. Much of the success, both of literary and moral education, will depend upon our seizing the happy moments for instruction; moments when knowledge immediately applies to what children are intent upon themselves; the step which is to be taken by the understanding, should immediately follow that which has already been secured. By watching the turn of mind, and by attending to the conversation of children, we may perceive exactly what will suit them in books; and we may preserve the connection of their ideas without fatiguing their attention. A paragraph read aloud from the newspaper of the day, a passage from any book which parents happen to be reading themselves, will catch the attention of the young people in a family, and will, perhaps, excite more taste and more curiosity, than could be given by whole volumes read at times when the mind is indolent or intent upon other occupations.

The custom of reading aloud for a great while together, is extremely fatiguing to children, and hurtful to their understandings; they learn to read on without the slightest attention or thought; the more fluently they read, the worse it is for them; for their preceptors, whilst words and sentences are pronounced with tolerable emphasis, never seem to suspect that the reader can be tired, or that his mind may be absent from his book. The monotonous tones which are acquired by children who read a great deal aloud, are extremely disagreeable, and the habit cannot easily be broken: we may observe, that children who have not acquired bad customs, always read as they speak, when they understand what they read; but the moment when they come to any sentence which they do not comprehend, their voice alters, and they read with hesitation, or with false emphasis: to these signals a preceptor should always attend, and the passage should be explained before the pupil is taught to read it in a musical tone, or with the proper emphasis: thus children should be taught to read by the understanding, and not merely by the ear. Dialogues, dramas, and well written narratives, they always read *well*, and these should be their exercises in the art of reading: they should be allowed to put down the book as soon as they are tired; but an attentive tutor will perceive when they ought to be stopped, *before* the utmost point of fatigue. We have heard a boy of nine years old, who had never been taught elocution by any reading master, read simple pathetic passages, and natural dialogues in "Evenings at Home," in a manner which would have made even Sterne's critic forget his stop-watch.

By reading much at a time, it is true that a great number of books are run through in a few years; but this is not at all our object; on the contrary, our greatest difficulty has been to find a sufficient number of books fit for children to read. If they early acquire a strong taste for literature, no matter how few authors they may have perused. We have often heard young people exclaim, "I'm glad I have not read such a book—I have a great pleasure to come!"—Is not this better than to see a child yawn over a work, and count the number of tiresome pages, whilst he says, "I shall have got through this book by and by; and what must I read when I have done this? I believe I never shall have read all I am to read! What a number of tiresome books there are in the world! I wonder what can be the reason that I must read them all! If I were but allowed to skip the pages that I don't understand, I should be much happier, for when I come to any thing entertaining in a book, I can keep myself awake, and then I like reading as well as any body does."

Far from forbidding to skip the incomprehensible pages, or to close the tiresome volume, we should exhort our pupils never to read one single page that tires, or that they do not fully understand. We need not fear, that, because an excellent book is not interesting at one period of education, it should not become interesting at another; the child is always the best judge of what is suited to his present capacity. If he says, "Such a book tires me," the preceptor should never answer with a forbidding, reproachful look, "I am surprised at that, it is no great proof of your taste; the book, which you say tires you, is written by one of the best authors in the English language." The boy is sorry for it, but he cannot help it; and he concludes, if he be of a timid temper, that he has no taste for literature, since the best authors in the English language tire him. It is in vain to tell him, that the book is "universally allowed to be very entertaining."

"If it be not such to me,
What care I how fine it be!"

The more encouraging and more judicious parent would answer upon a similar occasion, "You are very right not to read what tires you, my dear; and I am glad that you have sense enough to tell me that this book does not entertain you, though it is written by one of the best authors in the English language. We do not think at all the worse of your taste and understanding; we know that the day will come when this book will probably entertain you; put it by until then, I advise you."

It may be thought, that young people who read only those parts of books which are entertaining, or those which are selected for them, are in danger of learning a taste for variety, and desultory habits, which may prevent their acquiring accurate knowledge upon any subject, and which may render them incapable of that literary application, without which nothing can be well learned. We hope the candid preceptor will suspend his judgment, until we can explain our sentiments upon this subject more fully, when we examine the nature of invention and memory. [111]

The secret fear, that stimulates parents to compel their children to constant application to certain books, arises from the opinion, that much chronological and historical knowledge must at all events be acquired during a certain number of years. The knowledge of history is thought a necessary accomplishment in one sex, and an essential part of education in the other. We ought, however, to distinguish between that knowledge of history and of chronology which is really useful, and that which is acquired merely for parade. We must call that useful knowledge, which enlarges the view of human life and of human nature, which teaches by the experience of the past, what we may expect in future. To study history as it relates to these objects, the pupil must have acquired much previous knowledge; the habit of reasoning, and the power of combining distant analogies. The works of Hume, of Robertson, Gibbon, or Voltaire, can be properly understood only by well informed and highly cultivated understandings. Enlarged views of policy, some knowledge of the interests of commerce, of the progress and state of civilization and literature in different countries, are necessary to whoever studies these authors with real advantage. Without these, the finest sense, and the finest writing, must be utterly thrown away upon the reader. Children, consequently, under the name of fashionable histories, often read what to them is absolute nonsense: they have very little motive for the study of history, and all that we can say to keep alive their interest, amounts to the common argument, "that such information will be useful to them hereafter, when they hear history mentioned in conversation."

Some people imagine, that the memory resembles a store-house, in which we should early lay up facts; and they assert, that, however useless these may appear at the time when they are laid up, they will afterwards be ready for service at our summons. One allusion may be fairly answered by another, since it is impossible to oppose allusion by reasoning. In accumulating facts, as in amassing riches, people often begin by believing that they value wealth only for the use they shall make of it; but it often happens, that during the course of their labours, they learn habitually to set a value upon the coin itself, and they grow avaricious of that which they are sensible has little intrinsic value. Young people who have accumulated a vast number of facts, and names, and dates, perhaps intended originally to make some good use of their treasure; but they frequently forget their laudable intentions, and conclude by contenting themselves with the display of their nominal wealth. Pedants and misers forget the real use of wealth and knowledge, and they accumulate without rendering what they acquire useful to themselves or to others.

A number of facts are often stored in the mind, which lie there useless, because they cannot be found at the moment when they are wanted. It is not sufficient, therefore, in education, to store up knowledge; it is essential to arrange facts so that they shall be ready for use, as materials for the imagination, or the judgment, to select and combine. The power of retentive memory is exercised too much, the faculty of recollective memory is exercised too little, by the common modes of education. Whilst children are reading the history of kings, and battles, and victories; whilst they are learning tables of chronology and lessons of geography by rote, their inventive and their reasoning faculties are absolutely passive; nor are any of the facts which they learn in this manner, associated with circumstances in real life. These trains of ideas may with much pains and labour be fixed in the memory, but they must be recalled precisely in the order in which they were learnt by rote, and this is not the order in which they may be wanted: they will be conjured up in technical succession, or in troublesome multitudes.—Many people are obliged to repeat the alphabet before they can recollect the relative place of any given letter; others repeat a column of the multiplication table before they can recollect the given sum of the number they want. There is a common rigmarole for telling the number of days in each month in the year; those who have learnt it by heart, usually repeat the whole of it before they can recollect the place of the month which they want; and sometimes in running over the lines, people miss the very month which they are thinking of, or repeat its name without perceiving that they have named it. In the same manner, those who have learned historical or chronological facts in a technical mode, must go through the whole train of their rigmarole associations before they can hit upon the idea which they want. Lord Bolingbroke mentions an acquaintance of his, who had an amazing collection of facts in his memory, but unfortunately he could never produce one of them in the proper moment; he was always obliged to go back to to some fixed landing place, from which he was accustomed to take his flight. Lord Bolingbroke used to be afraid of asking him a question, because when once he began, he went off like a larum, and could not be stopped; he poured out a profusion of things which had nothing to do with the point in question; and it was ten to one but he omitted the only circumstance that would have been really serviceable. Many people who have tenacious memories, and who have been ill educated, find themselves in a similar condition, with much knowledge baled up, an incumbrance to themselves and to their friends. The great difference which appears in men of the same profession, and in the same circumstances, depends upon the application of their knowledge more than upon the quantity of their learning.

With respect to a knowledge of history and chronologic learning, every body is now nearly upon a level; this species of information cannot be a great distinction to any one; a display of such common knowledge, is considered by literary people, and by men of genius especially, as ridiculous and offensive. One motive, therefore, for loading the minds of children with historic dates and facts, is likely, even from its having universally operated, to cease to operate in future. Without making it a laborious task to young people, it is easy to give them such a knowledge of history, as will preserve them from the shame of ignorance, and put them upon a footing with men of good sense in society, though not, perhaps, with men who have studied history for the purpose of shining in conversation. For our purpose, it is not necessary early to study voluminous philosophic histories; these should be preserved for a more advanced period of their education. The first thing to be done, is to seize the moment when curiosity is excited by the accidental mention of any historic name or event. When a child hears his father talk of the Roman emperors, or of the Roman people, he naturally inquires who these people were; some short explanation may be given, so as to leave curiosity yet unsatisfied. The prints of the Roman emperors' heads, and Mrs. Trimmer's prints of the remarkable events in the Roman and English history, will entertain children. Madame de Silleri, in her Adela and Theodore, describes historical hangings, which she found advantageous to her pupils. In a prince's palace, or a nobleman's palace, such hangings would be suitable decorations, or in a public seminary of education it would be worth while to prepare them: private families would, perhaps, be alarmed at the idea of expense, and at the idea, that their house could not readily be furnished in proper time for the instruction of children. As we know the effect of such apprehensions of difficulty, we forbear from insisting upon historical hangings, especially as we think that children should not, by any great apparatus for teaching them history, be induced to set an exorbitant value upon this sort of knowledge, and should hence be excited to cultivate their memories without reasoning or reflecting. If any expedients are thought necessary to fix historic facts early in the mind, the entertaining display of Roman emperors, and British kings and queens, may be made, as madame de Silleri recommends, in a magic lantern, or by the Ombres Chinoises. When these are exhibited, there should be some care taken not to introduce any false ideas. Parents should be present at the spectacle, and should answer each eager question with prudence. "Ha! here comes queen Elizabeth!" exclaims the child; "was she a good woman?" A foolish show-man would answer, "Yes, master, she was the greatest queen that ever sat upon the English throne!" A sensible mother would reply, "My dear, I cannot answer that question; you will read her history yourself, you will judge by her actions, whether she was, or was not, a good woman." Children are often extremely impatient to settle the precise merit and demerit of every historical personage, with whose names they become acquainted; but this impatience should not be gratified by the short method of referring to the characters given of these persons in any common historical abridgment. We should advise all such characters to be omitted in books for children; let those who read, form a judgment for themselves: this will do more service to the understanding, than can be done by learning by rote the opinion of any historian. The good and bad qualities; the decisive, yet contradictory, epithets, are so jumbled together in these characters, that no distinct notion can be left in the reader's mind; and the same words recur so frequently in the characters of different kings, that they are read over in a monotonous voice, as mere concluding sentences, which come of course, at the end of every reign. "King Henry the Fifth, was tall and slender, with a long neck, engaging aspect, and limbs of the most elegant turn. **********. His valour was such as no danger could startle, and no difficulty could oppose. He managed the dissentions amongst his enemies with such address as spoke him consummate in the arts of the cabinet. He was chaste, temperate, modest, and devout, scrupulously just in his administration, and severely exact in the discipline of his army, upon which he knew his glory and success in a great measure depended. In a word, it must be owned that he was without an equal in the arts of war, policy, and government. His great qualities were, however, somewhat obscured by his ambition, and his natural propensity to cruelty."

Is it possible that a child of seven or eight years old can acquire any distinct, or any just ideas, from the perusal of this character of Henry the fifth? Yet it is selected as one of the best drawn characters from a little abridgment of the history of England, which is, in general, as well done as any we have seen. Even the least exceptionable historic abridgments require the corrections of a patient parent. In abridgments for children, the facts are usually interspersed with what the authors intend for moral reflections, and easy explanations of political events, which are meant to be suited to *the meanest capacities*. These reflections and explanations do much harm; they instil prejudice, and they accustom the young unsuspicious reader to swallow absurd reasoning, merely because it is often presented to him. If no history can be found entirely free from these defects, and if it be even impossible to correct any completely, without writing the whole over again, yet much may be done by those who hear children read. Explanations can be given at the moment when the difficulties occur. When the young reader pauses to think, allow him to think, and suffer him to question the assertions which he meets with in books, with freedom, and that minute accuracy which is only tiresome to those who cannot reason. The simple morality of childhood is continually puzzled and shocked at the representation of the crimes and the virtues of historic heroes. History, when divested of the graces of eloquence, and of that veil which the imagination is taught to throw over antiquity, presents a disgusting, terrible list of crimes and calamities: murders, assassinations, battles, revolutions, are the memorable events of history. The love of glory atones for military barbarity; treachery and fraud are frequently dignified with the names of prudence and policy; and the historian, desirous to appear moral and sentimental, yet compelled to produce facts, makes out an inconsistent, ambiguous system of morality. A judicious and honest preceptor will not, however, imitate the false tenderness of the historian for the dead; he will rather consider what is most advantageous to the living; he will perceive, that it is of more consequence that his pupils should have distinct notions of right and wrong, than that they should have perfectly by rote all the Grecian, Roman, English, French, all the fifty volumes of the Universal History. A preceptor will not surely attempt, by any sophistry, to justify the crimes which sometimes obtain the name of heroism; when his ingenious indignant pupil verifies the astonishing numeration of the hundreds and thousands that were put to death by a conqueror, or that fell in one battle, he will allow this astonishment and indignation to be just, and he will rejoice that it is strongly felt and expressed.

Besides the false characters which are sometimes drawn of individuals in history, national characters are often decidedly given in a few epithets, which prejudice the mind, and convey no real information. Can a child learn any thing but national prepossession, from reading in a character of the English nation, that "boys, before they can speak, discover that they know the proper guards in boxing with their fists; a quality that, perhaps, is peculiar to the English, and is seconded by a strength of arm that few other people can exert? *This* gives their soldiers an infinite superiority in all battles that are to be decided by the bayonet screwed upon the musket." [112] Why should children be told, that the Italians are *naturally* revengeful; the French *naturally* vain and perfidious, excessively credulous and litigious; that the Spaniards are *naturally* jealous and haughty? [113] The patriotism of an enlarged and generous mind cannot, surely, depend upon the early contempt inspired for foreign nations.—We do not speak of the education necessary for naval and military men—with this we have nothing to do; but surely it cannot be necessary to teach national prejudices to any other class of young men. If these prejudices are ridiculed by sensible parents, children will not be misled by partial authors; general assertions will be of little consequence to those who are taught to reason; they will not be overawed by nonsense wherever they may meet with it.

The words whig and tory, occur frequently in English history, and liberty and tyranny are talked of—the influence of the crown—the rights of the people. What are children of eight or nine years old to understand by these expressions? and how can a tutor explain them, without inspiring political prejudices? We do not mean here to enter into any political discussion; we think, that children should not be taught the principles of their preceptors, whatever they may be; they should judge for themselves, and, until they are able to judge, all discussion, all explanations, should be scrupulously avoided. Whilst they are children, the plainest chronicles are for them the best histories, because they express no political tenets and dogmas. When our pupils grow up, at whatever age they may be capable of understanding them, the best authors who have written on each side of the question, the best works, without any party considerations, should be put into their hands; and let them form their own opinions from facts and arguments, uninfluenced by passion, and uncontrolled by authority.

As young people increase their collection of historic facts, some arrangement will be necessary to preserve these in proper order in the memory. Priestley's Biographical Chart, is an extremely ingenious contrivance for this purpose; it should hang up in the room where children read, or rather where they live, for we hope no room will ever be dismally consecrated to their studies. Whenever they hear any celebrated name mentioned, or when they meet with any in books, they will run to search for these names in the biographical chart; and those who are used to children, will perceive, that the pleasure of this search, and the joy of the discovery, will fix biography and chronology easily in their memories. Mortimer's Student's Dictionary, and Brookes's Gazetteer, should, in a library or room which children usually inhabit, be always within the reach of children. If they are always consulted at the very moment they are wanted, much may be learned from them; but if there be any difficulty in getting at these dictionaries, children forget, and lose all interest in the things which they wanted to know. But if knowledge becomes immediately useful, or entertaining to them, there is no danger of their forgetting. Who ever forgets Shakespeare's historical plays? The arrangements contrived and executed by others, do not always fix things so firmly in our remembrance, as those which we have had some share in contriving and executing ourselves.

One of our pupils has drawn out a biographical chart upon the plan of Priestley's, inserting such names only as he was well acquainted with; he found, that in drawing out this chart, a great portion of general history and biography was fixed in his memory. Charts, in the form of Priestley's, but without the names of the heroes, &c. being inserted, would, perhaps, be useful for schools and private families.

There are two French historical works, which we wish were well translated for the advantage of those who do not understand French. The chevalier Meheghan's Tableau de l'Histoire Moderne, which is sensibly divided into epochs; and Condillac's View of Universal History, comprised in five volumes, in his "Cours d'Etude pour l'Instruction du Prince de Parme." This history carries on, along with the records of wars and revolutions, the history of the progress of the human mind, of arts, and sciences; the view of the different governments of Europe, is full and concise; no prejudices are instilled; yet the manly and rational eloquence of virtue, gives life and spirit to the work. The concluding address, from the preceptor to his royal pupil, is written with all the enlightened energy of a man of truth and genius. We do not recommend Condillac's history as an elementary work; for this it is by no means fit; but it is one of the best histories that a young man of fifteen or sixteen can read.

It is scarcely possible to conceive, that several treatises on grammar, the art of reasoning, thinking, and writing, which are contained in M. Condillac's course of study, were designed by him for elementary books, for the instruction of a child from seven to ten years old. It appears the more surprising that the abbé should have so far mistaken the capacity of childhood, because, in his judicious preface, he seems fully sensible of the danger of premature cultivation, and of the absurdity of substituting a knowledge of words for a knowledge of things. As M. Condillac's is a work of high reputation, we may be allowed to make a few remarks on its practical utility, and this may, perhaps, afford us an opportunity of explaining our ideas upon the use of metaphysical, poetical, and critical works, in early education. We do not mean any invidious criticism upon Condillac, but in "Practical Education" we wish to take our examples and illustrations from real life. The abbé's course of study, for a boy of seven years old, begins with metaphysics. In his preface he asserts, that the arts of speaking, reasoning, and writing, differ from one another only in degrees of accuracy, and in the more or less perfect connection of ideas. He observes, that attention to the manner in which we acquire, and in which we arrange our knowledge, is necessary equally to those who would learn, and to those who would teach, with success. These remarks are just; but does not he draw an erroneous conclusion from his own principles, when he infers, that the first lessons which we should teach a child, ought to be metaphysical? He has given us an abstract of those which he calls preliminary lessons, on the operations of the soul, on attention, judgment, imagination, &c.—he adds, that he thought it useless to give to the public the conversations and explanations which he had with his pupil on these subjects. Both parents and children must regret the suppression of these explanatory notes; as the lessons appear at present, no child of seven years old can understand, and few preceptors can or will make them what they ought to be. In the first lesson on the different species of ideas, the abbé says,

"The idea, for instance, which I have of Peter, is singular, or individual; and as the idea of man is general relatively to the ideas of a nobleman and a citizen, it is particular as it relates to the idea of animal." [114]

"Relatively to the ideas of a nobleman and a citizen." What a long explanation upon these words there must have been between the abbé and the prince! The whole view of society must have been opened at once, or the prince must have swallowed prejudices and metaphysics together. To make these things familiar to a child, Condillac says, that we must bring a few or many examples; but where shall we find examples? Where shall we find proper words to express to a child ideas of political relations mingled with metaphysical subtleties?

Through this whole chapter, on particular and general ideas, the abbé is secretly intent upon a dispute began or revived in the thirteenth century, and not yet finished, between the Nominalists and the Realists; but a child knows nothing of this.

In the article "On the Power of Thinking," an article which he acknowledges to be a little difficult, he observes, that the great point is to make the child comprehend what is meant by attention; "for as soon as he understands that, all the rest," he assures us, "will be easy." Is it then of less consequence, that the child should learn the habit of attention, than that he should learn the meaning of the word? Granting, however, that the definition of this word is of consequence, that definition should be made proportionably clear. The tutor, at least, must understand it, before he can hope to explain it to his pupil. Here it is:

"*** when amongst many sensations which you experience at the same time, *the direction of the organs* makes you take notice of one, so that you do not observe the others any longer, this sensation becomes what we call *attention*." [115]

This is not accurate; it is not clear whether the direction of the organs be the cause, or the effect, of attention; or whether it be only a concomitant of the sensation. Attention, we know, can be exercised upon abstract ideas; for this objection M. Condillac has afterwards a provisional clause, but the original definition remains defective, because the direction of the organs is not, though it be stated as such, essential: besides, we are told only, that the sensation described becomes (devient) what we call attention. What attention actually is, we are still left to discover. The matter is made yet more difficult; for when we are just fixed in the belief, that attention depends "upon our remarking one sensation, and not remarking others which we may have at the same time," we are in the next chapter given to understand, that "in comparison we may have *a double attention, or two attentions*, which are only two sensations, which make themselves be taken notice of equally, and consequently comparison consists only of sensations." [116]

The doctrine of simultaneous ideas here glides in, and we concede unawares all that is necessary to the abbé's favourite system, "that sensation becomes successively attention, memory, comparison, judgment, and reflection; [117] and that the art of reasoning is reducible to a series of identic propositions." Without, at present, attempting to examine this system, we may observe, that in education it is more necessary to preserve the mind from prejudice, than to prepare it for the adoption of any system. Those who have attended to metaphysical proceedings, know, that if a few apparently trifling concessions be made in the beginning of the business, a man of ingenuity may force us, in the end, to acknowledge whatever he pleases. It is impossible that a child can foresee these consequences, nor is it probable that he should have paid such accurate attention to the operations of his own mind, as to be able to detect the fallacy, or to feel the truth, of his tutor's assertions. A metaphysical catechism may readily be taught to children; they may learn to answer almost as readily as Trenck answered in his sleep to the guards who regularly called to him every night at midnight. Children may answer expertly to the questions, "What is attention? What is memory? What is imagination? What is the difference between wit and judgment? How many sorts of ideas have you, and which are they?" But when they are perfect in their responses to all these questions, how much are they advanced in real knowledge?

Allegory has mixed with metaphysics almost as much as with poetry; personifications of memory and imagination are familiar to us; to each have been addressed odes and sonnets, so that we almost believe in their individual existence, or at least we are become jealous of the separate attributes of these ideal beings. This metaphysical mythology may be ingenious and elegant, but it is better adapted to the pleasures of poetry than to the purposes of reasoning. Those who have been accustomed to respect and believe in it, will find it difficult soberly to examine any argument upon abstract subjects; their favourite prejudices will retard them when they attempt to advance in the art of reasoning. All accurate metaphysical reasoners have perceived, and deplored, the difficulties which the prepossessions of education have thrown in their way; and they have been obliged to waste their time and powers in fruitless attempts to vanquish these in their own minds, or in those of their readers. Can we wish in education to perpetuate similar errors, and to transmit to another generation the same artificial imbecility? Or can we avoid these evils, if with our present habits of thinking and speaking, we attempt to teach metaphysics to children of seven years old?

A well educated, intelligent young man, accustomed to accurate reasoning, yet brought up without any metaphysical prejudices, would be a treasure to a metaphysician to cross examine: he would be eager to hear the unprejudiced youth's evidence, as the monarch, who had ordered a child to be shut up, without hearing one word of any human language, from infancy to manhood, was impatient to hear what would be the first word that he uttered. But though we wish extremely well to the experiments of metaphysicians, we are more intent upon the advantage which our unprejudiced pupils would themselves derive from their judicious education: probably they would, coming fresh to the subject, make some discoveries in the science of metaphysics: they would have no paces [118] to show; perhaps they might advance a step or two on this difficult ground.

When we object to the early initiation of novices into metaphysical mysteries, we only recommend it to preceptors not to teach; let pupils learn whatever they please, or whatever they can, without reading any metaphysical books, and without hearing any opinions, or learning any definitions by rote; children may reflect upon their own feelings, and they should be encouraged to make accurate observations upon their own minds. Sensible children will soon, for instance, observe the effect of habit, which enables them to repeat actions with ease and facility, which they have frequently performed. The association of ideas, as it assists them to remember particular things, will soon be noticed, though not, perhaps, in scientific words. The use of the association of pain or pleasure, in the form of what we call reward and punishment, may probably be early perceived. Children will be delighted with these discoveries if they are suffered to make them, and they will apply this knowledge in their own education. Trifling daily events will recall their observations, and experience will confirm, or correct, their juvenile theories. But if metaphysical books, or dogmas, are forced upon children in the form of lessons, they will, as such, be learned by rote, and forgotten.

To prevent parents from expecting as much as the abbé Condillac does from the comprehension of pupils of six or seven years old upon abstract subjects, and to enable preceptors to form some idea of the perfect simplicity in which children, unprejudiced upon metaphysical questions, would express themselves, we give the following little dialogues, word for word, as they passed:

1780. *Father.* Where do you think?

$A--$. (Six and a half years old.) In my mouth.

$Ho--$. (Five years and a half old.) In my stomach.

Father. Where do you feel that you are glad, or sorry?

$A--$. In my stomach.

$Ho--$. In my eyes.

Father. What are your senses for?

$Ho--$. To know things.

Without any previous conversation, Ho— — (five years and a half old) said to her mother, "I think you will be glad my right foot is sore, because you told me I did not lean enough upon my left foot." This child seemed, on many occasions, to have formed an accurate idea of the use of punishment, considering it always as pain given to cure us of some fault, or to prevent us from suffering more pain in future.

April, 1792. H— —, a boy nine years and three quarters old, as he was hammering at a work-bench, paused for a short time, and then said to his sister, who was in the room with him, "Sister, I observe that when I don't look at my right hand when I hammer, and only think where it ought to hit, I can hammer much better than when I look at it. I don't know what the reason of that is; unless it is because I think in my head."

M——. I am not sure, but I believe that we do think in our heads.

H——. Then, perhaps, my head is divided into two parts, and that one thinks for one arm, and one for the other; so that when I want to strike with my right arm, I think where I want to hit the wood, and then, without looking at it, I can move my arm in the right direction; as when my father is going to write, he sometimes sketches it.

M——. What do you mean, my dear, by sketching it?

H——. Why, when he moves his hand (flourishes) without touching the paper with the pen. And at first, when I want to do any thing, I cannot move my hand as I mean; but after being used to it, then I can do much better. I don't know why.

After going on hammering for some time, he stopped again, and said, "There's another thing I wanted to tell you. Sometimes I think to myself, that it is right to think of things that are sensible, and then when I want to set about thinking of things that are sensible, I *cannot*; I can only think of that over and over again."

M——. You can only think of what?

H——. Of those words. They seem to be said to me over and over again, till I'm quite tired, "That it is right to think of things that have some sense."

The childish expressions in these remarks have not been altered, because we wished to show exactly how children at this age express their thoughts. If M. Condillac had been used to converse with children, he surely would not have expected, that any boy of seven years old could have understood his definition of attention, and his metaphysical preliminary lessons.

After these preliminary lessons, we have a sketch of the prince of Parma's subsequent studies. M. Condillac says, that his royal highness (being not yet eight years old) was now "perfectly well acquainted with the system of intellectual operations. He comprehended already the production of his ideas; he saw the origin and the progress of the habits which he had contracted, and he perceived how he could substitute just ideas for the false ones which had been given to him, and good habits instead of the bad habits which he had been suffered to acquire. He had become so quickly familiar with all these things, that he retraced their connection without effort, quite playfully." [119]

This prince must have been a prodigy! After having made him reflect upon his own infancy, the abbé judged that the infancy of the world would appear to his pupil "the most curious subject, and the most easy to study." The analogy between these two infancies seems to exist chiefly in words; it is not easy to gratify a child's curiosity concerning the infancy of the world. Extracts from L'Origine des Loix, by M. Goguet, with explanatory notes, were put into the prince's hands, to inform him of what happened in the commencement of society. These were his evening studies. In the mornings he read the French poets, Boileau, Moliere, Corneille, and Racine. Racine, as we are particularly informed, was, in the space of one year, read over a dozen times. Wretched prince! Unfortunate Racine! The abbé acknowledges, that at first these authors were not understood with the same ease as the preliminary lessons had been: every word stopped the prince, and it seemed as if every line were written in an unknown language. This is not surprising, for how is it possible that a boy of seven or eight years old, who could know nothing of life and manners, could taste the wit and humour of Moliere; and, incapable as he must have been of sympathy with the violent passions of tragic heroes and heroines, how could he admire the lofty dramas of Racine? We are willing to suppose, that the young prince of Parma was quick, and well informed for his age; but to judge of what is practicable, we must produce examples from common life, instead of prodigies.

S— —, a boy of nine years old, of whose abilities the reader will be able to form some judgment from anecdotes in the following pages, whose understanding was not wholly uncultivated, when he was between nine and ten years old, expressed a wish to read some of Shakespeare's plays. King John was given to him. After the book had been before him for one winter's evening, he returned it to his father, declaring that he did not understand one word of the play; he could not make out what the people were about, and he did not wish to read any more of it. His brother H— —, at twelve years old, had made an equally ineffectual attempt to read Shakespeare; he was also equally decided and honest in expressing his dislike to it; he was much surprised at seeing his sister B— —, who was a year or two older than himself, reading Shakespeare with great avidity, and he frequently asked what it was in that book that could entertain her. Two years afterwards, when H— — was between fourteen and fifteen, he made another trial, and he found that he understood the language of Shakespeare without any difficulty. He read all the historical plays with the greatest eagerness, and particularly seized the character of Falstaff. He gave a humorous description of the figure and dress which he supposed Sir John should have, of his manner of sitting, speaking, and walking. Probably, if H— — had been pressed to read Shakespeare at the time when he did not understand it, he might never have read these plays with real pleasure during his whole life. Two years increase prodigiously the vocabulary and the ideas of young people, and preceptors should consider, that what we call literary taste, cannot be formed without a variety of knowledge. The productions of our ablest writers cannot please, until we are familiarized to the ideas which they contain, or to which they allude. [120]

Poetry is usually supposed to be well suited to the taste and capacity of children. In the infancy of taste and of eloquence, rhetorical language is constantly admired; the bold expression of strong feeling, and the simple description of the beauties of nature, are found to interest both cultivated and uncultivated minds. To understand descriptive poetry, no previous knowledge is required, beyond what common observation and sympathy supply; the analogies and transitions of thought, are slight and obvious; no labour of attention is demanded, no active effort of the mind is requisite to follow them. The pleasures of simple sensation are, by descriptive poetry, recalled to the imagination, and we live over again our past lives without increasing, and without desiring to increase, our stock of knowledge. If these observations be just, there must appear many reasons, why even that species of poetry which they can understand, should not be the early study of children; from time to time it may be an agreeable amusement, but it should not become a part of their daily occupations. We do not want to retrace perpetually in their memories a few musical words, or a few simple sensations; our object is to enlarge the sphere of our pupil's capacity, to strengthen the habits of attention, and to exercise all the powers of the mind. The inventive and the reasoning faculties must be injured by the repetition of vague expressions, and of exaggerated description, with which most poetry abounds. Childhood is the season for observation, and those who observe accurately, will afterwards be able to describe accurately: but those, who merely read descriptions, can present us with nothing but the pictures of pictures. We have reason to believe, that children, who have not been accustomed to read a vast deal of poetry, are not, for that reason, less likely to excel in poetic language. The reader will judge from the following explanations of Gray's Hymn to Adversity, that the boy to whom they were addressed, was not much accustomed to read even the most popular English poetry; yet this is the same child, who a few months afterwards, wrote the translation from Ovid, of the Cave of Sleep, and who gave the extempore description of a summer's evening in tolerably good language.

Jan. 1796. S— — (nine years old) learned by heart the Hymn to Adversity. When he came to repeat this poem, he did not repeat it well, and he had it not perfectly by heart. His father suspected that he did not understand it, and he examined him with some care.

Father. "Purple tyrants!" Why purple?

S— —. Because purple is a colour something like red and black; and tyrants look red and black.

Father. No. Kings were formerly called tyrants, and they wore purple robes: the purple of the ancients is supposed to be not the colour which we call purple, but that which we call scarlet.

> "When first thy sire to send on earth
> Virtue, his darling child, design'd,
> To thee he gave the heavenly birth,
> And bade to form her infant mind."

When S— — was asked who was meant in these lines by "thy sire," he frowned terribly; but after some deliberation, he discovered that "thy sire" meant Jove, the father, or sire of Adversity: still he was extremely puzzled with "the heavenly birth." First he thought that the heavenly birth was the birth of Adversity; but upon recollection, the heavenly birth was to be trusted to Adversity, therefore she could not be trusted with the care of herself. S— — at length discovered, that Jove must have had two daughters, and he said he supposed that Virtue must have been one of these daughters, and that she must have been sister to Adversity, who was to be her nurse, and who was to form her infant mind: he now perceived that the expression, "Stern, rugged nurse," referred to Adversity; before this, he said, he did not know who it meant, whose "rigid lore" was alluded to in these two lines, or who bore it with patience.

> "Stern, rugged nurse, thy rigid lore
> With patience many a year she bore."

The following stanza S— — repeated a second time, as if he did not understand it.

> "Scared at thy frown, terrific fly
> Self pleasing follies, idle brood,
> Wild laughter, noise, and thoughtless joy,
> And leave us leisure to be good.
> Light they disperse, and with them goThe summer friend,
> the flattering foe;
> By vain prosperity receiv'd,
> To her they vow their truth, and are again believ'd."

Father. Why does the poet say *wild* laughter?

S— —. It means, not reasonable.

Father. Why is it said,

> "By vain prosperity receiv'd,
> To her they vow their truth, and are again believ'd?"

S——. Because the people, I suppose, when they were in prosperity before, believed them before, but I think that seems confused.

> "Oh gently on thy suppliant's head,
> Dread goddess, lay thy chastening hand."

S—— did not seem to comprehend the first of these two lines; and upon cross examination, it appeared that he did not know the meaning of the word *suppliant*; he thought it meant "a person who supplies us."

> "Not in thy Gorgon terrors clad,
> Nor circled by the vengeful band,
> As by the impious thou art seen."

It may appear improbable, that a child who did not know the meaning of the word suppliant, should understand the Gorgon terrors, and the vengeful band, yet it was so: S—— understood these lines distinctly; he said, "Gorgon terrors, yes, like the head of Gorgon." He was at this time translating from Ovid's Metamorphoses; and it happened that his father had explained to him the ideas of the ancients concerning the furies; besides this, several people in the family had been reading Potter's Æschylus, and the furies had been the subject of conversation. From such accidental circumstances as these, children often appear, in the same instant almost, to be extremely quick, and extremely slow of comprehension; a preceptor who is well acquainted with all his pupil's previous knowledge, can rapidly increase his stock of ideas by turning every accidental circumstance to account: but if a tutor persists in forcing a child to a regular course of study, all his ideas must be collected, not as they are wanted in conversation or in real life, but as they are wanted to get through a lesson or a book. It is not surprising, that M. Condillac found such long explanations necessary for his young pupil in reading the tragedies of Racine; he says, that he was frequently obliged to translate the poetry into prose, and frequently the prince could gather only some general idea of the whole drama, without understanding the parts. We cannot help regretting, that the explanations have not been published for the advantage of future preceptors; they must have been almost as difficult as those for the preliminary lessons. As we are convinced that the art of education can be best improved by the registering of early experiments, we are very willing to expose such as have been made, without fear of fastidious criticism or ridicule.

May 1, 1796. A little poem, called "The Tears of Old May-day," published in the second volume of the World, was read to S——. Last May-day the same poem had been read to him; he then liked it much, and his father wished to see what effect it would have upon this second reading. The pleasure of novelty was worn off, but S— — felt new pleasure from his having, during the last year, acquired a great number of new ideas, and especially some knowledge of ancient mythology, which enabled him to understand several allusions in the poem which had before been unintelligible to him. He had become acquainted with the muses, the graces, Cynthia, Philomel, Astrea, who are all mentioned in this poem; he now knew something about the Hesperian fruit, Amalthea's horn, choral dances, Libyan Ammon, &c. which are alluded to in different lines of the poem: he remembered the explanation which his father had given him the preceding year, of a line which alludes to the island of Atalantis:

> "Then vanished many a sea-girt isle and grove,
> Their forests floating on the wat'ry plain;
> Then famed for arts, and laws deriv'd from Jove,
> My Atalantis sunk beneath the main."

S— —, whose imagination had been pleased with the idea of the fabulous island of Atalantis, recollected what he had heard of it; but he had forgotten the explanation of another stanza of this poem, which he had heard at the same time:

> "To her no more Augusta's wealthy pride,
> Pours the full tribute from Potosi's mine;
> Nor fresh blown garlands village maids provide,
> A purer offering at her rustic shrine."

S— — forgot that he had been told that London was formerly called Augusta; that Potosi's mines contained silver; and that pouring the tribute from Potosi's mines, alludes to the custom of hanging silver tankards upon the May-poles in London on May-day; consequently the beauty of this stanza was entirely lost upon him. A few circumstances were now told to S— —, which imprinted the explanation effectually in his memory: his father told him, that the publicans, or those who keep public houses in London, make it a custom to lend their silver tankards to the poor chimney-sweepers and milk-maids, who go in procession through the streets on May-day. The confidence that is put in the honesty of these poor people, pleased S— —, and all these circumstances fixed the principal idea more firmly in his mind.

The following lines could please him only by their sound, the first time he heard them:

> "Ah! once to fame and bright dominion born,
> The earth and smiling ocean saw me rise,

With time coeval, and the star of morn,
The first, the fairest daughter of the skies.

"Then, when at heaven's prolific mandate sprung
The radiant beam of new-created day,
Celestial harps, to airs of triumph strung,
Hail'd the glad dawn, and angel's call'd me May.

"Space in her empty regions heard the sound,
And hills and dales, and rocks and valleys rung;
The sun exulted in his glorious round,
And shouting planets in their courses sung."

The idea which the ancients had of the music of the spheres was here explained to S— —, and some general notion was given to him of the *harmonic numbers*.

What a number of new ideas this little poem served to introduce into the mind! These explanations being given precisely at the time when they were wanted, fixed the ideas in the memory in their proper places, and associated knowledge with the pleasures of poetry. Some of the effect of a poem must, it is true, be lost by interruptions and explanations; but we must consider the general improvement of the understanding, and not merely the cultivation of poetic taste. In the instance which we have just given, the pleasure which the boy received from the poem, seemed to increase in proportion to the exactness with which it was explained. The succeeding year, on May-day 1797, the same poem was read to him for the third time, and he appeared to like it better than he had done upon the first reading. If, instead of perusing Racine twelve times in one year, the young prince of Parma had read any one play or scene at different periods of his education, and had been led to observe the increase of pleasure which he felt from being able to understand what he read better each succeeding time than before, he would probably have improved more rapidly in his taste for poetry, though he might not have known Racine by rote quite so early as at eight years old.

We considered parents almost as much as children, when we advised that a great deal of poetry should not be read by very young pupils; the labour and difficulty of explaining it can be known only to those who have tried the experiment. The Elegy in a country church-yard, is one of the most popular poems, which is usually given to children to learn by heart; it cost at least a quarter of an hour to explain to intelligent children, the youngest of whom was at the time nine years old, the first stanza of that elegy. And we have heard it asserted by a gentleman not unacquainted with literature, that perfectly to understand l'Allegro and Il Penseroso, requires no inconsiderable portion of ancient and modern knowledge. It employed several hours on different days to read and explain Comus, so as to make it intelligible to a boy of ten years, who gave his utmost attention to it. The explanations on this poem were found to be so numerous and intricate, that we thought it best not to produce them here. Explanations which are given by a reader, can be given with greater rapidity and effect, than any which a writer can give to children: the expression of the countenance is advantageous, the sprightliness of conversation keeps the pupils awake, and the connection of the parts of the subject can be carried on better in speaking and reading, than it can be in written explanations. Notes are almost always too formal, or too obscure; they explain what was understood more plainly before any illustration was attempted, or they leave us in the dark the moment we want to be enlightened. Wherever parents or preceptors can supply the place of notes and commentators, they need not think their time ill bestowed. If they cannot undertake these troublesome explanations, they can surely reserve obscure poems for a later period of their pupil's education. Children, who are taught at seven or eight years old to repeat poetry, frequently get beautiful lines by rote, and speak them fluently, without in the least understanding the meaning of the lines. The business of a poet is to please the imagination, and to move the passions: in proportion as his language is sublime or pathetic, witty or satirical, it must be unfit for children. Knowledge cannot be detailed, or accurately explained, in poetry; the beauty of an allusion depends frequently upon the elliptical mode of expression, which passing imperceptibly over all the intermediate links in our associations, is apparent only when it touches the ends of the chain. Those who wish to instruct, must pursue the opposite system.

In Doctor Wilkins's Essay on Universal Language, he proposes to introduce a note similar to the common note of admiration, to give the reader notice when any expression is used in an ironical or in a metaphoric sense. Such a note would be of great advantage to children: in reading poetry, they are continually puzzled between the obvious and the metaphoric sense of the words. [121] The desire to make children learn a vast deal of poetry by heart, fortunately for the understanding of the rising generation, does not rage with such violence as formerly. Dr. Johnson successfully laughed at infants lisping out, "Angels and ministers of grace, defend us." His reproof was rather ill-natured, when he begged two children who were produced, to repeat some lines to him, "Can't the pretty dears repeat them both together?" But this reproof has probably prevented many exhibitions of the same kind.

Some people learn poetry by heart for the pleasure of quoting it in conversation; but the talent for quotation, both in conversation and in writing, is now become so common, that it cannot confer immortality. [122] Every person has by rote certain passages from Shakespeare and Thomson, Goldsmith and Gray: these trite quotations fatigue the literary ear, and disgust the taste of the public. To this change in the fashion of the day, those who are influenced by fashion, will probably listen with more eagerness, than to all the reasons that have been offered. But to return to the prince of Parma. After reading Corneille, Racine, Moliere, Boileau, &c. the young prince's taste was formed, as we are assured by his preceptor, and he was now fit for the study of grammar. So much is due to the benevolent intentions of a man of learning and genius, who submits to the drudgery of writing an elementary book on grammar, that even a critic must feel unwilling to examine it with severity. M. Condillac, in his attempt to write a rational grammar, has produced, if not a grammar fit for children, a philosophical treatise, which a well educated young person will read with great advantage at the age of seventeen or eighteen. All that is said of the natural language of signs, of the language of action, of pantomimes, and of the institution of M. l'Abbé l'Epée for teaching languages to the deaf and dumb, is not only amusing and instructive to general readers, but, with slight alterations in the language, might be perfectly adapted to the capacity of children. But when the Abbé Condillac goes on to "Your highness knows what is meant by a system," he immediately forgets his pupils age. The reader's attention is presently deeply engaged by an abstract disquisition on the relative proportion, represented by various circles of different extent, of the wants, ideas, and language of savages, shepherds, commercial and polished nations, when he is suddenly awakened to the recollection, that all this is addressed to a child of eight years old: an allusion to the prince's little chair, completely rouses us from our reverie.

"As your little chair is made in the same form as mine, which is higher, so the system of ideas is fundamentally the same amongst savage and civilized nations; it differs only in degrees of extension, as after one and the same model, seats of different heights have been made." [123]

Such mistakes as these, in a work intended for a child, are so obvious, that they could not have escaped the penetration of a great man, had he known as much of the practice as he did of the theory of the art of teaching.

To analyze a thought, and to show the construction of language, M. Condillac, in this volume on grammar, has chosen for an example a passage from an *Eloge* on Peter Corneille, pronounced before the French academy by Racine, on the reception of Thomas Corneille, who succeeded to Peter. It is in the French style of academical panegyric, a representation of the chaotic state in which Corneille found the French theatre, and of the light and order which he diffused through the dramatic world by his creative genius. A subject less interesting, or more unintelligible to a child, could scarcely have been selected. The lecture on the anatomy of Racine's thought, lasts through fifteen pages; according to all the rules of art, the dissection is ably performed, but most children will turn from the operation with disgust.

The Abbé Condillac's treatise on the art of writing, immediately succeeds to his grammar. The examples in this volume are much better chosen; they are interesting to all readers; those especially from madame de Sevigné's letters, which are drawn from familiar language and domestic life. The enumeration of the figures of speech, and the classification of the flowers of rhetoric, are judiciously suppressed; the catalogue of the different sorts of *turns*, phrases proper for maxims and principles, turns proper for sentiment, ingenious turns and quaint turns, stiff turns and easy turns, might, perhaps, have been somewhat abridged. The observations on the effect of unity in the whole design, and in all the subordinate parts of a work, though they may not be new, are ably stated; and the remark, that the utmost propriety of language, and the strongest effect of eloquence and reasoning, result from the greatest possible attention to the connection of our ideas, is impressed forcibly upon the reader throughout this work.

How far works of criticism in general are suited to children, remains to be considered. Such works cannot probably suit their taste, because the taste for systematic criticism cannot arise in the mind until many books have been read; until the various species of excellence suited to different sorts of composition, have been perceived, and until the mind has made some choice of its own. It is true, that works of criticism may teach children to talk well of what they read; they will be enabled to repeat what good judges have said of books. But this is not, or ought not to be, the object. After having been thus officiously assisted by a connoisseur, who points out to them the beauties of authors, will they be able afterwards to discover beauties without his assistance? Or have they as much pleasure in being told what to admire, what to praise, and what to blame, as if they had been suffered to feel and to express their own feelings naturally? In reading an interesting play, or beautiful poem, how often has a man of taste and genius execrated the impertinent commentator, who interrupts him by obtruding his ostentatious notes — "The reader will observe the beauty of this thought." "This is one of the finest passages in any author, ancient or modern." "The sense of this line, which all former annotators have mistaken, is obviously restored by the addition of the vowel i." &c.

Deprived, by these anticipating explanations, of the use of his own common sense, the reader detests the critic, soon learns to disregard his references, and to skip over his learned truisms. Similar sensations, tempered by duty or by fear, may have been sometimes experienced by a vivacious child, who, eager to go on with what he is reading, is prevented from feeling the effect of the whole, by a premature discussion of its parts. We hope that no keen hunter of paradoxes will here exult in having detected us in a contradiction: we are perfectly aware, that but a few pages ago we exhibited examples of detailed explanations of poetry for children; but these explanations were not of the criticising class; they were not designed to tell young people what to admire, but simply to assist them to understand before they admired.

Works of criticism are sometimes given to pupils, with the idea that they will instruct and form them in the art of writing: but few things can be more terrific or dangerous to the young writer, than the voice of relentless criticism. Hope stimulates, but fear depresses the active powers of the mind; and how much have they to fear, who have continually before their eyes the mistakes and disgrace of others; of others, who with superior talents have attempted and failed! With a multitude of precepts and rules of rhetoric full in their memory, they cannot express the simplest of their thoughts; and to write a sentence composed of members, which have each of them names of many syllables, must appear a most formidable and presumptuous undertaking. On the contrary, a child who, in books and in conversation, has been used to hear and to speak correct language, and who has never been terrified with the idea, that to write, is to express his thoughts in some new and extraordinary manner, will naturally write as he speaks, and as he thinks. Making certain characters upon paper, to represent to others what he wishes to say [124] to them, will not appear to him a matter of dread and danger, but of convenience and amusement, and he will write prose without knowing it.

Amongst some "Practical Essays," [125] lately published, "to assist the exertions of youth in their literary pursuits," there is an essay on letter-writing, which might deter a timid child from ever undertaking such an arduous task as that of writing a letter. So much is said from Blair, from Cicero, from Quintilian; so many things are requisite in a letter; purity, neatness, simplicity; such caution must be used to avoid "exotics transplanted from foreign languages, or raised in the hot-beds of affectation and conceit;" such attention to the mother-tongue is prescribed, that the young nerves of the letter-writer must tremble when he takes up his pen. Besides, he is told that "he should be extremely reserved on the head of pleasantry," and that "as to sallies of wit, it is still more dangerous to let them fly at random; but he may repeat the smart sayings of others if he will, or relate *part* of some droll adventure, to enliven his letter."

The anxiety that parents and tutors frequently express, to have their children write letters, and good letters, often prevents the pupils from writing during the whole course of their lives. Letter-writing becomes a task and an evil to children; whether they have any thing to say or not, write they must, this post or next, without fail, *a pretty letter* to some relation or friend, who has exacted from them the awful promise of punctual correspondence. It is no wonder that school-boys and school-girls, in these circumstances, feel that necessity is *not* the mother of invention; they are reduced to the humiliating misery of begging from some old practitioner a beginning, or an ending, and something to say to fill up the middle.

Locke humorously describes the misery of a school-boy who is to write a theme; and having nothing to say, goes about with the usual petition in these cases to his companions, "Pray give me a little sense." Would it not be better to wait until children have sense, before we exact from them themes and discourses upon literary subjects? There is no danger, that those who acquire a variety of knowledge and numerous ideas, should not be able to find words to express them; but those who are compelled to find words before they have ideas, are in a melancholy situation. To form a style, is but a vague idea; practice in composition, will certainly confer ease in writing, upon those who write when their minds are full of ideas; but the practice of sitting with a melancholy face, with pen in hand, waiting for inspiration, will not much advance the pupil in the art of writing. We should not recommend it to a preceptor to require regular themes at stated periods from his pupils; but whenever he perceives that a young man is struck with any new ideas, or new circumstances, when he is certain that his pupil has acquired a fund of knowledge, when he finds in conversation that words flow readily upon certain subjects, he may, without danger, upon these subjects, excite his pupil to try his powers of writing. These trials need not be frequently made: when a young man has once acquired confidence in himself as a writer, he will certainly use his talent whenever proper occasions present themselves. The perusal of the best authors in the English language, will give him, if he adhere to these alone, sufficient powers of expression. The best authors in the English language are so well known, that it would be useless to enumerate them. Dr. Johnson says, that whoever would acquire a pure English style, must give his days and nights to Addison. We do not, however, feel this exclusive preference for Addison's melodious periods; his page is ever elegant, but sometimes it is too diffuse.—Hume, Blackstone, and Smith, have a proper degree of strength and energy combined with their elegance. Gibbon says, that the perfect composition and well turned periods of Dr. Robertson, excited his hopes, that he might one day become his equal in writing; but "the calm philosophy, the careless inimitable beauties of his friend and rival Hume, often forced him to close the volume with a mixed sensation of delight and despair." From this testimony we may judge, that a simple style appears to the best judges to be more difficult to attain, and more desirable, than that highly ornamented diction to which writers of inferior taste aspire. Gibbon tells us, with great candour, that his friend Hume advised him to beware of the rhetorical style of French eloquence. Hume observed, that the English language, and English taste, do not admit of this profusion of ornament.

Without meaning to enter at large into the subject, we have offered these remarks upon style for the advantage of those who are to direct the taste of young readers; what they admire when they read, they will probably imitate when they write. We objected to works of criticism for young children, but we should observe, that at a later period of education, they will be found highly advantageous. It would be absurd to mark the precise age at which Blair's Lectures, or Condillac's Art d'Ecrire, ought to be read, because this should be decided by circumstances; by the progress of the pupils in literature, and by the subjects to which their attention happens to have turned. Of these, preceptors, and the pupils themselves, must be the most competent judges. From the same wish to avoid all pedantic attempts to dictate, we have not given any regular course of study in this chapter. Many able writers have laid down extensive plans of study, and have named the books that are essential to the acquisition of different branches of knowledge. Amongst others we may refer to Dr. Priestley's, which is to be seen at the end of his Essays on Education. We are sensible that order is necessary in reading, but we cannot think that the same order will suit all minds, nor do we imagine that a young person cannot read to advantage unless he pursue a given course of study. Men of sense will not be intolerant in their love of learned order.

If parents would keep an accurate list of the books which their children read, of the ages at which they are read, it would be of essential service in improving the art of education. We might then mark the progress of the understanding with accuracy, and discover, with some degree of certainty, the circumstances on which the formation of the character and taste depend. Swift has given us a list of the books which he read during two years of his life; we can trace the ideas that he acquired from them in his Laputa, and other parts of Gulliver's travels. Gibbon's journal of his studies, and his account of universities, are very instructive to young students. So is the life of Franklin, written by himself. Madame Roland has left a history of her education; and in the books she read in her early years, we see the formation of her character. Plutarch's Lives, she tells us, first kindled republican enthusiasm in her mind; and she regrets that, in forming her ideas of universal liberty, she had only a partial view of affairs. She corrected these enthusiastic ideas during the last moments of her life in prison. Had the impression which her study of the Roman history made upon her mind been known to an able preceptor, it might have been corrected in her early education. When she was led to execution, she exclaimed, as she passed the statue of Liberty, "Oh Liberty, what crimes are committed in thy name!" [126]

Formerly it was wisely said, "Tell me what company a man keeps, and I will tell you what he is;" but since literature has spread a new influence over the world, we must add, "Tell me what company a man has kept, and what books he has read, and I will tell you what he is."

[101] V. Academie della Crusca.

[102] Marmontel. "On ne se guérit pas d'un dêfaut qui plait."

[103] We have heard that such a translation was begun.

[104] V. Hor. 2 Epist. lib. ii.

[105] V. Sympathy and Sensibility.

[106] V. A letter of Mr. Wyndham's to Mr. Repton, in Repton, on Landscape Gardening.

[107] The Critic.

[108] Professor Stewart.

[109] Berquin.

[110] V. Sympathy and Sensibility.

[111] Chapter on Invention and Memory.

[112] V. Guthrie's Geographical, Historical, and Commercial Grammar, page 186.

[113] Ibid, page 398.

[114] L'idée, par exemple, que j'ai de Pierre, est singuliére ou individuelle, et comme l'idée d'homme est générale par rapport aux idées de noble et de roturier, elle est particuliére par rapport à l'idée d'animal. Leçons Préliminaires, vol. i. p. 43.

[115] Ainsi lorsque, de plusieurs sensations qui se font en même temps sur vous, la direction des organs vous en fait

remarquer une, de maniére que vous ne remarquez plus les autres, cette sensation devient ce que nous appellons *attention*. Leçons Préliminaires, page 46.

[116] "La comparaison n'est donc qu'une double attention. Nous venons de voir que l'attention n'est qu'une sensation qui se fait remarquer. Deux attentions ne sont donc que deux sensations qui se font remarquer également; et par conséquent il n'y a dans la comparaison que des sensations." Leçons Préliminaires, p. 47.

[117] V. Art de Penser, p. 324.

[118] V. Dunciad.

[119] Motif des études qui ont été faites aprés Leçons Préliminaires, p. 67. Lejeune prince connoissoit déja le systême des operations de son ame, il comprenoit la génération de ses idées, il voyoit l'origine et le progrès des habitudes qu'il avoit contractées, et il concevoit comment il pouvoit substituer des idées justes aux idées fausses qu'on lui avoit données, et de bonnes habitudes aux mauvaises qu'on lui avoit laissé prendre. Il s'ètoit familiarié si promptement avec toutes ces choses, qu'il s'en retraçoit la suite sans effort, et comme en badinant.

[120] As this page was sent over to us for correction, we seize the opportunity of expressing our wish, that "Botanical Dialogues, by a Lady," had come sooner to our hands; it contains much that we think peculiarly valuable.

[121] In Dr. Franklin's posthumous Essays, there is an excellent remark with respect to typography, as connected with the art of reading. The note of interrogation should be placed at the beginning, as well as at the end of a question; it is sometimes so far distant, as to be out of the reach of an unpractised eye.

[122] Young.

[123] Comme votre petite chaise est faite sur le même modèle que la mienne qui est plus élevée, ainsi le système des idées est le même pour le fond chez les peuples sauvages et chez les peuples civilisés; il ne differe, qui parce qu'il est plus on moins etendu; c'est un même modele d'apres lequel on a fait des sieges de différent hauteur.—Grammaire.

[124] Rousseau.

[125] Milne's Well-bred Scholar.

[126]

"Oh Liberté, que de forfaits on commet en ton nom!"

V. Appel à l'Impartielle Postérité.